I0661820

John Cranston

Cultural Directions for the Rose

With full descriptions of all the newest and best roses in cultivation, selections

adapted to various circumstances and situations and a calender of operations to be

performed each month throughout the year. Seventh Edition

John Cranston

Cultural Directions for the Rose
With full descriptions of all the newest and best roses in cultivation, selections adapted to various circumstances and situations and a calender of operations to be performed each month throughout the year. Seventh Edition

ISBN/EAN: 9783337213237

Printed in Europe, USA, Canada, Australia, Japan

Cover: Foto ©Lupo / pixelio.de

More available books at **www.hansebooks.com**

CULTURAL DIRECTIONS

FOR

THE ROSE,

WITH FULL DESCRIPTIONS OF ALL THE NEWEST AND BEST ROSES IN CULTIVATION, SELECTIONS ADAPTED TO VARIOUS CIRCUMSTANCES AND SITUATIONS, AND

A CALENDAR OF OPERATIONS.

To be performed during each Month throughout the Year.

ALSO A

COMPLETE CATALOGUE OF ROSES INTRODUCED UP TO THE PRESENT TIME.

BY

JOHN CRANSTON,

KING'S ACRE NURSERIES,

NEAR HEREFORD.

SEVENTH EDITION. REVISED.

1888.

H. M. POLLETT & Co.,
HORTICULTURAL AND GENERAL STEAM PRINTERS,
FANN STREET, ALDERSGATE STREET,
LONDON, E.C.

CONTENTS.

———

PART I.

PART II.

3

PREFACE.

———

It is now thirty years since I published the first edition of "Cultural Directions for the Rose," and the last and sixth edition has been for some time out of print.

I have long been called upon by a very large circle of Rosarians and friends to publish a new edition of my Rose book. I do so in the hope that it may prove to be of some service to the amateur in the cultivation of the Rose.

In bringing out this, the seventh edition, it has been my object to make it as practicable and useful as possible to the amateur, giving what further experience I have gained in the cultivation of this beautiful and most popular of all English flowers.

I have also taken considerable pains in the selection of varieties recommended for cultivation, and have been careful to select only the most reliable, taking both old and new Roses, which have been introduced up to the present time.

In addition, I have given at the end of my book a complete catalogue of Roses introduced up to this date, and containing upwards of 2,000 varieties, with the class or family to which each belongs, the raiser's name, the date (representing the year of introduction), colour, size, and habit of growth. There are obvious difficulties to encounter in preparing such a list, and in placing it at the service of my readers, I do so in the hope that it will be found valuable and interesting. I have taken great pains and trouble to make the list as complete as possible, and as far as reliable information is obtainable I have endeavoured to make it the most comprehensive and exhaustive catalogue of Roses published up to the present time.

NURSERIES,

KING'S ACRE, NR. HEREFORD.

April, 1888.

CULTURAL DIRECTIONS

FOR

THE ROSE.

PART I.

THERE is no flower so well adapted to our changeable climate as the Rose, and certainly none with equal beauty possessing so many valuable properties. In the Rose may be found almost every shade of colour, endless varieties of form, size, etc., a delicious fragrance not to be met with in any other flower, considerable diversity of habit, and a hardiness of constitution that admits of its adaptation to every purpose for which it may be required in the flower garden.

To contrast the wonderful difference existing in the habit and character of Roses, would alone open a subject for long contemplation. Take for instance the miniature China or Fairy Roses, which grow only a few inches in height, and compare them with the rambling Ayrshire and other climbing Roses, which often attain a height of twenty to thirty feet ; the characteristic distinctions between the Moss and the Gallica Roses, the Tea-scented and the Hybrid Perpetual, the summer and the autumnal ; the variations in form, colour, and size to be met with in each of these families are alike equally remarkable, and form a striking instance of the wonderful works of the Creator.

With so vast a difference as is here to be met with, the almost endless number of varieties is not so much to be wondered at.

With the exception of the introduction of a few distinct species, this work has been accomplished by hybridizing and cross breeding; and with a flower so very popular as the Rose, and which bears seed so freely, it is natural to suppose that the work of raising seedlings would be taken in hand by all who are fond of this most interesting pursuit.

Until of late years little has been accomplished by English amateurs and cultivators, which has often surprised me. With the French it has been otherwise, and to them we are indebted for nearly all our finest Roses, and if we may judge by the quantity of new varieties annually introduced, they doubtless find it profitable as well as interesting.

It may be said, and that justly, that our climate is not so suitable for raising seedlings as that of France (especially the south). This, however, would apply more to tender kinds, which certainly do not mature their seed thoroughly in this country unless artificial means are adopted. Nevertheless, we have hardy seed-bearing Roses in abundance, which are quite as prolific with us as in France, and in favourable seasons ripen their seed as well. My opinion is, that if the crossing and raising of seedlings were taken up by English amateurs and cultivators with the same amount of energy which has been displayed by the French, the constitution of our Roses would be much improved.

Of late, too many of our new Roses have been deficient in two most important properties, viz., freedom of growth and hardiness of constitution, and it more frequently happens than otherwise that a first-class Rose of exquisite form and colour is either of bad habit, or too delicate to withstand our cold season. This delicacy has doubtless been produced by crossing the hardier perpetuals too freely with the Tea-scented and other tender sorts.

In crossing and raising new varieties, more regard should be paid to the habit and constitution of the plants. Too many varieties crossed with the tender Tea-scented Roses have of late been introduced, and many of these rarely withstand a very severe winter ; it is therefore necessary that the habit and constitution of our Roses should be improved, and never will this be accomplished until the task is taken up spiritedly by English amateurs and florists.

Botanists have divided the Rose into sections, and again into species and sub-species, although the original species of each section is not easily defined, nor, in fact, has the origin of all been ascertained. So numerous has been the production of garden varieties, that florists have thought it necessary to make divisions and sub-divisions, taking the original species for the type, wherever it could be correctly ascertained ; but in too many instances a slight difference in the leaf or habit produced by cross breeding appears to have justified the adoption of a new section or family. It therefore often becomes a difficult matter to know, even by those well experienced in such matters, how to arrange the varieties correctly, according to their respective divisions, and few agree entirely as to the location of certain varieties which properly belong as much to one class as to another. It will be well, therefore, in all cases where practicable, to diminish rather than to increase the number of families or divisions.

All Roses may be included in one or other of two great divisions, viz., Summer-blooming and Perpetual-blooming. The Summer-blooming are varieties which bloom only once during the season, though they vary as to the duration and time of flowering, some commencing earlier and lasting only a short time in bloom, others commencing later and lasting two or three weeks : thus, with a collection of the Summer-blooming Roses, a succession of flower may be had for five or six weeks.

The autumnal or perpetual-blooming Roses are such as, in the open air, bloom from June till November, or with the assistance of glass may be had in bloom nearly the whole of the year.

Roses may be grown in a great variety of forms, and their habit and character are such as to admit of their being adapted to a variety of purposes in the garden. Hence we have what are called Standard Roses, Half-standard, Dwarf-standard, Dwarf, Weeping, Climbing, Pillar or Pole Roses, Pot Roses, &c.

Standard Roses are usually from four to five feet high. The height of the stem should be adjusted according to the vigour of the variety, the object being to form a head to the plant, which, when grown would appear in unison with the height of the stem.

Half-standard Roses are budded upon stems from two to two-and-a-half feet in height, varieties of less vigorous habit being used than are required for standard Roses.

Dwarf-standard Roses have stems from one foot to fifteen inches in height; these are rarely used for other than the most dwarf and delicate-growing kinds, such as the dwarf-growing Hybrid Perpetual and Bourbon Roses. The Tea-scented Roses succeed admirably upon these low stems, either for planting out or for pot culture.

Dwarf Roses are either budded or grafted upon stocks a few inches in height, or struck by cuttings or layers; this mode of growing Roses is suitable to varieties of every description, whatever their habit of growth may be, and can be made to assume various forms.

Weeping Roses are varieties of the climbing or other vigorous-growing sorts, budded upon stems of the Dog Rose, four, five to six feet in height, and trained so as to form pendulous trees. These are very beautiful objects, but unless in sheltered situations, require to be securely tied to strong stakes, otherwise during a heavy gale of wind they are almost sure to be blown down.

Pillar or Pole Roses.—This form of growing Roses is considered by many to be the most natural and beautiful. Certainly, no plant can be more handsome than a well-grown and properly trained pillar Rose. It is not all Roses that can be made to assume this form, and it would be useless to make the attempt with such sorts as are not suitable. To form handsome pillar Roses six to eight feet in height, such varieties must be chosen as are vigorous or robust in habit, yet not too rambling. Many of the Hybrid Chinas and Hybrid Bourbons are suitable ; so are many of the stronger growers of the Hybrid Perpetuals, Bourbons, Noisettes, &c. The climbing Roses are sometimes used for this purpose, for which they are well adapted, provided the poles are of sufficient height, which should not be less than from ten to twelve feet, and made thoroughly secure.

A good support for pillar Roses may be obtained in larch poles, which are very durable ; and if they can be procured with portions of the roots attached, these will assist in keeping them firm in the ground. The yew is perhaps the best of all, and certainly no other is so durable. Having occasion to destroy some old yew tree hedges, which had been growing more than sixty years, I had them taken up with some portions of their roots left on, and the side branches projecting six or nine inches ; these have a very rustic appearance, and the snags which are left on are useful for the purpose of training the shoots tied to them.

Climbing Roses are the most vigorous of all

Roses, and are used whenever a considerable space is to be covered in a short time. They are very suitable for covering old buildings, rough banks, old roots, and trunks of trees, arbours, archways, &c. ; also for avenues and festoons, &c. Some of the best varieties are used for training against houses. Wherever planted, they thrive and make rapid growth, and when allowed to grow in a wild and natural form in dingles or upon sloping ground, have a very picturesque and beautiful appearance. Bedding Roses are varieties of dwarf Roses, which are used for planting in groups or beds. Varieties of the most decided and attractive colours are usually used for this purpose, and these when planted in large masses (distinct varieties being used for each group) are very effective ; indeed, nothing can possibly be more beautiful than large groups of Roses of one kind when in full bloom. Suitable varieties for this as well as selections for other purposes will be found towards the end of this book.

THE ROSARIUM AND ITS ARRANGEMENT.—The form or design of a Rosarium should be as simple and uniform as possible. A geometrical figure with gravel walks and box or tile edging is best. The beds may be parallelograms, ovals, or circles, arranged according to the form of the ground and other circumstances. In no instance, however, should the beds be more than seven or eight feet in width, and the walks three to four feet if the Rosarium is on a large scale, and the beds eight feet in width; the main walks should not be less than five feet.

A terrace or mound should be formed on one or more sides, where the whole can be seen from one point: the effect when viewed from above, when all the plants are in full bloom, is very striking and beautiful, and will amply repay this extra expense. It will likewise form an excellent boundary, which should in all cases be made to separate the Rosarium from the other parts of the garden.

The beds being of moderate width and a path to correspond, will allow each plant to be examined, tended, and the flowers gathered without inconvenience, or the beds being trampled upon, which in wet weather would be injurious.

If the situation to be appropriated to the Rosarium is exposed to the north-east or north-west winds, an evergreen fence should be planted to afford protection. Though of slow growth (unless plants of large size can be obtained), nothing would harmonise so well or be so well suited to the purpose as a yew or holly hedge. A quicker-growing hedge would be the Thuja occidentalis or Thuja Lobbii, which will bear clipping, and will form a serviceable and handsome fence. Walls are very ugly, nor are they nearly so good as hedges. A powerful wind will soon find its way over the highest wall, but a thick fence will break and distribute the current. If walls are used, they should be covered with climbing Roses. An embankment or terrace upon one side, and a nicely kept yew or holly fence upon the other three, would have a very pleasing effect.

Some of the choicest evergreens, such as the berry-bearing varieties of Aucubus, Daphne, the varieties of Heath, Escallonia, the varieties of variegated and other Holly, Laurestinus, Rhododendrons, nicely arranged and grouped round the Rosarium have a very pleasing effect, and during the winter season especially add greatly to ornament and take away the bare appearance which, during a few months of the year, the Rosarium does undoubtedly possess.

In the Rosarium every form in which the Rose is capable of being grown can be brought into practice; for instance, pillar or weeping Roses can be used with good effect for the centre of circular or oval beds, or for dividing any portion of the ground. Festoons may likewise be formed for the same purpose, and for dividing the summer-blooming from the perpetual Roses, which should never be mixed promiscuously in a Rosarium. The summer Roses, having but one season of flowering, would not harmonise well with the perpetuals when the former are gone out of bloom. A separate portion should therefore be appropriated solely to their growth. A temple in the centre of a Rosarium, when well designed and covered with climbing Roses, has a good effect. Climbing Roses can also be used as archways at the entrance of the Rosarium, and for arching walks, &c. Groups of dwarf Roses can likewise be freely introduced, and with the best effect; in fact, with a well-arranged design, no Roses, of whatever habit or form of growth, need be excluded. Groups of dwarf Roses are perhaps more telling and effective when well introduced about the pleasure ground, but here the beds should be of large size and well brought out.

SITUATION.—This is rather a difficult subject to treat, for everyone who has a garden, whether it be in the smoky atmosphere of a manufacturing town, in wet, low, or high situations, must have Roses; and, indeed, what flower garden is complete without them? If there is a possibility of choice, select an open, airy situation, on ground rather elevated than otherwise, in a pure, free air, far away from all smoke, and remote from the shade and roots of large trees. In such a spot, with the help of anything like good soil, the Rose can be grown in the highest perfection, and the amateur may treat himself with every variety, whatever its habit of growth may be. But the proportion possessing these favoured localities is necessarily limited. Where such localities are not to be had, a greater amount of care and attention will be required in cultivation, and this will be increased in confined situations, more particularly where there is much smoke.

Nothing is so hurtful to the Rose as smoke. This is apparent from the difficulty experienced in growing Roses in the immediate neighbourhood of large manufacturing towns. But even here the amateur need not despair, for, with a proper selection of sorts and a little extra attention, they may be cultivated with considerable success. For such localities good, hardy, free-growing sorts must be selected, freedom of growth with ample foliage being of equal importance to hardiness, and in many cases much more so. Very many of the most hardy Roses are so diminutive in growth that they are less suitable than several of the more tender kinds, which possess freedom of growth. It will be well in such situations to have the plants as low standards or dwarfs, and to avoid as much as possible growing them on tall standards. Many kinds do best when grown upon their own roots, or worked low upon the Manetti or Briar stock.

In all cases let the syringe be used freely throughout the growing season, keeping the foliage clean and in a healthy condition, for upon this the chances of success mainly depend. Leaves to a plant are as lungs to an animal; so long as they are clogged with soot or filth of any description, proper respiration cannot go on, and the plant will soon decline and die. Apply the syringe morning and evening, and adopt every means to keep up a healthy growth. Syringing during the growing season will also assist in keeping down green-fly.

In Part II. will be found a select list of varieties best adapted for growing in the neighbourhood of towns. When, however, the more tender kinds are desired, recourse must be had to conservatories, greenhouses, or other glass structures. The plants may either be grown in pots or planted out in prepared beds or borders.

Low, damp situations, with a wet soil, are also most unfavourable to Roses; by draining and slightly elevating the ground these evils may be overcome and good Roses can be grown. To attempt to grow them in such situations without first of all providing efficient drainage is labour in vain, and nothing but disappointment can be the result.

Elevated situations, not too much exposed to high winds, are favourable to the growth of Roses, and the tender kinds are less injured by frost than in low grounds ; but the prevalence of high winds is hurtful as well as troublesome, and where these are common, screens of plantations or fences should be contrived, and no plants higher than half-standards grown.

SELECTING VARIETIES.—This is a most important matter though rarely attended to, and is, I doubt not, a more frequent cause of failure to the amateur than any other. The first thing the amateur generally does is to fix upon the varieties he wishes to grow, and for this purpose the catalogue is taken in hand, and those varieties described as being the most beautiful and perfect in form are chosen, without any regard to the habit or the hardiness of the kind or nature of the soil in which they are to be grown. Their destination may be a smoky atmosphere, and a light porous soil, or perhaps a cold, wet, tenacious soil, in combination with a damp atmosphere. In many instances the sorts which are chosen are not at all suited to the soil or the climate, their constitution possibly being of the most tender kind, and such as should only be grown in the most favourable soils and situations ; the result is, as may be expected, that nearly the whole

of them die, or, if they survive the operation of
planting, fail to produce a bloom, and are quite gone
before the next season comes round. The amateur,
of course, is much disappointed, and wants to know
" the reason why" his Roses do not grow ; and not
unfrequently the nurseryman is blamed for having
supplied poor plants, and has to take the whole
brunt of the burden upon his own shoulders. Now
if due precaution had been exercised in selecting
varieties of good constitution, suited to the situation
where they were to be grown, the result would have
been totally different. There are hundreds of fine
Roses which will grow in almost any soil with an
ordinary amount of attention. It may be said that
it is impossible to gain this information and to make
a suitable selection from a printed catalogue with a
voluminous list of names, a part only of which are
fully described, or sufficiently so to enable the
amateur to make a satisfactory selection, which
would in every instance suit his purpose. Being
quite prepared to admit that there is some truth in
this objection, it will be my object to remove, as far
as possible, the difficulty by which the amateur is
beset ; this, in fact, is the chief object in the publica-
tion of the present edition. To accomplish this, I
shall not only give a select list of sorts, adapted to
certain soils and climates, but selections for every
purpose to which the Rose may be appropriated,
either in the flower garden, conservatory, or forcing
house, likewise a descriptive list of such Roses
only as I consider are worthy of being placed in a
collection.

Another important matter to be attended to in making selections is to apportion the height of the stock upon which the plant is to be grown to the habit of the variety. We frequently see tender, dwarf and weak-growing sorts budded and grown upon tall standards, three to four feet in height, and often more; when so treated they always do badly, and even if they live, look meagre and out of proportion. A standard Rose, to look well, should form a head sufficiently large to appear in unison with the height of the stock; or, in other words, the diameter of the head should equal, as nearly as may be, the height of the stem. Let the vigorous and free-growing kinds, therefore, be worked on full standards, and the moderate and dwarf kinds, as half-standards, dwarf-standards, and dwarfs; it is an established fact, that when adapted thus, the weaker-growing kinds do infinitely better than in any other way. It is also necessary to determine in what form and to what purpose the plant is to be grown: and to carry out this satisfactorily it is important that such sorts are selected as will attain the desired object. For instance, it often happens that sorts are fixed upon to be grown as pillar or pole Roses that will not attain a height of three feet in as many years; and the same may be said of wall Roses, bedding Roses, or for whatever other purpose they are intended. Proper selections for the object in view must in every instance be made, and to do so it will be necessary that the habit and character of the variety be previously ascertained.

Soil.—The Rose is capable of being grown in a

variety of garden soils, but that is best which contains the greatest proportion of loam ; and a deep stiff loam is what Roses most delight in. The worst of all is the black porous soil, usually met with in town gardens, and which contains a super-abundance of humus or decomposed organic matter ; here the Rose will rarely thrive without a liberal admixture of stiff loam, or even clay. Sharp gravelly and light sandy soils are also bad for Roses. In many localities, and especially by the sea-side (where the latter soil usually prevails), it is often a difficult matter to grow any but the most robust and free-growing sorts. Rich peat soils are not at all unfavourable ; and good Roses may be grown in boggy soils, provided they are thoroughly drained. There is, however, no description of soil to equal a deep rich loam, rather retentive than otherwise, having somewhat of a greasy tendency ; and if such is well drained, there will be little or no difficulty in growing the most choice and delicate Roses. As, however, all cannot possibly possess these advantages, we must suit our Roses to the soil, and our soil to the Roses as best we can ; and so happy and ready is the Rose to yield to our will, and to become attached to our soil and locality, that little difficulty will be experienced in improving what Nature has given us to its advantage.

I will now make a few observations on the preparing of soils. Commencing with loamy soils the first thing to look to in this, as well as all others, is to see that it is thoroughly drained. This matter is of so vast an importance to cultivation of plants

of every description, and now so generally acknow-
ledged and understood, that few gardens or new
grounds are now made without this first and all-
important work being well carried out ; therefore it
is necessary to be done in cases where it has been
previously neglected.

After being assured that the drainage of the soil
is perfect, let the ground intended for the Rosery be
trenched to the depth of eighteen inches to two feet,
and thrown up into ridges as the operation proceeds.
If this is performed in the autumn, a few frosts and
drying winds during winter will soon make the
stiffest soil friable and in good working condition ;
when it has become dry, mellow, and pulverised, let
it be levelled down and formed into beds, or other-
wise properly arranged for the reception of the
plants. Good rotten manure will then be all that
is required to be added, and of this let a good
thick dressing be well incorporated with the soil
where the Roses are to be planted.

With ordinary black garden soils, spoken of as
being prevalent in town gardens, mix the stiffest
loam that can be procured, and less of stable manure,
for this latter will tend to lighten the soil, which we
want to make as stiff as possible. If the loam has a
tendency to clay, it will be all the better, and
instead of stable manure let liquid manures be used
during the growing season. This kind of soil should
be trodden as firm as possible, and the plants would
be greatly benefited by a mulching of manure placed
upon the surface.

Gravelly soils will require to be loosened to the

depth, if possible, of eighteen inches, but should the subsoil be of a very gravelly nature, it should not be brought to the surface. This description of soil soon eats away or exhausts a quantity of manure, hence the term a "hungry soil." Liberal dressings must be given, and those which are the most lasting and cooling are the best, such as cow dung and pig dung. A mixture also of stiff loam and decayed vegetable matter of any kind will greatly improve them.

Sandy soils will require somewhat similar treatment to the above, but if very light and shallow will demand a greater abundance of loam, or clay would be preferable. They would also be greatly benefited by having the manure placed upon the surface, which would prevent excessive evaporation during hot weather. Whatever manure is mixed with the soil should be well decayed, and, if possible, use cow dung or night soil. The soil should be loosened to the depth of eighteen inches, and loam or clay mixed with it to the depth of twelve or fifteen inches; afterwards make it as firm as possible. Peat and bog soils are both much improved by an admixture of loam. Trench as recommended for loamy soils. Burnt clay may be here used with the greatest advantage — indeed, it is serviceable to every description of soil; and perhaps few materials improve old, worn-out soils so much as burnt earth, wood ashes, and wood charcoal. In low, damp situations it will be well, in preparing the ground, to elevate the soil in the beds six or eight inches above the surface level. In the bottom of the bed a layer of old mortar and brickbats placed a few inches in thickness would tend to keep the soil dryer, and consequently less liable to become sodden.

In preparing for the Tea-scented and China Roses to be grown upon their own roots, a little more care and forethought will be necessary, not only in the preparation of the soil, but also in the situation to be chosen. A warm south border, in front of a green-house, vinery, or wall, is to be preferred. If such cannot be had, and there be no alternative but allowing them to take a place with other Rose beds upon the lawn or in the Rosery, let there be at least six or eight inches of drainage in the bottom of the beds, consisting of any rubble at hand. In stiff loamy soils use a liberal quantity of sand and leaf-mould, and let the soil, in every instance where Roses are to be grown upon their own roots (whether Tea-scented, Hybrid Perpetual, Bourbon, or otherwise), be made more friable and less reten-tive by a liberal admixture of leaf-mould, sand, and well rotted manure.

MANURE.—I have found, after repeated trials for some years, that pig dung is the best of all manures for Roses, and next night soil, cow dung and horse dung ; these should stand in a heap from one to three months, but not sufficiently long to become exhausted of their ammonia and salts. Pig dung should be put on the ground during winter or early spring, and forked in at once. In using night soil, mix with burnt earth, sand, charcoal dust, or other dry substances. Apply a small portion of the mixture to each plant or bed during winter, and let it be forked in at once. Soot is a good manure, especially for the Tea-scented and other Roses upon their own roots, so are wood ashes and charcoal. Bone dust or half-inch bones form an excellent and most lasting manure; a liberal mixture with the soil in preparing beds for the Tea-scented, China, or other kinds upon their own roots, is most beneficial. Guano and superphosphate of lime are both good manures for Roses, but require to be used cautiously; if too freely applied, the result will be gross wood and foliage, to the injury and sacrifice of the bloom. Perhaps the better way to apply them is in a liquid state, and then, when judiciously employed, they are most beneficial, particularly upon light, sandy, and gravelly soils. Liquid manure of all kinds should be used in the spring when the plants are in a growing state, and again to the perpetuals after the first bloom is over. The drainage from dung heaps and stables is most efficacious, and good liquid manure may be made with either horse, cow, sheep, or pig dung.

PLANTING.—All kinds of Roses which are worked upon the Briar or other stocks, may be planted in the autumn, say from the middle of October to the end of December; but where grounds cannot be so early prepared, or the weather is too wet for planting at that season, it is better to defer it until February. In very many instances it will be found absolutely necessary to do so, and this delay will be far preferable to planting when the ground is at all wet, or not otherwise in proper condition to receive the plants. I believe that, with proper management, equally good results are obtained in both instances, though some prefer the autumn, and others the spring; but by no means let it be deferred later than the end of March with the hardier and worked kinds, otherwise many failures and much weak growth will be the result, for no plant suffers more from late planting than the Rose. The Tea-scented and other tender kinds should not be planted out before the end of March or the beginning of April. Plants upon their own roots, whether Tea-scented, China, Hybrid Perpetual, or Bourbon, should never be planted out before April. It is not unfrequently the custom with many amateurs to plant all their Roses, whether worked plants or otherwise, at the same time; the result is, that those upon their own roots, if planted in the autumn or during winter, are almost sure to perish before spring. As soon as these latter are received, let them be placed in a cold frame or plunged underneath a north wall or hedge, where they can be screened and protected during the more severe weather.

It may not be out of place here, to mention that all who are about to purchase plants should do so as early as possible in the autumn; even if the plants are not required for planting till the spring, it will nevertheless be better, and indeed necessary, to do so in order to secure good plants, for if deferred until the spring, the chances are that many of the newest and best kinds will have been sold out, and, as a matter of course, the best plants have been selected for the earliest orders.

As soon as the plants are received from the nursery, let the roots be examined, and all injured portions and sucker roots removed, also shorten the long fibrous roots ; by no means allow the roots to become dry, but have them put into the ground as quickly as possible, and there let them remain until required for planting. All the Tea-scented, as well as the more tender varieties of the Noisette, should be put in beneath a wall where they can be protected by hanging a few mats before them in severe frosty weather; here they can remain until all the frost is over, say to the beginning or end of March, when they can be planted out wherever required. All hardy sorts may, of course, be planted out on the first favourable opportunity that offers after the ground is prepared.

Endeavour to choose a fine day, let the soil be sufficiently, though not too dry; this will be indicated by its being moist without sticking to the spade or shoe. Prepare the soil as previously recommended, then make the holes to receive the plants sufficiently large that the roots may be spread evenly and to their full extent ; but on no account allow those which are budded upon the Briar stock to be planted too deeply. Level the whole of the soil in, shaking the plant during the operation, so that the soil may pass well amongst the roots, then tread the mould firmly, holding the plant in one hand to prevent it from sinking deeper into the soil.

Dwarf Roses which have been budded upon the Manetti, Griffer, or Boursault stocks, will require to be planted deeper than is usual or advisable with sorts upon the Dog Rose or common Briar; they should, in fact, be planted so that the collar of the bud is entirely beneath the soil, and they will not succeed perfectly if this is not carefully attended to. The plants which are grown upon the Manetti stock are either budded or grafted quite low, to allow of them being planted so that the union of the bud with the stock may be readily covered. Let all standard Roses which are two feet in height and upwards, be securely fastened to stakes, to prevent their being disturbed by the wind.

PRUNING.—This operation will require to be performed during February, March, and April. At the time of pruning it is necessary to have in view the proper formation of the tree, so that when grown and in bloom it may assume the form desired. When fully grown it should appear equal on every side, somewhat conical, but wider at its base, so that when viewed from different positions it should present an uniform appearance. When in bloom every flower should be seen, and not hidden by leaves or shoots growing before them, neither should the tree be at all crowded, but each shoot should stand out at equal and regular distances.

I know it will be found somewhat difficult to obtain a proper and uniform shape with all kinds; there are some which will, in spite of all pruning, grow as close in the head as a besom, others will start off anyhow, one shoot frequently taking the lead, and if allowed, will grow to such an extent as to entirely rob all other parts of the tree, the plant soon becoming a one-sided rambling-looking object. To avoid this, examine at pruning time all such trees as are liable to grow into this form, and cut out entirely any shoots which are observed to be gross and over robust.

All shoots left after pruning should be as equal in size as possible ; this will ensure uniformity of growth upon all sides. If, however, as is sometimes the case, a vigorous and gross shoot should appear which cannot be well dispensed with, it should be stopped when it has grown six or eight inches ; the lateral shoots afterwards produced may be again stopped when two or three inches in length. The erect-growing kinds are again somewhat difficult to bring into shape, as no pruning will prevent their growing into a close compact head, with the flowers all at the top of the tree, so that they cannot be seen on a moderately tall standard ; such sorts are best grown as low bushes, or as standards of medium height. During the growing season, when they have become sufficiently hardened to bend without breaking, let the lower shoots be brought down and tied to small wooden or iron hoops placed underneath the head of the tree, and in like manner bring the middle and upper shoots down. After this has been practised for about two seasons the plant will have assumed a proper shape, and then can easily be kept so, and that without the assistance of the hoop or further tying.

Before commencing to prune, it is necessary to observe the habit of the plant, whether it be a vigorous, moderate, or dwarf-growing variety ; also to determine what kinds are required for exhibition purposes, as these will want somewhat more careful pruning and thinning.

Carefully thin out from the head of the plant by clearing away all small and crowded branches, likewise all gross unripe shoots, leaving such only as are composed of firm and well-ripened wood, and these at regular and equal distances. Prune down according to the strength of the shoot and habit of the variety, in some cases to two or three inches ; in others, where the habit is vigorous, one foot or even eighteen inches will not be too long for a shoot to be left ; but as this will depend upon the habit of the variety, and the shoot to be pruned, no absolute rule can be given. In shortening the shoots, cut close to an eye, observing where practicable to leave well swollen plump buds, which invariably produce the finest blooms ; likewise secure those having an outward tendency, and pointing in a direction proper for the handsome formation of the plant. Commence with the most hardy sorts, such as the French, Moss, Alba, Provence, Damask, and Austrian Roses. These for the most part have dormant-looking buds, and being less active than others, take a longer time to develop them, and being perfectly hardy, are not so liable to be injured by spring frosts should they happen to start prematurely into growth. With few exceptions, the whole of the varieties in the above six classes are of uniform and moderate growth, and many of the Moss as well as the French are dwarf in habit, producing short-jointed firm wood with rather dormant-looking eyes. All such sorts will require what is termed "close pruning," that is, the shoots of the previous year's growth to be cut down to within an inch or two of the old or two years' wood, leaving only two or three eyes at the base of the previous year's shoot; these will throw out one, two, or three shoots, with trusses or single blooms at the end of each. To form a conical-shaped plant, prune the centre shoots rather closer than the outer and lower ones; the centre will then grow up in advance of the sides, and give the plant a pyramidal shape. The vigorous growers in these classes will require a moderate pruning, say for the stronger shoots six inches, and for the weaker ones four inches.

The Hybrid China and Hybrid Bourbons are mostly very vigorous growers, and require more care in pruning than most sorts. An acquaintance with the varieties is necessary to enable the operator to prune these successfully. Many of the most vigorous often produce shoots six and seven feet long in a season, which if pruned close as recommended for the French and others, would not produce a single flower. These vigorous growers must be well thinned, and the strongest shoots left two feet and upwards in length, and the weak ones from one foot to eighteen inches. There are some sorts, such as Blairii, Triomphe de Boyeux, Brennus, Fulgens, and a few others, in which the vigorous shoots may be left nearly the full length; and to make them bloom abundantly this is often necessary. For the moderate growers in these two classes, six inches to one foot will be about the average length. It will be found that after long pruning has been repeated several years, the plants will have become somewhat exhausted; in fact, many of the shoots which at first grew five or six feet will now be often less than eighteen inches ; consequently, to give the plant more strength, it will require to be pruned down somewhat closer than was first recommended. In the course of years the plants which have undergone the long-pruning system will possibly become leggy, overgrown, and somewhat unsightly in appearance. It will therefore be found necessary, when such is the case, to cut them back hard, so as to form entirely new wood and better-shaped heads. Cut into the old wood as far back as may be thought necessary, new eyes will soon form, even in wood five or six years old, provided the plant is in good health ; by this means well-furnished plants with young wood are reproduced.

The Austrian Briar Roses require a system of pruning peculiar to themselves. If pruned as recommended for moderate or close pruning, they will produce but few, if any, blooms. Therefore, such as are required to bloom must be left unpruned with the exception of a little thinning, and merely the ends of the shoots being taken off. This treatment may be continued from year to year with the Harrisonii and a few others, but the Persian Yellow, to be kept in vigorous health, must be pruned down hard every alternate year ; otherwise it will soon become exhausted. When this is done, of course, no blooms are produced until the following season.

It is well, therefore, to grow several plants of this kind, pruning a few each year. Like other Roses that are required to form fine and handsome heads, they must be shortened down to four or five buds the first season of planting.

The Hybrid Perpetual, Damask Perpetual, Perpetual Moss, and Bourbon Roses may be pruned from the beginning to the end of March. By pruning a few at the beginning, and others towards the latter end of the month, the blooming season will be prolonged, and the same result may be obtained by adopting this system with the summer-blooming as well as all other kinds. The varieties of Hybrid Perpetual Roses are so numerous that there will naturally be found a very great difference in their habit of growth, some being quite dwarf, others robust, and a few even sufficiently vigorous to form pillar or pole Roses. The dwarf as well as the more moderate growers will require to be pruned down to two or three eyes, and the weak and crowded shoots to be taken out. The robust will require the same thinning out of superfluous wood, while the strong shoots must be pruned down to six or eight inches in length, and the smaller ones to four or five. As all perpetual Roses produce blooms upon every or nearly every shoot, it will be no difficult matter to prune these so as to have a continuous show of blooms ; but to have flowers of good size and quality, as well as to keep the plant in proper form, some little judgment must be exercised. The Damask Perpetual and Perpetual Moss may be pruned as recommended for the Hybrid Perpetuals.

The Tea-scented, China, and Noisette are the last sorts to be pruned, and should not be commenced before the end of March or the beginning of April. Few, if any, of these require close pruning. The Tea-scented and China especially should not be pruned too hard. Thin out the small weak wood, and shorten the other shoots one-half, and in some instances even less. The vigorous-growing Noisette requires long pruning, the strongest shoots being left even longer than recommended for the vigorous-growing Bourbons. The Cloth of Gold Rose, belonging to this section, is one of the most shy blooming of all, and yet one of the most beautiful. Its situation, when intended to be grown out of doors, should be against a south wall. It will then, if grown freely, bloom after the first year or two. Very little pruning, however, is required; the secret of making it bloom is to get it to grow freely, and for this ample space must be given. When it has become established and is making vigorous growth, it will bloom both in summer and autumn. It must, however, be manured highly every year, and no more pruning given than will suffice to keep the plant in a well-trained form. I have had standard plants of this Rose of unusually large size, and with nearly a hundred expanded blooms at one time, but of late years the severe winters have somewhat discouraged any attempt at growing it otherwise than against a south wall or in the conservatory.

Banksian Roses produce their blooms upon the small, weak, one or two years' old wood, but rarely until the plant has been established some three or

four years and their vigorous growth has become
somewhat exhausted. Whatever pruning is neces-
sary should be performed after the plant has
bloomed, which is generally towards the end of
May or beginning of June. Shorten the long,
vigorous shoots one-third or less, and secure all the
small, short-jointed, and thoroughly matured wood.
From these, blooms will be produced the following
season.

DISBUDDING.—Next to pruning, disbudding must
be considered the most important operation to be
performed. After the shoot-buds are fairly started,
look through the plant and rub off or cut out any
which are likely to take a wrong direction; likewise
thin out wherever they are too much crowded. It
will be found in some instances that at least one-
third of the shoots may be dispensed with, which, if
allowed to grow, would crowd the plant with small,
useless wood. By lessening these, such as remain
will consequently be much strengthened, producing
fine blooms, and the plant will assume a well-
regulated form, requiring much less attention at
pruning time.

Young plants require in all instances to be cut
down the first year to within a few inches of the
insertion of the bud, leaving from four to six eyes,
according to circumstances. This must be done to
all alike the first year of planting. I mention this
more particularly because I have repeatedly seen
one-year old Roses planted and allowed to grow
without receiving any shortening or pruning what-
ever. The proper time to cut them back is early

in spring, as soon as the sap rises and the buds are observed to be swelling. When the shoots are very long, it will often be necessary to shorten them a little at the time of planting, so as to prevent them from being blown about by the wind. Never allow them to be pruned closely down when newly planted.

PROTECTING. — Nearly the whole of the Tea-scented, China, and Noisette Roses will require protection during winter. Some of the most hardy will not require it unless the weather be very severe. The best and surest method to adopt with all the tenderest budded Roses grown on standards, is to have them taken up about November and planted underneath a south wall, here they can be readily and easily protected during severe frost. The plants being put in closely together, a few mats nailed to the wall will suffice to cover them. The mats need only to be put on during severe frost, but should it continue any length of time an extra covering should be provided with additional mats or straw. In favourable localities where frost is not so severe, sufficient protection might be given with coils of haybands being wound round the heads of the plants, first of all securely staking them, and drawing the branches up closely together.

For the tender sorts upon their own roots or budded low down, a good protection is afforded by placing half-decayed leaves and rotten manure two or three inches thick upon the surface of the beds. Moss may be used instead of leaves, but should be pegged down or otherwise secured to prevent the wind from blowing it away. A few fern branches will be sufficient protection for the head, as the loss of the top part of the plant is not of much importance; provided the roots and the lower parts or crown are preserved, there will generally be found a sufficient number of young shoots emitted from below. Nature often provides the best of all protections—snow, a good thick coating of which, during severe frost, is sufficient to protect the roots and crowns of all Roses on their own roots or budded low down upon the Manetti or other stocks.

INSECTS.—There are very many insects which are injurious and destructive to the Rose, but none more so than the Green Rose Chafer or Golden Rose Beetle, and the Antler Rose Sawfly, both of which feed upon the young leaves, shoots, and buds.

In the *Book of the Garden* we have the following excellent description of these two insects:—" The Green Rose Chafer or Gold Rose Beetle (*Cetonia aurata—Scarabæus auratus* of some entomologists) is one of our largest and most beautiful beetles, easily recognised by its bright green colour, sometimes reflecting a rich golden or copper tint. The wings are very long, of a brownish colour, folded under the horny wing cases, which have a few white lines placed transversely, resembling cracks, and scattered over them. On the under-side they are of a fine coppery tint, sometimes inclining to rose colour. The horns are short, the scutel forming an elongated triangle. They are readily found, enveloped in the petals of the Rose, and, from their

colour and size, cannot be easily overlooked. The
havoc they make in the Parisian Rose gardens is
fearful, compared with what we experience in
Britain. *Le Vere Blanc*, as they are there called,
is the greatest enemy the French Rose-growers have
to contend with. Their habits in many respects
resemble those of the Cockchafer. We know of no
means more likely to reduce the numbers of these
Rose-chafers than by capturing them in their beetle
state, which, from their large size and conspicuous
colours, is no difficult matter.

The Antler Rose Sawfly (*Cladius difformis
panza*).—Several species of *Cladius* attack the
Rose in their larva state, devouring not only the
foliage, but often the pith also. Their attacks on
the foliage are first observed in the shape of
innumerable small perforations, which daily in-
crease, portions of the margins being also devoured.
The cause of this is only discovered by turning up
the under-side of the leaf. In size they scarcely
exceed half an inch, nearly cylindrical, tapering a
little towards the tail. Their colour is bright green,
covered with short, erect hairs, with a darkish line
down the back, and one much darker on each side.
The head is brownish and horny, with two small
black dots on the sides. It is difficult to point out
any remedy, except what has been so often recom-
mended for caterpillars in general, viz., dusting the
plants with powdered hellebore, or with snuff,
watering with lime or soot water, shaking the
branches suddenly and catching the enemy on a
cloth spread below.

"Another destructive insect is the Sawfly of the Rose (*Selandria Ethiops*). During the month of June, the leaves of the Rose trees are often found assuming a withered brown colour, as if scorched by fire. The cause of this may be traced, by the aid of a microscope, to the destructive effects of this insect. The upper circle of the leaf will be found nearly eaten away, while the under-side remains perfectly entire. A closer examination will show the enemy itself, in colour so nearly resembling the foliage that its detection by the naked eye is almost impossible. In its larva state it is nearly half-an-inch long, of a cylindrical form, with a dark line down the middle of the back. The head is orange colour, with a small black spot on each side. The larvæ change their skins several times before arriving at their full size, and then descend into the earth, where they form elliptical shells, highly polished on the inside ; in these they pass the winter, and eventually become transformed, first into the pupa state, and afterwards, towards spring, into perfect insects. Syringing the Roses with water in which hot lime and soot have been steeped, is one of the best remedies for the suppression of all tender-skinned insects on Roses and other plants."

The Rose Aphis (*Aphis Rosæ*) is a great pest amongst Roses, and especially in situations where air cannot circulate freely amongst the plants ; in such confined places much difficulty is often experienced in keeping these troublesome insects under, and generally the weakest and most delicate sorts are those worst attacked. Numerous recipes are given for the destruction of these aphides, but whatever means are adopted should be taken in time and before the plants get smothered with them. I have found the following remedy answer in every instance where applied :—To one pound of tobacco, and two pounds of soft soap. add six quarts of boiling water ; let this stand a short time, then strain through a piece of coarse canvas ; to the filtered liquor add nine or ten gallons of water, and with this diluted fluid syringe the infested plants, or otherwise dip the branches into it, wetting the whole of the foliage. If necessary, repeat the operation two or three times, always syringing the plants over afterwards with clean water. A decoction of quassia is frequently used, in the proportion of one ounce of the chips to a quart of water. Fumigating with tobacco is perhaps the best and most effectual way of destroying them, where appliances can be had so as to confine the smoke. In hothouses and greenhouses this is readily done, and is the best means that can be adopted.

APHIS VESTATOR.—This, the Rose cultivator's friend, should never be destroyed ; it feeds upon and destroys all other aphides, and is a most valuable ally for such purposes. The ladybirds are also useful in destroying these small insects, so are many kinds of birds, and none more so than the so-called mischievous tomtit and sparrow. The sparrows are especially valuable ; not only do they feed upon the aphides, but the Rose-chafer, and other enemies to the Rose. I have often watched their early morning avocations amongst the Roses ; a dozen or two sparrows will clear some thousands of insects during the day, and woe be to the Rose-chafer that comes within their sight.

DISEASES.—*Mildew.* This fungus is the most troublesome of all diseases to which the Rose is subject, and of late years has been much more prevalent than formerly. The late Mr. Knight, in writing upon it, says, " The secondary and intermediate cause of this disease has long appeared to me to be the want of sufficient moisture from the soil, and excess of humidity in the air, particularly if the plant is exposed to a temperature below that to which they have been accustomed. If damp and cloudy weather in July succeeded that which was warm and bright, without the intervention of sufficient rain to moisten the ground to some depth, the crop is generally much injured by mildew."

There can be no doubt as to the truth of these observations, but latterly this disease appears to have become more prevalent, and seems to baffle all our skill to ward it off, much more to eradicate it. Some sorts of Roses are much more liable to it than others, and some are even so badly affected by it, that it is next to impossible to keep them in health and free from it throughout the season. A good remedy is flour of sulphur. This should be applied the very moment the least sign of the disease makes its appearance, otherwise it will not arrest its progress. The best instrument for applying it is the sulphurator; this excellent little machine will distribute it evenly throughout every part of the plant, which it is impossible to do with a dredger. If the dredger be used, syringe the plants over with a little water, and apply it to every part affected. The sulphur should not be applied to the young foliage whilst the sun is powerful, or it will sometimes be injurious ; no harm will result from applying it in the evening, and it may remain on for a day or two, when it should be syringed off. The quantity used has been from two-and-a-half to three ounces to the gallon of water. The plants affected are syringed or well wetted with the mixture, and if the shoots are at all tender, they must be syringed over with clear water in a few hours afterwards. One or two applications, in most instances, will be sufficient, but when the disease has been allowed to establish itself, it must be applied weekly until it is cured. Various nostrums are frequently advertised and recommended for this disease, but I should advise all to be cautious what they apply to their Roses, for the remedy will oftentimes prove worse than the disease.

Red Fungus or rust, as it is sometimes called, seldom appears before August, or until the wood and foliage are pretty well matured; its consequence, therefore, at this season is not of much importance, nor is the damage at all serious. It should, however, be prevented by the application of sulphur, as recommended for mildew, or freshly slaked lime to the parts affected will, in some instances, destroy it.

Green Centres.—These must be considered a disease, though prevalent only among certain sorts of Roses. Its cause may be attributed to too much manure, or the use of it in a raw or green state. This should be avoided with all kinds subject to this disease, and where manure is applied let it be thoroughly decayed.

STOCKS.—Roses are grown upon several varieties of stocks; those most in use are the wild Dog Rose, the Manetti, Grifferæ, Celini, and the Black Boursault. The Dog Rose, procured from hedge-rows and woods, is the only suitable kind on which standard or half-standard Roses can be grown. For dwarfs, the Manetti and Grifferæ are preferable, especially for light soils. Stocks for budding should be procured in the autumn, the roots pruned close, and the stem shortened to the height required. Standards will require to be left three to four feet in length, half-standards two to three feet, and dwarfs six to eighteen inches. These should be planted out in rows three feet apart; the following summer they will be fit for budding. The Manetti is a vigorous variety of Hybrid China Rose, introduced nearly forty years ago from Italy by Mr. Rivers. For dwarf Roses this is a most excellent stock; it is alike suitable for stiff as for light soils. In many light, shallow soils, where the Dog Rose will scarcely live, this succeeds admirably. It is very hardy and enduring, and will last as long as, or perhaps longer, than any other; it requires, how-ever, somewhat different treatment to other stocks, both as regards its preparation before as well as after budding. My practice is to prepare the cuttings in the autumn, say from nine to twelve inches in length, taking out all the eyes excepting three at the top of the cutting; they are then planted six to eight inches deep. Here they remain until the following autumn, when they are taken up and planted out into rows from eighteen inches to two feet apart. The following summer they will be fit for budding; this is done by inserting a bud in the stem which formed the cutting two inches or more below the surface, the soil being previously cleared away to enable the operation to be performed. The following spring, when the bud shows signs of starting in growth, cut down the upper part of the stock to within an inch of the buds: by the end of the summer they will have formed fine large plants. When the plants are taken up to be transplanted into the Rosery, it will be necessary to plant them quite over the collar of the bud, so that the union of the stock and bud is quite covered; the plants being budded so very low, there will be little difficulty in planting them thus.

This stock, be it observed, is not adapted to standards or half-standards, or, in fact, to any other than dwarfs treated as described above. There are few Roses which refuse to grow upon it. Since the introduction of this stock, Roses upon their own roots (excepting the Tea-scented and China) have not been so much sought after, for the reason that, to have a bed of Roses upon their own roots, well filled and in a good blooming condition, requires two if not three years before it can be accomplished; whereas, with the same sort budded upon the Manetti stock, a fine bed can be obtained the first year of planting, with, perhaps, double the quantity of bloom that would ever be produced by plants grown upon their own roots.

For pot culture this is also a valuable stock. For pillar Roses it is remarkably well adapted. Strong-growing kinds will often grow from six to eight feet the first season, and will ultimately make the finest plants possible. I have some examples of pillar Roses, both summer and perpetual, which are eight to ten feet in height, and beautifully furnished from the bottom upwards.

The Persian Yellow and Harrisonii may be instanced as two summer Roses, forming large and beautiful pillar Roses, resembling more the size of young Apple trees than Roses.

The seedling Briar or cultivated Briar stock is the wild Dog Rose, raised either from seed or struck from cuttings in the same manner as the Manetti. This stock has of late become much more into general use than formerly. It is specially adapted for the Tea-scented and Noisette Roses, and it is undoubtedly better suited than the Manetti for all the yellow Roses, either for out-door or pot culture.

The Grifferæ is a variety of the Multiflora Rose, and is used as a stock for the Noisette Roses, or any vigorous-growing varieties. Maréchal Niel and Cloth of Gold do admirably upon this stock. It is not, perhaps, so hardy as the Manetti, but all tender varieties, such as the Tea-scented and Noisette, take more freely upon it.

The Black Boursault and the Celini are used by some for the Tea-scented and Noisette Roses, but I do not consider they are so lasting or so good as either of the preceding.

PROPAGATION.—Roses are propagated by budding, grafting, cuttings, layering, and by suckers (either or all of these modes are in practice for the purpose of increasing a given variety); and by seed to obtain new varieties.

Budding.—This is by far the most ready and easy system by which the Rose can be propagated, and is that most generally practised. It offers many advantages over other modes of propagating, as by its adoption a weak kind is increased in vigour by bringing it to grow upon a stock which is more hardy and more vigorous in habit. By adopting this mode of propagating, Roses are wrought into a variety of forms which otherwise could not be done. The mode of operation is so simple, and has been so often described, that a few words will suffice by way of explanation. The usual time for budding is July and August, but the proper time to be chosen must be determined by the state of the scion, as well as the stock which is to be budded. In no case will it answer to bud until the sap flows freely, both in the stock and the plant from whence the buds are to be taken. The scion must be firm and well ripened, otherwise the buds are apt to perish. If the bark does not rise freely on the stock, the operation should be deferred for a few days, or until the sap is induced to flow, which may be hastened by giving a few copious waterings. The buds should be taken from ripe shoots of the current year; the fact of the plant being in bloom will generally indicate that the wood is ripe and thoroughly matured. In taking off the leaves, let a portion of the leaf-stalk be left at the base of the eye, it will be an assistance when inserting the bud, and will help to shade and protect the bud after it is inserted. As soon as possible after the incision is made in the stock, the bud (which must be previously cut and taken out) should be inserted, and immediately bound up with cotton or matting, so as to exclude the air and wet until the bark is united. In about three weeks, the matting or cotton will require to be loosened, and in a few weeks afterwards may be taken entirely off. A few inches should be taken off the end of the Briar which has been budded ; the sap will consequently flow more directly to the bud at the base of the shoot.

Grafting.—Early in spring is the usual time for grafting Roses ; but with the assistance of propagating pits or house where artificial heat can be obtained, this operation can be performed at various seasons of the year, provided the stock and the scion are both in proper condition. The stock to be grafted should be rather in advance of the scion, and taken when the sap is in active motion. The scion should consist of hard, well-ripened wood, and not too far advanced. Any of the modes of grafting usually practised, such as whip grafting, saddle grafting, or cleft grafting, may be adopted. Whip or tongue grafting is the most simple and the most expeditious, and will answer every purpose.

The Manetti and the Seedling Briar or Dog Rose are the kinds most in use for stocks, to graft both hybrids and the Tea-scented Roses. The stocks should be taken up and potted into small pots one season before being required for grafting ; they can then be plunged out of doors. If potted during March and April they will be ready for grafting the following November or December. The stocks should be taken into the propagating frames a few weeks before being required. After they are grafted, let them be plunged into the same bottom heat as before, and here they should be kept rather close and shaded when necessary until the grafts have fairly taken and the plants have commenced growing, they may then receive a little air or be removed to a cooler house or frame. Avoid too high a temperature ; the Rose being very impatient of heat, should always be forced steadily. A temperature of 65' to 75' by day, and 55' or 65° by night should not be exceeded. When watering, do not wet the graft, nor allow too much moisture to settle near to the junction of the graft ; to prevent this, a little clay or wax may be placed around the junction. With a little attention to these minor matters a good practitioner will be as successful with this mode of propagating as with more simple and generally practised systems of budding. I have not spoken of grafting Roses out of doors, nor do I recommend the practice ; the chance of success are so uncertain that it rarely answers to risk them, especially when we have a more safe and certain method in the one described above.

Layering.—This mode of propagating may be applied to most of the free-growing Roses, but it is only practised with sorts which are required to be grown upon their own roots, and which do not strike freely from cuttings ; for instance, the old and other Moss, the Provence and Austrian Roses, &c. To obtain proper shoots for layering, the plant should be cut down to the surface of the ground every year ; young shoots will then be produced. These should be layered about June or July, or as soon as the shoots become sufficiently hardened to bend without breaking. An incision must be made at an eye upon the side of the shoot, and gently twisted so that the incision be kept open. The shoot should then be secured in its position by a peg, and covered with earth to the depth of three or four inches. In the following spring most of these will have formed roots, and may then be taken off and planted out ; those not rooted must remain down another season.

Cuttings. — With the exception of the Moss, Austrian, and a few other varieties, nearly all may be struck from cuttings ; and to obtain plants on their own roots this is the most expeditious and best system. This mode of propagating Roses may be practised throughout spring, summer, and autumn ; but the shoot which is to form the cutting should in all instances be matured and well ripened. The cuttings should be made from three to four inches in length, and if a small portion of the old wood can be taken off with it, so as to form a heel, the cutting will strike more freely. The two or three upper leaves should be allowed to remain on the cutting until they fall off, when they should be removed to prevent their damping. Take five or six-inch pots and fill with a compost of friable loam, leaf-mould, and sand, pressing it moderately firm ; plant with a small pin from six to eight cuttings evenly around the sides of the pot, making the soil firm about them; water with a fine rose to settle the soil, and place the pots at once into a frame with a gentle bottom-heat, where they can be kept close and constantly shaded from the sun. Sprinkle them over with a fine rose, or syringe daily for the first week or nine days. In about three or four weeks the cuttings will have rooted, when they should be potted singly into three-inch pots, and again placed in a frame with a gentle bottom heat. Here they should remain nine days or a fortnight, being shaded and watered as required. When rooted round their pots, they should be removed into a cold frame to harden, previous to being placed out of doors.

Many hardy kinds, such as the Hybrid Perpetuals, Bourbons, &c., may be struck out of doors under hand - glasses. About the end of September or beginning of October prepare a border with light soil upon the north side of a hedge or wall ; let the cuttings be made five or six inches in length, choosing firm, well-ripened wood, taken off with a small portion of old wood to form a heel ; without this the cuttings will not strike so readily. Put the cuttings in thickly, pressing them firmly into the soil; well water, and place over them small hand or cap glasses ; these must remain on until the cuttings are struck in the spring. An occasional watering with clear lime-water should be given ; this will destroy the worms, which are often troublesome and disturb the cuttings. In the spring, when the cuttings are found to be rooted, take them up and pot singly into small pots ; put them into a cold frame where they can be shaded from the sun until sufficiently hardened to be planted out of doors. Some of the hardy, vigorous - growing summer Roses will strike, if planted in a shady border, without the assistance of hand-glasses ; but when this is done the cuttings require to be made nine to twelve inches in length and planted at least six to eight inches deep, and the soil trodden firmly about them.

Suckers.—This mode of propagating is practised but seldom, and then only with a few kinds, such as the Scotch and Austrian Roses. The former emit suckers freely, which are taken off and planted out during the spring or autumn ; these suckers have generally some small fibrous roots attached.

By Seed. — The object of raising Roses from seed is to obtain new varieties. Although somewhat uncertain as to the result, it is, nevertheless, a very pleasant and interesting occupation. There has long been an idea prevalent that good varieties of Roses cannot be raised from seed in England, and that we must go to warmer climates for anything of sterling merit. This, however, is not entirely so, as some excellent varieties recently raised in this country testify.

The tender varieties, however, seldom if ever mature seed in our climate, but even the ripening of seed can be accomplished artificially, and, with the assistance of glass and hot water, we may reckon our advantages equal to those in the South of France or Italy. The seed pods should become thoroughly ripe upon the tree before they are gathered. When taken off, place each sort separately into small pots, mixing with them fine sand. They may be stored away in this manner until February, care being taken to keep them out of the way of mice, which will very soon destroy the lot if the opportunity be given them.

Early in February take them out and break up the pods, and rub the whole until the seeds are all separated ; they may then be sown in shallow pans, pots, or boxes, using light soil with a liberal admixture of sand, and cover with same to the depth of an inch. Place them in a frame having a northern aspect, or otherwise in a shady or sheltered spot, where an uniform temperature and moisture can be maintained. About April or May many of the seedlings will begin to make their appearance, but this will depend upon the quality of the seed ; if it was well ripened when gathered, a large portion will vegetate the first season, but in most instances the greater portion will not vegetate till the following spring. The seedling plants should be removed when sufficiently strong to bear transplanting. In taking them up care should be taken not to disturb the dormant seeds or others just beginning to vegetate. The seedlings which are removed from the seed pans during the spring and summer should be pricked out into other pans, and afterwards placed in a cold frame, where they can be shaded from the hot sun, and occasionally watered. If allowed to grow in the seed pans until the autumn, they may then be transplanted into the open ground in a well-sheltered border, and there allowed to remain until they bloom. Many of the seedlings will bloom the first year, but little more than the colour can be ascertained until the plant has been established at least two years. Those which produce very thin petals, or which are deficient in colour, or single, may safely be discarded at once, retaining only such as have good outline, decided and distinct colour, petals of good substance, and the flowers, if not full, somewhat more than semi-double. If all, or any of these properties exist, they will improve under cultivation.

Crossing or Hybridising.—By crossing varieties of opposite characters, the colour, habit, and form are changed, and new varieties are obtained; thus we are constantly receiving flowers of increased size and more perfect form. To perform this operation with any chance of success, a judicious selection of the varieties to be crossed must be made. Choose for the parent plants such sorts as bear seeds freely; upon a dry fine day, when the bloom is fully expanded, remove the anthers from the flower with a pair of scissors, to prevent self-impregnation, then take the pollen of another variety of opposite character, or one possessing some property that it is desirable to impart, and place on the pistil of the parent plant. This will require to be done with great care, and at a time of the day when the farina is observed to be most abundant. After the flower is impregnated, enclose it with a gauze bag, to prevent insects from disturbing the pollen until it has taken effect. The seed pod which has been fertilized should be marked so as to be known at the time of gathering, and should be noted down, so that the realisation of the object aimed at may be watched in the seedling plants. Much time and patience will be required during and after the performance of this work. To those who have time to devote to it, nothing can be more pleasing or interesting, and it is the only sure means of bringing out any desired properties in new varieties.

A more easy plan, though not so certain in its results, is to plant side by side varieties of opposite characters, and to allow fertilization to be effected by the action of the winds, insects, or other causes. There need be no restriction as to crossing one group with another; and so distinct and opposite are the properties of many varieties, even in the same group or family, that no limit can be placed to the possible results.

Before fertilizing, it will be necessary to become acquainted with what kinds will bear seed freely, and these must be selected from the seed bearers. A great many varieties of Roses never produce mature seed. The following may be taken as good seed - bearers:—Moss : Alice Leroy, Baronne de Wassenaër, Celina, Clemence Beaugrand, Comtesse de Murinais, Luxembourg, and Marie de Blois.

Hybrid China: Blairii No. 2, Brennus, Chénédolé, Fulgens, Double-margined Hip, and Magna Rosea. Hybrid Bourbons: Charles Lawson, Coupe d'Hébé, Paul Ricaut, and Paul Perras. Austrian: Harrisonii. Ayrshire: Ruga, Bennett's Seedling. Hybrid Perpetual: Abel Carrière, Annie Wood, Baronne Prévost, Centifolia Rosea, Charles Lefebvre, Dr. Andry, Duc de Rohan, Duc de Wellington, Duke of Edinburgh, Fisher Holmes, Géant des Batailles, Genéral Jacqueminot, John Hopper, Jules Chretien, Jules Margottin, La France, Lord Macaulay, Madame Charles Crapelet, Mdlle. Bonnaire, Marguerite de St. Amand, Marie Beauman, Monsieur Etienne Levet, Prince Camille de Rohan, Sénateur Vaisse, and Victor Verdier. Bourbon: Sir Joseph Paxton. China: Mrs. Bosanquet. Many of the Tea-scented Roses bear seed freely, but unless in very favourable situations and in warm seasons, the seed rarely ripens. To rear seedlings of this class, as well as some of the Noisette and China Groups, the plants require to be brought under glass to mature their seed.

Forcing.—Few plants are more impatient of a high artificial temperature than the Rose, and as little assistance can be expected from nature throughout the cold sunless months of December, January, and February (the time when forcing is most active), a considerable amount of care and attention, as well as skill, must be exercised. Houses or pits of proper construction, with efficient heating appliances, must be provided. The best are low span-roof houses or pits, with platforms or raised beds on each side, and the path along the centre. This will allow of the plants being placed within ten or twelve inches from the glass, so that they may receive the full benefit of the light and sun. The platform or raised beds should be constructed so that the pots can be plunged in leaves or tan, and so arranged that the plants can be plunged more deeply as they increase in height, always endeavouring to keep them about ten or twelve inches from the glass. Air should be admitted throughout the bottom and top of the house, but not so as to come in direct contact with the plants. If hot-water pipes are used, not less than a double row of four-inch pipe for a house twelve feet in width will be sufficient. The temperature by day should not rise higher than 60° or 75°, nor fall lower than 50° by night. The plants intended for forcing must be established at least one year in pots, varying from seven to twelve inches in diameter according to the size and strength of the plant, which may be either worked on the Manetti, Dog Rose, or upon their own roots.

To prepare all the hardy kinds let the plants be taken up in the autumn. Carefully trim the roots, and put into eight or nine-inch pots, using good turfy loam, and a liberal admixture of rotten dung and leaf-mould. After potting, let them be watered and placed upon a sheltered border, where they can be plunged in coal-ashes, leaves, or tan. In the spring cut them back rather close, and as they commence growing, disbud and tie the shoots out, so as to form well-shaped plants. Any flower buds which appear should be taken off before they become fully matured.

The Tea-scented and other tender sorts should be potted into seven or eight-inch pots, about March or April, and either grown under glass, being plunged in a gentle bottom heat, or otherwise grown out of doors upon a hotbed, where a genial bottom heat can be obtained throughout the summer. Early in October the plants should be re-potted, taking pots according to the size of the plants, say from eight to nine inches in diameter; a portion of the old soil should be removed, but this should be done without injuring or disturbing the roots. After potting, place them in a sheltered situation until about the end of November; they may then be pruned, and if they have been properly disbudded, and the shoots have been trained during the previous growth, little more than shortening the shoots down to three or four eyes will be necessary. The Tea-scented sorts will not require to be cut so hard, in fact they should receive only moderate pruning. The plants may now be taken into the forcing house, the pots being plunged to their full depth in prepared beds of leaves or tan; here they should remain for the first fortnight without any artificial heat being applied, after which begin gently, increasing the temperature gradually as the plants are commencing to grow. The plants being brought up rather close to the glass, to receive all the benefit to be derived from sun and light, will be somewhat exposed to sudden changes of temperature; to provide against this, protection must be given by covering the outside of the house with mats or canvas during frosty weather. When the plants commence growing, examine them frequently for the grub, and upon the first appearance of green-fly, fumigate with tobacco ; and this will possibly require to be repeated every nine days or fortnight. Water the paths occasionally to keep up a moist atmosphere, and in the morning during fine weather let the plants be syringed over, and air admitted on all favourable occasions. If the least signs of mildew is observed, let sulphur be applied immediately, for should this disease once get thoroughly established, there will be some difficulty in eradicating it. The syringing must be discontinued when the plants are about to bloom.

If it is desired to remove any plants to flower in the greenhouse or conservatory, let this be done a week or nine days before the blooms are likely to expand, when they will have somewhat recovered the change of temperature by the time they come into bloom, and will last much longer in flower in consequence. If allowed to bloom in the forcing house, shading must be provided and applied when necessary ; air must also be admitted more abundantly, and less fire heat used. Plants which were brought into the forcing house in December will bloom about the middle of March. To keep up a succession, introduce another supply in January and again in February, they may then be had in bloom from March till June.

After the plants are gone out of bloom, harden

them off for a few weeks in a cold house or pit before turning them out of doors. When ready to be taken out, top-dress with rich soil, and plunge all the hardy kinds in an open airy situation, there to remain until required for the next season's work. About September or October let them be re-potted, take off a portion of the old soil, trim the roots, and pot into rich compost as before recommended. The same plants may be forced annually for several years, provided they are carefully attended to, and not allowed to be forced or bloom more than once during the same season.

The French accomplish much in the way of forced Roses and their mode of growing them in small-sized pots for market is very clever. The plants which they use for this purpose are all budded upon the Dog Rose, of all heights, from dwarfs to standards, and the pots in which they are grown are rarely more than seven or eight inches in diameter, and many are grown in five or six-inch pots. The plants have a very unique appearance, and are usually loaded with deliciously fragrant flowers. With few exceptions, the gardens or nurseries where these are grown are small and untidy, and the glass houses of the rudest description, having the most poverty-stricken appearance; nevertheless, the healthy growth of the plants therein show that they have been well tended, and that the growers know full well how to manage them.

One of the largest establishments for forced Roses have ever seen, and which, I believe, is the largest in France, is that of M. Laurent, near Paris. He had when I visited his establishment some years ago three or four acres entirely covered with low span-roof and lean-to houses and pits, specially for forcing Roses and Lilacs, these being the only two plants he cultivated. I am quite afraid to say the number of Roses which are here forced annually, but I should judge there could not have been much less than twenty or thirty thousand.

It was early in February when I saw them, when the houses and pits were all full, and many thousand plants outside ready to take the place of the early forced Roses, as soon as their blooms were over. The blooms are gathered every morning, and sent to Paris for bouquets and decoration, for which there is always a large demand. The plants from this establishment are not sold. M. Laurent is also celebrated for forcing Lilacs. His method of producing white flowers from the purple Lilac is not generally known or practised, nor am I thoroughly in the secret, but it is nevertheless a fact that he depends entirely upon the purple Lilac to produce the finest white blooms throughout the winter.

GROWING ROSES IN POTS FOR THE GREENHOUSE OR FOR EXHIBITION.—The treatment necessary for preparing Roses for greenhouse culture, as well as for exhibition, will be somewhat the same in both instances, though perhaps more care and attention will be required for the latter, both in training as well as after treatment. Commence with young healthy plants worked upon the Manetti stock. Plants established in eight or nine-inch pots, of the most suitable kinds for pot culture, are generally to be had at the nurseries, and these being specially prepared for the purpose a season will be gained by commencing with them. Early in the autumn the plants may be potted into seven, eight, or nine-inch pots, the largest sized plants requiring the latter size. The compost should consist of strong turfy loam and an equal quantity of rotted cow-dung or horse-dung. The Tea-scented and China sorts will require the addition of leaf-mould and a small quantity of sand. The pots must be thoroughly well drained, using two or three inches of potsherds; upon these place a few inches of charcoal and bones, and again a few lumps of the turf from the compost, which, by-the-bye, should not be sifted or broken too fine. If the plants are in small pots, loosen the ball of earth gently without disturbing the roots ; in potting, press the soil firmly round the plant, and afterwards give a gentle watering, but not too copious at first, as the soil is apt to set hard on the surface by so doing. The hardy sorts can be plunged out of doors in an open situation, using tan or coal-ashes as a plunging material. The Tea-scented and other tender kinds must be placed in a frame, where they will be better plunged in tan ; and if this be in sufficient quantity to create a genial warmth, it will greatly assist them, and the roots will soon commence to grow. Towards spring, the hardy worked plants which are plunged out of doors will require to be pruned down rather closely the first year, and this can be done a few

weeks after potting. About the middle of May,
prepare a gentle hotbed, in an open sunny situation,
with manure which has been turned several times
previously, in which case the heat will be retained
for a much longer period ; upon this, place all the
Tea-scented or other Roses which it is desired to
grow on as rapidly as possible ; let them be plunged
to the rim of the pot in sawdust or tan. Here with
a gentle bottom heat and free access of air upon all
sides, they will make rapid and robust growth.
Let all buds be taken off as they appear. Give a
supply of manure water once a week. In the
course of three or four weeks the heat of the
hotbed will be partially exhausted, when it should
be turned over, adding some fresh manure to renew
the heat ; the plants are then to be replaced and
plunged as before. About the end of October
remove them into the greenhouse or frame. The
hardy sorts can be plunged out of doors and
protected during severe weather. Early in
February the plants will require re-potting ; those
which have been growing in seven or eight-inch
should be shifted into nine-inch, and those from
nine-inch into ten-inch pots.

As soon as the potting is finished, let the plants
be pruned. The Tea-scented and China must not
be cut in too close. Select the best shoot near the
centre to train for the leading stem, and shorten it
about one-third ; prune the other shoots one half or
three parts their length ; these should be carefully
tied up, which is most easily done by placing wire
round the pot, underneath the rim. Let the shoots

be drawn as near to the edges of the pot as can safely be done without breaking them, then make fast with small pieces of bast matting to the wire. If it is desired to grow the plants for exhibition, they must be carefully watched, and the shoots tied out as they advance in growth. The best form is that of a pyramid. To keep the plants equally balanced on all sides, a little skilful training will be requisite. Any gross shoots which appear should be stopped; the weak ones consequently will be encouraged. The second year the plants will be better if grown in a low house where they can be placed near to the glass, and receive an abundance of air at all favourable seasons. To obtain plants of larger size suitable for exhibition, three years must elapse before they can be brought into proper form and size.

Rose Conservatories.—Nothing can possibly be more delightful and beautiful than a large conservatory filled entirely with the choicest kinds of Tea-scented, Noisette, and China Roses. The temperature is delightful and most enjoyable at all seasons, but, perhaps, more so in the spring of the year, when cold, piercing, easterly winds prevail. Our conservatories thus possessing the genial temperature of Italy or the south of France, the frosts of winter cannot harm our Roses, neither can smoke nor dust stifle them; the whole being under easy control, can be tended at our pleasure. The green-fly, the greatest pest to Roses out of doors, is here easily destroyed; a few pounds of tobacco paper will bring a whole colony to grief in a very short time. These are only a few of the advantages derived from growing the delicate kinds of Roses under glass, and it is almost needless to attempt to picture to the Rose amateur the delightful and pleasurable occupation which a Rose conservatory affords at all seasons of the year, for it can more easily be imagined than described.

I had long contemplated the idea, as well as the necessity, of having conservatories in which to plant out all tender kinds of Roses, but not until the destruction occasioned by the severe winter of 1860-61, was I fully determined to carry out this object. During that season nearly every Tea-scented, China, and Noisette Rose not under glass was totally killed, this disaster being attributable as much, perhaps, to the cold, wet, sunless summer preceding, as the the severity of the winter. I then determined to erect a large conservatory, wherein to plant out all Tea-scented, China, and Noisette Roses. This conservatory is 140 feet in length, 24 feet in width, and has a well-prepared bed, 11 feet wide, made the entire length of the house, with $3\frac{1}{2}$ feet walks passing round, upon either side of which are tan pits, 3 feet wide, for growing specimen plants in pots. The centre bed is divided into seven rows, the centre row being planted with Maréchal Niel, Lamarque, Climbing Devoniensis, Reine Marie Henriette, Cheshunt Hybrid, Gloire de Dijon, Celine Forestier, William Allen Richardson, Belle Lyonnaise, &c. ; these are trained upon iron-wire pillars to the top of the house, which by-the-bye, is 16 feet in height. The other rows are planted with

standard and dwarf-standard Tea-scented Roses,
from 4 feet graduating to 1 foot; the whole is
surrounded by a neat garden-tile edging.

PROPERTIES OF A GOOD ROSE.—The first and most
essential point to constitute a good Rose, is that the
variety be hardy, and of a healthy and moderately
robust habit, combining ample foliage, for, be its
bloom ever so good, if it refuses to grow under
proper treatment it is almost worthless. Next to
these are fine form, fullness, large size, good
substance, fragrance, freedom to bloom, and decided
and distinct colour. The form of the flower,
whether it be cupped, globular, or expanded, should
be symmetrical; the petals even and regularly
placed, smooth and free from all indentures, full but
not crowded, the outer row being broad and closely
folded to enable the flower to stand firm for several
days; they should be thick and leathery in texture,
and not (as we too frequently see them) thin and
flimsy, and either faded or fallen to pieces after an
hour's sun. The colour, whatever it is, should be
decided and lasting, and not changing to a dull
cloudy or objectionable shade. The flower stem
should be stout to hold the bloom partly erect, so
that it may be seen without the necessity of applying
the hand. Every Rose should be fragrant, and the
more highly so the better. Whether summer-
blooming only or perpetual, it should be free to
flower, in the former case yielding abundance of
blooms throughout June and July, and in the latter
from June till November, allowing for an occasional
rest for each period of flowering. A perpetual

Rose to justify its name should always produce blooms at the end of each shoot. As examples of finely formed and perfect Roses the following may be instanced :—Cupped : Baroness Rothschild. Globular : Alfred Colomb, Pierre Notting. Expanded : Souvenir de la Malmaison. Compact or Imbricated : A. K. Williams, Mdlle. Marie Cointet.

There is another class of Roses which must not be overlooked, nearly if not quite as useful as the above, and to some much more so. These are hardy, free-blooming, attractive varieties for garden decoration, many of which have not a single property to recommend them as show flowers, but which for grouping and general effect in the flower garden are most beautiful and attractive. The properties most to be desired in these are freedom and uniformity of growth, profusion of bloom, and brilliancy combined with durability of colour.

EXHIBITING AND CUTTING ROSES FOR SHOW.— The method of showing now most generally adopted is in trusses, either singly or in groups of three ; in the latter case each truss is placed in a separate tube, so as to exhibit as small as possible the habit and characteristic properties of the variety. This is, undoubtedly, the best and most natural way of showing blooms.

The blooms are usually shown in boxes, painted green, which should all be of uniform size. The dimensions required by the Horticultural Society are 6 inches in height at back, 4 inches in front, and 18 inches in width, and any convenient length, say from 3 to 4 feet. The lids are made so that they can be taken off when the flowers are staged for exhibition. The boxes are filled with green moss, into which zinc tubes holding water are inserted for the reception of blooms. The tubes may be from 3 to $3\frac{1}{2}$ inches deep, and about $\frac{3}{4}$ inch wide. When three trusses of each variety are to be exhibited, the tubes are placed in a triangular form, each to hold one stem.

When cutting blooms, choose, if possible, the early part of the morning, before the dew is off. Blooms gathered at this time will continue fresh throughout the day, but if cut when the sun is upon them, many of the thin-petaled varieties will fade in a few hours. When they cannot be gathered in the morning, let it be done late in the evening, putting the stems into water immediately. In gathering and selecting the blooms, some little practice and skill, as well as an acquaintance with the varieties, will be necessary to enable the exhibitor to form a correct judgment as to the precise stage in which a flower should be when cut, so as to show the real character of the variety, and to be preserved perfect throughout the day of the show. If it be necessary to gather the flowers the morning before the day of the show, many of the thin-petaled varieties must not be more than half expanded; the stiff and thick-petaled kinds may be nearly fully so. In very hot weather it will not be safe to depend upon any blooms which have been fully expanded and exposed to the sun for even a few hours. In the autumn or in cool weather this is not so important. If the blooms can be gathered upon the morning of the show, many of the flowers may be fully, and others three parts expanded. From four to five inches of the stem should be cut with the bloom, and all, or nearly all, the foliage allowed to remain. In arranging the blooms, some taste will be necessary; the largest blooms should be placed in the back row, and the smallest brought to the front. The colours should contrast as much as possible, for on this the general effect of the stand will much depend. The blooms should always present a nice fresh appearance, and to keep them so a little water should be occasionally sprinkled upon the foliage; they require also to be kept in as cool and shady a place as possible until the time for staging.

LABELS.—Every Rose tree should be labelled; not only does a knowledge of its name add to the interest of the flower, but it is also a guide at pruning time, for a successful pruner will invariably look to the name of his Rose before commencing operations. Knowing this, he will call to mind the habit of the variety, and prune accordingly. The best kind we can recommend is the Acme Label; nothing can be more desirable in the way of a label. They are neat, clear, and simple, and practically everlasting, the letters being raised in hard rolled zinc; they can be obtained from the manufacturer, J. Pinches, 27, Oxenden Street, London, S.W.

PART II.

A Choice Selection of the most esteemed Varieties of Roses
in cultivation, with Short Descriptions and Notes
on their Origin.

IN this collection, I have selected and described
such varieties of Roses as are most worthy of
cultivation, omitting all second rate, or doubtful
sorts. There may possibly be some omissions of a
few good old varieties, but the selection will, I think,
be found of ample service. The new Roses of quite
recent introduction I have purposely omitted, simply
through not having proved them sufficiently to be
enabled to give a reliable opinion of their merits.
It requires at least one season to test the properties
of a new Rose, and those who jump at hasty con-
clusions upon the quality of this or that flower, are
often misled, and by so doing mislead others. All
I have described are from my own personal observa-
tion, and may be depended upon as being reliable.

The following abbreviations are used to describe the habit of
growth :—*vig., vigorous ; rob., robust ; mod., moderate.*

SUMMER ROSES.

FLOWERING IN MAY, JUNE, AND JULY.

THE PROVENCE OR CABBAGE ROSE.
(*Rosa centifolia.*)

The Old Provence or Cabbage Rose is supposed
to have been introduced in 1596. All the varieties
are perfectly hardy and deliciously fragrant, mostly

of moderate or dwarf habit of growth, requiring
rich soil and close pruning. They thrive best when
grown upon their own roots, and a bed of the Old
Cabbage Rose should be in every Rosarium. The
De Meaux, or Pompon, is a most interesting and
beautiful little Rose ; for a small bed, or for an
edging to larger beds, nothing can be better or more
beautiful. Few of the kinds are suitable for tall
standards ; they will, however, thrive well upon half
and dwarf standards.

Cabbage Provence, or *Old Cabbage Rose :* flowers rose colour, the
outer petals changing to paler rose, form globular, very large and
full, highly fragrant ; *mod.*

Cristata, or *Crested* (Vibert, 1827): bright rose colour, large and
full, with crested calyx ; *mod.*

De Meaux, or *Pompon* (O. Taunton, 1825): flowers rosy pink
and lilac, very small and compact habit, quite dwarf ; a most
beautiful little Rose ; *mod.*

Spong : pale rose, flowers small ; a pretty free-flowering Rose,
and useful for edging or for a small bed ; *mod.*

Unique, or *White Provence* (Grimwood, 1777): flowers paper-
white, perhaps the purest white Rose grown, form cupped, moderate
size and full, though the petals are not very evenly disposed, habit
moderate ; a most beautiful Rose ; *mod.*

THE MOSS ROSE.

(*Rosa centifolia muscosa.*)

The original or Old Moss Rose is supposed to
have been introduced from Holland in 1596, but as
to its origin no satisfactory account has ever been
given. It is, however, generally believed to be a
sport from the Old Provence, and from the close
resemblance which the flowers bear to each other
(with the addition of the mossy buds of the former),

this is doubtless correct. Although several hundred varieties of the Moss Rose have been raised since the introduction of the original, none are superior, if equal to it, in point of beauty or fragrance ; its long handsome buds covered with tufts of the most beautiful mossy excrescence make it interesting and beautiful in all stages. The Crested Moss Rose, or, as it is sometimes called, Crested Provence, is most peculiar and beautiful ; the beauty of its bud alone should claim a place for it in every garden. The Moss Roses are mostly of delicate growth, though some are vigorous and robust in habit, and form good standards, but as a rule they all succeed best when grown upon low stocks, or otherwise upon their own roots; the latter mode is best suited to the Old Moss, and no garden wherever Roses are grown should be without a bed or two of this old favourite. They require rather high cultivation and close pruning, and generally speaking rather better treat-ment than ordinary kinds. In wet or cold damp soils they do not thrive, a warm dry soil being required, and this well supplied annually with manure. If at any time they appear to decline in health, they should be taken up and replanted into fresh loamy soil, and cut hard back.

Alice Leroy (Trouillard, 1842): rosy pink, good mossy buds, free blooming, good habit ; *mod.*

Baronne de Wassenaer (Verdier, 1854) : deep rose, very large, double and showy ; *vig.*

Celina (Robert, 1855) : velvety purple and crimson, very beau-tiful in bud, but delicate and weak-growing ; *mod.*

Colonel Robert le Fort (E. Verdier, 1884) : reddish purple, flower large, very double and very fragrant ; *mod.*

Common, or *Old:* pale rose, globular, very large and excellent ; *mod*.

Comtesse du Murinais (Vibert, 1843) : generally white, some- times flesh ; a distinct robust-growing kind ; *rob*.

Crested (Vibert, 1827): pale rosy pink, buds beautifully crested ; very handsome and distinct ; *mod*.

Gloire des Mousseuses (Laffay, 1852) : pale rose, outer petals whitish ; most distinct and beautiful Moss Rose ; *vig*.

Gracilis, or *Prolific* (Shailler, 1796) : deep pink, globular, large, full, and of good shape ; an excellent kind ; *vig*.

John Cranston (E. Verdier, 1861) : shaded violet-crimson, colour rich and good ; *vig*.

Julie de Mersant : rose, pretty moss buds ; *vig*.

Laure (Laffay, 1845) : deep brilliant rose, a beautiful round handsome bud ; one of the best Moss Roses grown ; *vig*.

Little Gem (W. Paul & Son, 1880) : a miniature Moss Rose ; it forms compact bushes, densely covered with small double crimson flowers, beautifully mossed, distinct ; *vig*.

Luxembourg : purplish crimson ; a good pillar Rose ; *vig*.

Marie de Blois (Moreau-Robert, 1852) : bright rose, large and full; an excellent Rose, with well-mossed and handsome buds; *mod*.

Princess Alice (Paul, 1853): blush, pink centre, good habit, buds well mossed ; *mod*.

White Bath (Salter, 1810) : paper-white, beautiful, large and full ; the best white Moss Rose ; *vig*.

THE FRENCH ROSE.
(*Rosa Gallica.*)

The French Rose, or Rosa Gallica, is supposed to have been introduced into England about the six- teenth century, and until the introduction of the Perpetual-blooming varieties was the favourite Rose of our English gardens. Upwards of one thousand varieties of this family alone have been cultivated ; such, however, has been the increase of Perpetual Roses during the last twenty years, that the Gallica and other summer-blooming Roses (excepting the very choicest kinds) have long been thrown out of cultivation. There are, however, many varieties of this family, possessing a brilliancy and richness of colour, together with flowers of perfect form and chaste outline combined with delicious fragrance, which for Garden Roses cannot be dispensed with. They are all perfectly hardy, and will grow in any ordinary garden soil, though improved by, and well deserving of liberal cultivation. They are all suitable for growing as standards or dwarf bushes, and no Roses bloom more abundantly, nor produce a finer show throughout June and July. Moderate close pruning is necessary, the heads being kept well thinned out of the small and weak wood.

Belle des Jardins (Guillot fils, 1872) : violet-red, striped pure white, flowers medium size, full ; *mod*.

Blanchfleur (Vibert, 1846) : white, slightly tinted with flesh colour ; *mod*.

Boula de Nanteuil : rich crimson and purple, very large and full ; *rob*.

Commandante Beaurepaire (Moreau-Robert, 1875) : bright rose colour, striped purple and violet, mottled with white, large and full ; *rob*.

D'Aguesseau : crimson, shaded with purple, large and full ; *mod*.

Duchess of Buccleuch : dark rose colour, margin blush, beautiful ; *vig*.

Kean, or *Shakespeare* : rich velvety purple, centre scarlet ; *vig*.

La Tour d'Auvergne : bright rose, slightly mottled, and finely shaped ; *vig*.

Œillet Flamand (Vibert, 1845) : rose colour, striped with white and red ; *mod*.

Œillet Parfait (Foulard, 1841) : pure white, striped with rosy crimson, very double, beautiful ; one of the best striped Roses ; *mod*.

Old : velvety crimson, rich colour, beautiful flowers, large and finely shaped ; *rob.*

Perle des Panachées : white, finely striped with rose, pretty and distinct ; *mod.*

Village Maid : white and crimson striped, pretty, but only semi-double ; *mod.*

THE HYBRID CHINA ROSE.
(*Rosa indica hybrida*).

The Hybrid China Roses are hybrids between the French and the Provence, crossed with the China and Noisette Roses. They are most robust growers, with ample foliage and showy flowers. Their vigorous growth and hardy constitution make them the most desirable of all for forming large handsome pillar Roses ; and certainly nothing can be more beautiful than Blairii No. 2, Chénédolé, Fulgens, Leopold de Bauffremont, Madame Plantier, Magna Rosea, &c., when grown six to eight feet in height, and trained to rough poles ; in this form they are usually one mass of flower from bottom to top. They are also adapted for standards, especially where tall standards are required, and the most vigorous sorts may be trained to form umbrella-shaped heads. In pruning, do not shorten the strong shoots upon the vigorous growers too close ; thin out the heads, and prune the strong shoots down to 18 inches or 2 feet, and the weak ones to 9 or 12 inches.

Blairii No. 2 (Blair, 1845) : rosy blush, fine large petals, very handsome foliage ; fine pillar or weeping Rose ; *vig.*

Brennus (Laffay, 1830) : deep carmine ; a handsome old variety, which forms a noble standard or pillar ; *vig.*

Chenedolé (Thierry): brilliant glowing crimson, very showy, and a superb variety ; forms a noble standard or pillar Rose ; *vig.*

Comtesse de Lacepede : silvery blush, very distinct and beautiful ; *vig.*

Double Margined Hip : creamy white, beautifully edged with pink : a very pretty Rose ; *vig.*

Fulgens (Malton) : bright scarlet-crimson, colour exquisite ; a fine old Rose, very showy, and an exquisite pillar or weeping Rose ; *vig.*

Leopold de Bauffremont : fresh rosy pink, shape perfect ; a beautiful, compact, free-blooming, and fine pillar Rose ; *vig.*

Madame Plantier (Plantier, 1835) : pure white ; an abundant bloomer, and a good pillar Rose ; *vig.*

Madame Rivière (Eug. Verdier fils, 1874) : very beautiful and delicate bright rose, very large, full, and well formed ; *vig.*

Magna Rosea : light blush, tinted with pink, very large and showy ; *vig.*

THE HYBRID BOURBON ROSE.

(*Rosa Bourbonica hybrida.*)

These are hybrids between the Gallica and Provence, and the Bourbon Roses ; the foliage, which is large, handsome, and shining, partakes much of the latter kind, the flowers resembling the Hybrid Chinas. They are nearly all of vigorous or robust growth, forming handsome standards, and some make good pillar Roses. A few are good show Roses, in fact, Charles Lawson, Coupe d'Hebe, and Paul Ricaut, are equal to any in cultivation.

Catherine Bonnard (E. Verdier, 1871) : cerise-crimson flowers moderate size, full, and well formed ; a good pillar Rose ; *vig.*

Charles Lawson (Lawson, 1853) : bright rose shaded, very large and double ; a fine Rose ; *vig.*

Coupe d'Hebe (Laffay, 1840) : delicate rosy flesh, large and double ; one of the most beautiful of summer Roses ; *rob.*

Juno (Laffay, 1847) : pale rose, globular, very large and full ; a handsome Rose, and good for a pillar ; *vig.*

Madame Isaac Pereire (Margottin fils, 1880) : beautiful vivid carmine, full, of immense size, perfect imbricated form, blooming all the season, growth very vigorous ; a first-class variety ; *vig.*

Madame Jeanne Joubert (Margottin, 1877) : fine carmine, large and imbricated, blooming late in the autumn ; a good garden Rose ; *mod.*

Paul Perras : pale rose, very large and handsome ; makes a fine standard or pillar Rose ; *vig.*

Paul Ricaut (Portemer, 1845) : brilliant carmine, very large, most exquisitely formed, and very beautiful ; *vig.*

Souvenir de Mons. Faivre (Levet, 1879) : fine scarlet-red, with slaty reflex, very large, full, and well formed ; *vig.*

Vivid (W. Paul & Son, 1853) : vivid crimson, showy ; a fine pillar or climbing Rose ; *vig.*

THE ALBA OR WHITE ROSE.

(*Rosa alba*.)

The Alba Roses are distinguished by their light glossy foliage, and white, blush, or delicately pink flowers. They are a very distinct group, of moderate growth, with flowers of moderate size. They are all abundant bloomers, and form good standards, half-standards, or dwarf bushes. They require close pruning.

Belle de Segur : soft rosy flesh colour, with blush edges, medium size, and full ; *mod.*

Celestial, or *Maiden's Blush :* flesh colour, beautifully tinted with the most delicate pink ; *mod.*

Félicité Parmentier : blush, with pink centre, large and full ; *mod.*

Madame Legras : creamy white, large and full, free bloomer ; *mod.*

THE DAMASK ROSE.
(*Rosa Damascena.*)

The introduction of the Damask Rose dates as far back as 1573, when, as is supposed, it was introduced from Syria. The leaves are pubescent and of pale green colour, by which the group is readily distinguished. They are all deliciously fragrant ; this, and the interest attached to the early introduction of the species, will always obtain admirers of the Damask Rose. They are mostly of moderate growth, and require rather close pruning and rich soil.

La Ville de Bruxelles (Vibert, 1836) : bright glossy rose, full and very handsome ; a robust-growing Rose ; makes a good pillar or standard ; *rob.*

Leda, or *Painted Damask :* blush, edged with pink, pretty and distinct ; *mod.*

Madame Hardy (Hardy, 1832): pure white, large and full ; an excellent old white Rose, of moderate though good habit ; *mod.*

Madame Stoltz : pale lemon, nicely formed, distinct and pretty ; *vig.*

Madame Zoutman : the palest flesh, often white, shape perfect ; the most beautiful of all white Roses ; *mod.*

York and Lancaster : red and white, striped, large and full; *vig.*

THE AUSTRIAN BRIAR.
(*Rosa lutea.*)

The Austrian Briar was introduced from the South of Europe in 1596. The different varieties form a beautiful and distinct group, containing the deepest and purest yellow Roses in cultivation—the Persian Yellow especially ; this was introduced from Persia in 1838.   Harrisonii is also a beautiful free-flowering Rose.   These Roses, after the first or second year, require little or no pruning ; let the heads be kept well thinned, and merely the ends taken off the long shoots.   They are, perhaps, more impatient of a smoky atmosphere than any other Roses, and to grow them successfully they must have pure air and a warm dry soil.

Austrian Yellow : flowers single, colour bright yellow ; succeeds best grown upon its own roots ; *mod.*

Austrian Copper : flowers reddish copper, single, striking and beautiful ; succeeds best upon its own roots : *mod.*

Harrisonii (Harrison, 1830) : fine golden yellow, semi-double, flowers of moderate size ; a very free grower, and a most abundant bloomer ; forms a good weeping or pillar Rose ; *rob.*

Persian Yellow (Willcock, 1838) : the deepest golden yellow, flowers large and full ; the finest of all double yellow Roses, hardy and free growing ; *rob.*

THE   SWEET   BRIAR.

(*Rosa rubiginosa*).

So delicious is the scent of the Sweet Briar that no Rose garden, nor in fact, any other garden of flowers should be without a bush or two, or a hedge of this native plant.   Many varieties have been raised, producing double flowers, all of which are more or less fragrant, but none whose leaves possess the delicious perfume of the common kind.   I consider but one variety worthy of cultivation for its flower alone, which is the Double Scarlet.

Double Scarlet : bright rosy crimson, flowers small, perfectly double and deliciously fragrant ; very pretty and free flowering, habit of growth moderate.

THE SCOTCH ROSE.
(*Rosa spinosissima.*)

The Scotch Rose is a native of the north of England and Scotland. Many interesting and pretty varieties have been raised, but as none of them possess the properties of a florist's flower, they have been thought but little of; nevertheless, they are very pretty and sweet scented, and blooming so early in spring, before any other Roses, are desirable and well worthy of cultivation. They form pretty hedges in the Rosarium, and may also be planted with good effect upon sloping banks or in rough situations. They are so thoroughly hardy that they will grow in the poorest soil. The following are a few of the best varieties:—

Argo : blush.
Arthur's Seat : pale blush.
Flora : deep rose.
Loch Ness : pale rose.
Pluto : lilac-rose.

Snowball : white.
Townsend : blush.
Yellow : straw, often only creamy white.

CLIMBING ROSES.

THE AYRSHIRE ROSE.
(*Rosa arvensis.*)

The Ayrshire Rose, a native of Britain, is one of the hardiest and most vigorous of Roses. From their rampant and quick growth, they are the most suitable for covering rough banks, archways, arbours, festoons, &c.; they also form beautiful objects when grown as weeping Roses, being budded upon tall standard Briars, eight to nine feet in height. No pruning (further than reducing their size when overgrown) is necessary.

Bennett's Seedling (Bennett, 1840): pure white, small flowers, blooms in immense large clusters; beautiful as climbing or weeping Rose; *vig.*

Dundee Rambler (Martin): white, tinged with pink, very vigorous; *vig.*

Myrrh-scented: white, tinged with pink, pretty, and very fragrant; *vig.*

Queen of the Belgians: creamy white, thick petals, large and double; *vig.*

Ruga: pale flesh, very fragrant and beautiful, double, free blooming; *vig.*

Splendens: white tinged with pink, very pretty; *vig.*

Thoresbyana (Bennett, 1840): *see Bennett's Seedling.*

HYBRID OF AYRSHIRE.

Madame Viviand-Morel (Schwartz, 1883): carmine-rose colour, tinted with cherry-red, reverse of the petals violet-white, of medium size, blooming in clusters, climbing habit; a seedling from *Cheshunt Hybrid*, and of an Ayrshire; *vig.*

THE MULTIFLORA ROSE.
(*Rosa multiflora.*)

The Multiflora Rose was introduced from China in 1804. From the original type some twenty or thirty varieties have sprung; out of these can be selected three excellent and distinct Roses, being all that are desirable from this group.

De La Griffera: deep rose colour, changing to blush, double; *vig.*

Laura Davoust: pink and lilac blush, blooms in immense large clusters; the most beautiful of all climbing Roses; *vig.*

Russelliana: rose colour, changing to lilac, flowers of medium size; a distinct and pretty Rose; *vig.*

THE EVERGREEN ROSE.
(*Rosa sempervirens.*)

The Evergreen Roses, correctly speaking, are only sub-evergreen ; although during a mild winter they often retain their foliage the greater part of the season. They are well furnished with ample foliage of dark green colour, and of most vigorous growth ; their flowers are small, produced in corymbs, and mostly fragrant. These Roses are natives of Italy.

Donna Maria : pure white, small and double ; *vig.*

Félicité Perpetue (Jacques, 1828) : creamy white, beautiful ; a good climbing Rose ; *vig.*

Rampant : pure white, double ; *vig.*

THE BOURSAULT ROSE.
(*Rosa alpina.*)

The Boursault Roses are a very distinct group, having very smooth reddish wood, quite free from thorns ; they are vigorous growers, making good climbing or pillar Roses. The original Rosa alpina, a single red Rose, is a native of the Alps, the name Boursault having been given to it by a French amateur of that name, who raised the first double variety, which is still in cultivation under the name of the Old or Red Boursault.

Amadis, or *Crimson* (Laffay, 1829) : brilliant purplish crimson, changing to purplish lilac ; a showy semi-double Rose, and one of the best ; *vig.*

Gracilis (Shailler, 1796) : bright rosy pink, large and full, superb ; *vig.*

Inermis (Lacharme, 1850) : rosy pink, changing to pale rose, flowers large and double ; a distinct and good kind ; *vig.*

Weeping Boursault : flowers blush colour, small and pretty, blooming most abundantly, habit quite pendulous ; a distinct and pretty Rose ; *vig.*

THE BANKSIAN ROSE.
(*Rosa Banksiæ*).

The White Banksian was introduced from China in 1807, and named in honour of Lady Banks. The Yellow Banksian Rose was introduced in 1827. They are rather tender sub-evergreen Roses, very vigorous in growth, with small and beautiful shining leaves. Their time of flowering is May; owing to this, and a somewhat tender habit, they can only be grown successfully against a south wall. The time to prune them is just after they have flowered, say in June; all gross shoots should be taken out, retaining all the small twiggy branches, for it is upon the points of these that the flowers are produced. A warm dry soil suits them best.

Alba, or *White* (1807): white, flowers small and very double, produced in large clusters, deliciously fragrant, having somewhat of the violet scent; *rig.*

Fortuniana (1850): white, large and very sweet. Introduced from China, by Mr. Fortune, in 1850; *rig.*

Lutea, or *Yellow* (1827): bright yellow, small, double and very pretty; flowers produced in clusters, in great abundance; *rig.*

Besides the above groups of climbing Roses, there are the hybrid climbing, two varieties only of which may be considered worthy of culture, viz., The Garland, white and pale lilac, and Madame d'Arblay, a pure white Rose of the most vigorous growth. Sir John Sebright, a hybrid Musk Rose, is also worthy of culture; flowers light crimson, small but showy. The Prairie Roses (Rosa rubifolia), of which there are some twenty varieties, are only of secondary merit; Queen of the Prairies is perhaps the best, and the only one at all worthy of notice.

AUTUMNAL ROSES.

THE PERPETUAL MOSS ROSE.
(*Rosa centifolia.*)

It is only within the last few years that any really fine perpetual Moss Roses have been raised; we have, however, now a few first-rate varieties in this class, possessing the properties of the Moss Rose, with the desirable addition of blooming in the autumn. Many of the varieties are somewhat difficult to propagate, and only the most vigorous do well upon the Dog Rose. I find, however, that all of them grow freely upon the Manetti stock, especially the moderate growers. They require rich soil and close pruning.

Alfred de Dalmas (Laffay, 1855): pink, flowers small; *rob.*

Blanche Moreau (Moreau-Robert, 1880): pure white, large, full, and of fine form, well furnished with deep green moss; one of the best; *vig.*

Eugénie Guinoisseau (Guinoisseau, 1864): cherry-red, large and full; *mod.*

Eugène de Savoie (Moreau-Robert, 1861): bright red, large and full; *vig.*

James Veitch (E. Verdier, 1864): deep violet, shaded red, large and double; one of the best; *vig.*

Madame Edouard Ory (Moreau-Robert, 1854): reddish crimson, globular, very large; a good Rose; *mod.*

Madame Moreau (Moreau-Robert, 1872): rose, edged with white, large, full and expanded; *vig.*

Madame William Paul (Moreau-Robert, 1869): bright rose, large and full, finely formed; a good free-blooming Rose; *vig.*

Mousseline (Moreau-Robert, 1881): rosy white, changing to pure white, large, globular; *vig.*

Perpetual White Moss (Laffay): white, blooming in clusters, very mossy ; *vig.*

Salet (Lacharme, 1854): bright rose, changing into light rose, large, full, and thoroughly perpetual ; *vig.*

Soupert et Notting (Pernet, 1875), bright rose, large, globular, very full ; one of the best ; *mod.*

Souvenir de Pierre Vibert (Moreau-Robert, 1867): dark red, shaded carmine and violet, large, full, and free blooming ; *vig.*

THE MICROPHYLLA ROSE.

(*Rosa microphylla.*)

The most important of the Microphylla Roses are the Rugosa, introduced some years ago from Japan. R. alba and R. rubra are splendid shrubs for borders. The flowers are succeeded by hips of large size, which are very attractive in the autumn.

Ma Surprise (Guillot, 1872): white, centre rosy peach, large, full, and sweetly scented ; *mod.*

Rugosa alba: white, large size, five petals, very fragrant ; a beautiful single Rose ; *mod.*

Rugosa rubra: deep rose, tinged with violet; the leaflets are nine in number, of dark colour, and very tough and durable ; *mod.*

Rugosa rubra flore pleno (*syn.* Himalayensis) : crimson, large, full and double ; *mod.*

THE DAMASK PERPETUAL ROSE.

The Damask Perpetual Roses have many claims for admiration ; their rich perfume is delicious, and their compact habit of growth, with a profusion of bloom throughout the summer and autumn, renders them most desirable Roses for bedding or grouping. Crimson Superb or Mogador is the best—a large bed of this should be grown by everyone ; it succeeds admirably upon the **Manetti** stock, but it does not grow freely upon the **Briar**. All the moderate growers in this class require close pruning, and to grow them successfully they must have rich soil annually replenished with manure.

Céliné Dubois (1850): white, slightly tinged with rose ; a sport from *Crimson (Rose du Roi)*; *mod.*

Crimson (Rose du Roi) (Souchet, 1819): brilliant crimson, large and full, deliciously fragrant ; *mod.*

Madame Knorr (Verdier, 1865): pale rose, medium, full, sweet-scented ; *mod.*

THE PERPETUAL SCOTCH ROSE.
(*Rosa spinosissima.*)

Stanwell Perpetual : this is the only variety of this group worthy of culture. The flowers are rosy blush, often tinted with pink, large and tolerably full. It is a free autumnal bloomer and deliciously fragrant ; a beautiful and distinct Rose ; *mod.*

THE MACARTNEY ROSE.
(*Rosa bracteata.*)

The old single Macartney Rose is a native of China, and was introduced in 1795. There are only two or three varieties worth growing. They are all somewhat tender, requiring protection during winter ; they succeed best when trained upon a wall.

Alba odorata (Levet, 1876) : flowers yellowish white, large and full; a good climber, and should be trained against a south wall ; *vig.*

Berberifolia Hardii : bright yellow, with chocolate centre ; flowers single, somewhat resembling the Cistus; *mod.*

Marie Leonida : white, centre blush, flowers large and double ; a very distinct Rose, and very pretty; *vig.*

THE MUSK ROSE.
(*Rosa Muscata.*)

One of the oldest family of Roses, somewhat resembling the Noisette Roses in habit, but having a peculiar musk-like scent. They flower freely through the autumn, but should have a sheltered situation, and protection during winter.

Fringed: white, petals serrated; cupped; *vig.*

Princesse de Nassau: cream, changing to pure white flowers, double and highly scented; *vig.*

Rivers': pink, shaded with buff; *vig.*

THE POLYANTHA ROSE.
(*Rosa Polyantha.*)

Anne Marie de Montravel (Veuve Rambaux, 1881): pure white, small, full and imbricated; flowers produced in clusters and in extraordinary quantities; *vig.*

Cécile Brunner (Veuve Ducher, 1881): bright rose, yellowish in centre, very sweet; *vig.*

Jeanne Drivon (Schwartz, 1884): white, edged and shaded with pink, very double, distinct; *mod.*

Mignonette (Guillot, 1882): soft rose changing to white; small and pretty, blooming in clusters; *mod.*

Perle d'Or (Dubreuil, 1884): nankeen-yellow, with orange centre; small and full, very beautiful; flowers very numerous and of good shape; *mod.*

Paquerette (Guillot, 1876): small and double, pure white, produced in panicles; *mod.*

Princesse Wilhelmine des Pays Bas (Soupert et Notting, 1886): pure white, imbricated, very sweet; *mod.*

THE HYBRID PERPETUAL ROSE.

These invaluable Roses have been obtained by crossing the Hybrid China with the Bourbon, China and Tea-scented Roses, thereby producing a hardy race flowering throughout the summer and autumn.

The Rose has perhaps undergone greater improvement within the last twenty years than it ever previously attained, and this improvement may be attributed in a great measure to the introduction of the class now under consideration, having opened a field for hybridising and raising seedlings to an almost endless extent. A better foundation to work upon there could not possibly have been, for certainly they are the most desirable of all Roses.

In this section we have varieties suited to any soil, climate, or situation, and also adapted to a variety of purposes. Although vigorous and hardy, nevertheless some discretion must be exercised in selecting for cold damp situations, for many Roses which in the south of England are beautiful, will scarcely open their flowers in the north.

Nearly all the Hybrid Perpetuals, excepting those described as of moderate habit, make good standards, but it will be well in every instance, when making selections, to bear in mind that the vigorous and robust make the best standards, and the moderate growers should be grown as dwarf bushes or dwarf standards only.

There are many fine varieties in this class which are admirably adapted for grouping in masses. The following are especially fine: La France, General Jacqueminot, Baroness Rothschild, Senateur Vaisse, &c. The vigorous growers make handsome pillar Roses; for this purpose they are best budded upon

the Manetti stock. So overwhelmed are we with
Roses of this class that the great difficulty now is
to make a choice selection, which, considering the
large number of varieties, may naturally be sup-
posed to be not a very easy task. I beg, however,
to submit the following, which I think will be found
to contain all the best sorts which have been intro-
duced up to the present time :—

Abel Carrière (E. Verdier, 1875): dark velvety crimson, colour
of *Prince Camille de Rohan*; large and well formed, good shape,
and one of the best dark Roses; *vig.*

Abel Grand (Damaizin, 1865): clear silvery pink, flowers large,
full, and well formed; a good Rose, and very sweet: *vig.*

Alexandrine Bachmeteff (Margottin, 1853): light cherry-red,
large and full; *vig.*

Alexander Dupont (Liabaud, 1883): purple velvety red, shaded
crimson; very large; *vig.*

Alfred Colomb (Lacharme, 1865): brilliant carmine-crimson,
flowers very large, full, and globular; superb; *vig.*

Alfred de Rougemont (Lacharme, 1863): purplish crimson,
shaded fiery red, large and full: *vig.*

Alfred K. Williams (Schwartz, 1877): fine carmine-red, large,
full, and imbricated; one of the most beautiful and perfect; *vig.*

Alice Dureau (Vigneron, 1867): rosy lilac, centre deep red
rose, flowers very full, globular: very fine and sweet-scented; *vig.*

Alphonse Soupert (Lacharme, 1884): pure vivid rose, the flower
in the way of *La Reine*: growth very vigorous, in the way of
Jules Margottin: first class for forcing; *vig.*

American Beauty (Bancroft, 1885): bright rosy carmine, large
and full, sweetly scented; a good Rose: *vig.*

André Gill (Barrault, 1883): bright carmine-red, large, full,
and well formed, globular; *vig.*

Anna Alexieff (Margottin, 1858): pretty rose colour, large, full,
and of good habit; flowers freely; *vig.*

Annie Laxton (Laxton, 1871): deep rose, beautifully shaded
with cherry-crimson; very early; *mod.*

Annie Wood (E. Verdier, 1866): brilliant crimson-scarlet, flowers double and perfectly imbricated; a first-rate Rose; *vig.*

Antoine Ducher (Ducher, 1866): very rich crimson-rose, large smooth thick petals, flowers large, full, deep, and well formed; *rob.*

Auguste Neumann (E. Verdier, 1869: rich velvety crimson and violet-purple, very dark, and colour stands well, full and of good size; a good Rose; *mod.*

Auguste Rigotard (Schwartz, 1871): clear brilliant crimson, petals large, even, and smooth, flowers cupped; a fine Rose: *vig.*

Baron Adolphe de Rothschild (Lacharme, 1862): fiery red, large and full: a well-shaped Rose: *vig.*

Baron de Bonstettin (Lialaud, 1871): rich velvety purple, in the way of and similar to *Monsieur Boncenne:* a fine Rose; *vig.*

Baron de Maynard (Lacharme, 1865): pure paper-white, flower of moderate size, full and well formed: *mod.*

Baron Haussmann (Leveque fils, 1867): clear carmine-crimson, flowers of good size, beautifully imbricated and full; a fine Rose; *vig.*

Baron Nathaniel de Rothschild (Leveque, 1883): bright crimson-red, large, full, fine form; *vig.*

Baronne Nathaniel de Rothschild (Pernet, 1885): delicate silvery rose, very large and nearly full, globular; *mod.*

Baronne Prevost (Desprez, 1843): brilliant rose, very large and full: forms a fine pillar Rose on the Manetti stock; *vig.*

Baroness Rothschild (Pernet, 1869): palest flesh, petals large and smooth, flowers large, double, and of fine globular form; very distinct and beautiful, and one of the best: *vig.*

Barthelemy Joubert (Moreau-Robert, 1877): bright cherry-red, large and full; fine: *vig.*

Beauty of Beeston (Frettingham, 1872): brilliant velvety crimson, full and fragrant; *mod.*

Beauty of Waltham (W. Paul, 1862): cherry-crimson, petals large and well disposed, flowers cupped, large and finely formed, very sweet; *vig.*

Bessie Johnson (Curtis, 1872): blush-white, flowers very large and full, and highly fragrant; a good light Rose; *vig.*

Boieldieu (Margottin, 1877): bright cherry, very large, full globular flower; *vig.*

Boule de Neige (Lacharme, 1867) : pure white, centre delicately shaded with cream, flowers of beautifully imbricated form : a good white Rose ; *mod.*

Brightness of Cheshunt (Paul & Son, 1881) : peculiarly vivid brick-red, a medium-sized flower of open imbricated form : very free and fine autumnal ; *vig.*

Brilliant (W. Paul & Son, 1886) : bright scarlet-crimson, petals of great substance ; good button-hole and garden Rose ; *vig.*

Camille Bernardin (Gautreau, 1865) : bright red, beautifully formed, large, full and deliciously sweet : *vig.*

Captain Christy (Lacharme, 1873) : blush, centre delicate flesh colour, flowers large, full and beautifully formed ; a superb Rose ; *mod.*

Centifolia rosea (Touvais, 1863) : rich rose-pink, flowers large and cupped : a very distinct and beautiful Rose, with abundant foliage : *vig.*

Charles Darwin (Laxton, 1879) : deep crimson, with brownish tint, and slightly shaded with violet ; a good autumnal bloomer and thoroughly distinct : *vig.*

Charles Dickens (W. Paul & Son, 1886) : rose colour, large and full ; a most profuse bloomer, hardy and free ; a grand garden and bedding Rose ; *vig.*

Charles Lamb (W. Paul & Son, 1884) : bright clear red, and full, handsome foliage ; *vig.*

Charles Lefebvre (Lacharme, 1861) : rich velvety shaded crimson, flowers large and of fine form ; a superb Rose ; *vig.*

Clara Cochet (Lacharme, 1886) : clear satin-rose, with brighter centre, very large and full ; *vig.*

Climbing Captain Christy (Ducher, 1881) : a sport from *Captain Christy* ; a good wall Rose ; *vig.*

Climbing Charles Lefebvre (Cranston, 1876) : a wonderful vigorous sport from that superb old Rose *Charles Lefebvre*, producing shoots 8 to 9 feet in a season ; as a perpetual climbing Rose this is a great acquisition ; *vig.*

Climbing Edouard Morren (Paul & Son, 1879) : same as *Edouard Morren*, but more vigorous ; *vig.*

Climbing Jules Margottin (Cranston, 1875) : a sport from *Jules Margottin*, with flowers exactly similar to its parent ; a free and vigorous climbing habit, not in a robust form, but branching as freely as an evergreen climbing Rose ; *vig.*

Climbing Victor Verdier (Paul & Son, 1871): bright cherry-red strong climbing habit ; a good pillar or climbing Rose ; *vig.*

Clovis (Ledechaux, 1868): violet-red, shaded, distinct and good ; *vig.*

Colonel Felix Breton (Schwartz, 1884): velvety grenata-red, large and full, regularly imbricated form, growth vigorous ; a new colour ; *vig.*

Comte de Mortemart (Margottin fils, 1881): fine clear rose, of very large size, full ; in the way of *Centifolia*, beautiful circular shelled form ; a very distinct variety in every way ; *mod.*

Comte Horace de Choiseul (Leveque, 1879): fiery vermilion, tinged velvety scarlet, large and full, very fragrant ; *vig.*

Comte de Paris (Leveque, 1887): poppy red, shaded with bright purple, brown, and vivid crimson, large, full and of good shape, very vigorous ; a good Rose ; *vig.*

Comtesse de Camondo (Leveque, 1880): fine bright rose, shaded with violet, very large, full, imbricated form ; extra ; *vig.*

Comtesse de Casteja (J. Margottin fils, 1883): rich deep scarlet, large, full, perfect imbricated form ; opens freely ; a first-class variety ; *vig.*

Comtesse Cecille de Chabrillant (Marest, 1858): beautiful satin-rose, flowers very compact and perfect, superb, very sweet ; *mod.*

Comtesse de Paris (E. Verdier, 1864): very bright clear red, and of fine form ; a good Rose ; *mod.*

Comtesse de Paris (Leveque, 1883): bright rose colour, large, full, and globulous, well formed ; *mod.*

Comtesse de Serenyi (Lacharme, 1874): blush centre, beautifully shaded rose, cupped and perfectly formed ; one of the best light Roses ; *vig.*

Constantin Fretiakoff (Jamain, 1877): flowers very large, very full, well formed, beautiful brilliant cerise-red, much deeper in the centre ; a superb Rose and sweet scented ; *vig.*

Coquette des Alpes (Lacharme, 1867): white, centre rose shaded, fine form, full, free bloomer ; *mod.*

Coquette des Blanches (Lacharme, 1871): pure white, globular, large and good ; *vig.*

Countess of Oxford (Guillot père, 1869): carmine, with soft violet shade, velvety, flowers large, full, and cupped, petals smooth ; a fine Rose ; *vig.*

Countess of Rosebery (W. Paul & Son, 1879): flowers brilliant carmine-rose, large, full, and finely cupped : a vigorous-growing variety, blooming freely all through summer and autumn : *vig.*

Crimson Bedder (Cranston, 1874): as a crimson bedding Rose, this variety surpasses every other for brilliancy of colour and continuous blooming; its habit of growth is moderate, and shoots short-jointed, producing a mass of flowers the whole season; colour scarlet and crimson, very effective and lasting, clean glossy foliage and free from mildew; excellent for forcing : *mod.*

Crown Prince (W. Paul & Son, 1880): flowers bright purple, the centre shaded with lurid crimson, very large and double : *vig.*

Dean of Windsor (Turner, 1878): clear rich vermilion, sometimes slightly shaded with crimson, large, full, and good symmetrical form ; free and constant ; *vig.*

Devienne Lamy (Leveque fils, 1888): deep carmine, a large full flower of imbricated form ; a very fine Rose : *mod.*

Dingée Conard (E. Verdier, 1875): rich velvety crimson, a well-formed compact flower, fine even petals, and good high centre; a fine dark Rose ; *mod.*

Directeur Alphand (Leveque et fils, 1884): deep blackish purple, large, full, and well formed ; growth very vigorous ; *vig.*

Docteur Andry (E. Verdier, 1864): rich rosy crimson, flowers large, fine smooth petals; a superb Rose : *vig.*

Docteur Baillon (Margottin père, 1878): bright crimson-red shaded with purple, large, full, and well formed ; *rob.*

Dr. Hogg (Laxton, 1880): deep violet, nearest to the blue colour sometimes desired in Roses, pretty shell-shaped petal, and very hardy ; *vig.*

Dr. Sewell (Turner, 1879): brilliant crimson-scarlet, shaded with purple, back of petals bright red, large, full, and finely cupped : *vig.*

Due de Montpensier (Leveque, 1875): rich velvety crimson, flowers large, full, and well formed ; a superb Rose ; *vig.*

Due de Rohan (Leveque, 1861): fine brilliant carmine, superb colour ; a good old Rose ; *mod.*

Due de Wellington (Granger, 1864): rich velvety crimson, flowers good size, cupped and well formed ; a first-rate Rose ; *mod.*

Duchesse de Caylus (C. Verdier, 1864): glowing rosy crimson, flowers large, full, and beautifully cupped, with high centre and fine outline ; *mod.*

Duchesse de Vallombrosa (Schwartz, 1875): blush, centre delicate flesh, flowers large, full, and cupped; an exquisitely formed and beautiful Rose; *vig.*

Duchess of Bedford (W. Paul & Son, 1879): flowers dazzling light scarlet-crimson, large, full, and of perfect globular shape; *vig.*

Duchess of Connaught (Noble, 1883): crimson shaded purple, large and full, very fine; *vig.*

Duchess of Edinburgh (Bennett, 1874): pale rose, flowers large and globular; a well formed flower, but not constant; *vig.*

Duke of Albany (W. Paul & Son, 1883): vivid crimson, changing darker, and shaded with velvety black, large and full; a good autumnal bloomer; *vig.*

Duke of Connaught (Paul & Son, 1878): velvety crimson and purple, rich deep colour; a compact well-formed, and very good Rose; *mod.*

Duke of Edinburgh (Paul & Son, 1868): rich velvety crimson, shaded, flowers large and very attractive; a superb Rose; *vig.*

Duke of Teck (Paul & Son, 1880): bright crimson-scarlet, clear and distinct; in the way of *Duke of Edinburgh*; *vig.*

Dupuy Jamain (Jamain, 1868): brilliant carmine-crimson, colour very fine, petals large, broad, and smooth, flowers well formed, luxuriant foliage; a good Rose; *vig.*

Earl of Beaconsfield (Christy, 1880): cherry-red, centre darker, large and full: *mod.*

Earl of Dufferin (Alex. Dickson & Sons, 1887): velvety crimson, shaded with maroon, flowers large, full and well formed; *vig.*

Earl of Pembroke (Bennett, 1882): velvety crimson, enlivened on margin of petals with bright red; very vigorous; *vig.*

Edouard Morren (Granger, 1868): brilliant glossy pink, large; a good Rose; *vig.*

Egeria (Schwartz, 1878): light silvery peach colour, large, full and well formed; *vig.*

Elie Morel (Boucharlet, 1867): rosy lilac, flowers large and of fine form; a beautiful Rose; *vig.*

Ella Gordon (W. Paul & Son, 1884): bright cherry-red, large, full and globular, petals smooth, thick and well rounded; *vig.*

Emilie Hausbury (Leveque, 1869): light rose changing to pale satin-rose, large and full, exquisitely formed; *vig.*

Emily Laxton (Laxton, 1877) : large full flower with globular pointed buds, flowers large and well formed ; a good Rose ; *vig.*

Emperor (Wm. Paul & Son, 1884) : very dark, almost black, small and neat for button-holes ; hardy and free, both in growth and flowering ; *vig.*

Empress (Wm. Paul & Son, 1884) : white with pink centre, small, neat and of perfect form ; a good button-hole Rose : a seedling from the *Maiden's Blush*, flowering in summer and autumn ; *vig.*

Empress of India (Laxton, 1876) : dark crimson and purple, well formed, moderate size ; *vig.*

Ernest Prince (Ducher, 1882) : clear red, deeper in the centre, very large, well formed and globulous ; *vig.*

Etendard de Lyon (Gonod, 1884) : a very striking pæony-red colour, large and distinct ; very effective : *mod.*

Eugène Appert (V. Trouillard, 1859) : bright scarlet and crimson, colour superb ; a fine pillar Rose ; *vig.*

Exposition de Brie (Grainger, 1865) : rich glowing crimson, flowers large and of good form ; very fine : *vig.*

Ferdinand Chaffolte (Pernet, 1879) : deep velvety crimson, colour very bright and beautiful, flowers large and full, outer petals smooth and shell-shaped ; *vig.*

Firebrand (Labruyere, 1873) : crimson, medium size, double and good ; very fragrant : *rob.*

Fisher Holmes (E. Verdier, 1865) : rich purplish crimson, flowers large, cupped, double and of fine imbricated form ; a superb Rose : *rob.*

Fontenelle (Moreau, Robert, 1877) : dark velvety crimson and purple, very large and full, blooms in clusters : *vig.*

François Fontaine (Fontaine, 1867) : dark rosy crimson, large globular form : a good late-blooming kind : *vig.*

François Levet (Levet, 1880) : Chinese rose, medium size : *vig.*

François Louvat (Touvais, 1861) : deep crimson, shaded with lilac, very large and fine cupped form ; a superb Rose ; *vig.*

Garden Favourite (W. Paul & Son, 1884) : bright pink, large and full ; fine decorative Rose, producing large quantities of flowers ; *vig.*

Géant des Batailles (Nerard, 1846) : brilliant crimson, large, full and very sweet : a well-known old Rose ; *mod.*

General Jacqueminot (Roussel, 1853): brilliant scarlet-crimson, most superb glowing colour, and a most abundant bloomer; a fine bedding Rose; *mod.*

George Baker (Paul & Son, 1881): a pure lake shaded with cerise, good form; *mod.*

Georges Moreau (Moreau-Robert, 1881): very bright shaded red, very large, opening well, globulous; *rig.*

Gloire de Bourg la Reine (Margottin père, 1879): fine brilliant scarlet-red and crimson, flower large and full; a superb Rose; *rig.*

Gloire de Ducher (Ducher, 1865): reddish purple, very large, full, and vigorous; *rig.*

Gloire de Rosomene (Vibert): brilliant crimson, semi-double; *rob.*

Gloire Lyonnaise (Guillot, 1885): very pale yellow, petals edged pure white, large and full, very vigorous: the first yellow Hybrid Perpetual yet raised; *rig.*

Gloire de Margottin (Margottin, 1888): rosy cerise colour, large, semi-double, beautiful in the bud; a good new Rose; *rig.*

Glory of Cheshunt (W. Paul & Son, 1880): this is a seedling from *Charles Lefebvre*, with flowers of a rich shaded crimson, very bright and vivid; *rig.*

Glory of Waltham (Vigneron, 1865): crimson, double, very sweet; a good climbing Rose; *rig.*

Grand Mogul (W. Paul & Son, 1887): deep brilliant crimson shaded with scarlet and black, sometimes approaching maroon, large, full, and of perfect form: a good new Rose; *rig.*

Grandeur of Cheshunt (Paul & Son, 1883): light crimson shaded with rose, peculiarly distinct, large flowers; *rig.*

Harrison Weir (Turner, 1879): beautiful rich velvety crimson, enlivened with scarlet, flowers large, full, very smooth; *rig.*

Helene Paul (Lacharme, 1882): very fine white, sometimes shaded with rose, very large, of globular form; *rig.*

Henrich Schultheis (Bennett, 1882): delicate pinkish rose colour, large, full, and sweet; a fine Rose; *rig.*

Henry Bennett (Lacharme, 1875): intense violet-crimson, colour very rich, flowers cupped, good even petals, but not sufficiently full; *rig.*

Henry Ledechaux (Ledechaux, 1868): clear cherry-red, large and globular; *mod.*

Her Majesty (Bennett, 1886): clear bright satiny rose, very large and full, finely formed petals, and handsome foliage ; *rob.*

Hyppolyte Flandrin (Damazin, 1865): rosy pink, colour glossy and good, petals large, smooth and firm, flowers very large and imbricated ; *mod.*

Hyppolyte Jamain (Lacharme, 1874): fine bright rose shaded with carmine, very large and full, flowers very even and well-formed : a fine Rose ; *vig.*

Horace Vernet (Guillot fils, 1866): rich brilliant velvety crimson, petals large and smooth, flowers large, full, and of a most perfectly imbricated form ; a truly superb Rose ; *mod.*

Inigo Jones (W. Paul & Son, 1886): flowers dark rose colour shaded with purple, large, full, and globular, of perfect form, free, and hardy ; a fine dark Rose ; *vig.*

Jean Cherpin (Liabaud, 1865): rich violet-plum, a superb colour, petals smooth and well formed, and the flowers cupped ; *mod.*

Jean Goujon (Margottin, 1862): dark rose colour, large, full, and cupped ; *vig.*

Jean Liabaud (Liabaud, 1875): fiery crimson, centre rich velvety crimson, flowers large, double and well formed ; one of the finest dark Roses ; *vig.*

Jean Soupert (Lacharme, 1875): plum-purple, almost black, flowers good size and evenly formed ; *mod.*

Jeanne Sury (Fauden, 1868) : bright claret and crimson ; a large handsome Rose ; *mod.*

John Bright (Paul & Son, 1878): pure glowing crimson, very bright ; effective and good ; *vig.*

John Hopper (Ward, 1862): centre brilliant rosy crimson, the outer petals lilac-rose, flowers cupped, full and well formed ; a first-class Rose ; *vig.*

John Stuart Mill (Turner, 1874): bright clear red, large, full and beautiful form, fine shell-like petal of good substance ; a good Rose ; *vig.*

Jules Chretien (Schwartz, 1877): bright crimson-red, shaded with purple, very large, full and well formed ; a superb Rose ; *vig.*

Jules Margottin (Margottin, 1853): brilliant glossy pink, a glowing flesh colour, flowers large ; a beautiful old variety ; *vig.*

Julius Finger (Lacharme, 1879): pure white, lightly tinted with rose at the end of the season, large, full and perfect form ; *vig.*

Julia Touvais (Touvais, 1868) : soft pink, with silvery rose tint, large, full and distinct; *vig.*

King's Acre (Cranston, 1864) : bright vermilion-rose, flowers of extra large size, globular ; a fine Rose for forcing ; *mod.*

La Duchesse de Morny (E. Verdier, 1863) : bright pleasing rose, flowers large, full, and beautifully formed, having petals of good substance ; *vig.*

Lady of the Lake (W. Paul & Son): peach colour, large, full and of fine globular form ; good and distinct, and very hardy ; *vig.*

Lady Sheffield (W. Paul & Son, 1881): brilliant rosy cerise, large and full ; *vig.*

La France (Guillot fils, 1867): satin-pink, outer petals pale flesh, flowers large and globular ; partakes somewhat of the China Rose ; very fragrant, distinct and beautiful ; *vig.*

La Reine (Laffay, 1843): brilliant glossy red, large and full: *mod.*

La Rosiere (Damaizin, 1874) : amaranth, large and full, somewhat resembling *Prince Camille de Rohan ;* a superb Rose ; *mod.*

La Ville de St. Denis (Thomas) : rosy carmine, flowers as large as those of *La Reine,* and exquisitely formed ; *mod.*

Leelia (Crozy, 1857): satin-rose ; a noble Rose with fine large smooth petals, and of exquisite form ; *vig.*

L'Espérance (Fontaine, 1871): rosy cerise, colour clear and satiny, flowers large, well formed and double, highly scented ; *mod.*

Le Havre (Eude, 1870) : brilliant vermilion, flowers smooth and well formed ; a fine Rose ; *vig.*

Le Rhone (Guillot fils, 1862): rich scarlet-crimson, medium, full ; very fragrant and vigorous ; *vig.*

Lecury-Dumesnil (E. Verdier fil, 1883) : dazzling red, strongly marbled and tinted with brown, crimson and violet ; flowers extra large, full and perfectly imbricated ; *vig.*

Longfellow (Paul & Son, 1885) : rich violet-crimson, fine ; in the way of *Charles Lefebvre,* but more violet in colour; *vig.*

Lord Bacon (W. Paul & Son, 1883): deep crimson, shaded velvety black, large and full ; *vig.*

Lord Beaconsfield (Bennett, 1878): blackish crimson, very fine large bold globular flower, of good habit ; *mod.*

Lord Clyde (W. Paul & Son, 1863): crimson and purple, deeply shaded, large and full ; *vig.*

Lord Frederick Cavendish (Frettingham, 1883): bright scarlet, large, full and globular ; a beautiful Rose ; *vig.*

Lord Macaulay (W. Paul & Son, 1863): rich dark velvety crimson, colour dense and glowing, flowers large, double and well formed ; a superb Rose ; *rob.*

Lord Raglan (Guillot père, 1854): deep crimson, changing to mottled crimson, large and superb ; *mod.*

Louise Peyronny (Lacharme, 1844): rose-pink colour, immense size and double ; *vig.*

Louis Van Houtte (Lacharme, 1869): deep red-amaranth shaded with dark claret, good and distinct, flowers cupped and well formed ; a fine distinct Rose, and very fragrant ; superb ; *mod.*

Mabel Morrison (Broughton, 1878): a sport of *Baroness Rothschild*, pure white, not sufficiently double ; *vig.*

Madame Alexandria Jullien (Vigneron, 1883): fine delicate fresh rose, large and full, beautiful elongated bud ; *vig.*

Ma Surprise (A. Levet, 1884): bright scarlet, sometimes violet, not always perpetual ; a seedling from *Eugène Appert* ; *mod.*

Madame Alice Dureau (Vigneron, 1869): clear rose colour, large and full, sweetly scented ; *mod.*

Madame Appoline Foulon (Vigneron, 1883): fine light salmon, shaded with lilac, flowers large and full ; *vig.*

Madame Bellenden Ker (Guillot père, 1866): white, in the way of *Mdlle. Bonnaire*, large and full ; a desirable white Rose ; *vig.*

Madame Bellon (Pernet, 1871): brilliant cerise, flowers very large, well formed and full ; a very fine Rose ; *mod.*

Madame Boutin (Jamain, 1861): cerise, a beautiful clear colour, flowers very large and full, petals broad and even ; *vig.*

Madame Bertha Mackart (E. Verdier, 1884): deep rose, reverse of petals silvery, flowers extra large, cup-shaped and somewhat globular: vigorous in growth, described as thoroughly perpetual ; *vig.*

Madame Caillat (E. Verdier, 1861): clear brilliant rose, flowers large and full, petals broad and even ; a first-rate Rose, and quite distinct ; *vig.*

Madame Charles Crapelet (Fontaine, 1859): rosy scarlet, large smooth petals, flowers beautifully formed ; a superb Rose ; *vig.*

Madame Charles Wood (E. Verdier, 1861): beautiful clear rosy crimson, petals large and of good substance, flowers very large, expanded, full and well formed ; *vig.*

Madame Clemence Joigneaux (Liabaud, 1861): brilliant rosy carmine, flowers very large, deep and very full, fine stout petals; a superb Rose; *viy.*

Madame Ducher (Levet, 1879): bright carmine, very large, flowers evenly and well formed; a superb Rose; *mod.*

Madame Eugène Verdier (E. Verdier, 1878): light silvery rose, clear and good, of large fine-petalled globular shape; *rob.*

Madame F. Bruel (Levet, 1882): carmine-rose, large and full; a seedling from *Comtesse d'Oxford*; *mod.*

Madame Ferdinand Jamain (Ledechaux, 1875): rosy claret, deep petals, large and bold flower; distinct and good, very fragrant; *viy.*

Madame Fillion (Gonod, 1865): fresh rosy pink, flowers large, full, and of good form; very fragrant; *viy.*

Madame François Pettit (Lacharme, 1877): beautiful white, form globular; *viy.*

Madame Furtado (V. Verdier, 1860): brilliant carmine-rose, colour fresh and beautiful, flowers globular, of great depth and fine outline, highly scented, delicate habit; *mod.*

Madame Gabriel Luizet (Liabaud, 1877): fine satin-rose, a very delicate and beautiful tint, large, full and well formed; a distinct and very beautiful Rose, very sweet; *viy.*

Madame Georges Schwartz (Schwartz, 1871): glossy rose with soft lavender shade, flowers large, full and cupped; a fine deep flower and a superb Rose; *viy.*

Madame Hippolyte Jamain (Garcon, 1871): white, slightly tinged with rose; extra large, and a very fine show flower; *mod.*

Madame John Twombly (Schwartz, 1882): deep currant-red, large, full and well formed; in the way of *Alfred Colomb*; *viy.*

Madame Julie Daran (Touvais, 1861): violet-crimson, flowers cupped, beautiful form, large smooth petals, of good quality; *viy.*

Madame la Marquise d'Herrey (Vigneron, 1877): violet-red shaded with bluish slate, large and full; this is the nearest approach to a blue Rose; *viy.*

Madame Lacharme (Lacharme, 1873): white, centre the palest blush, cupped, exquisitely formed and highly scented; a beautiful white Rose; *viy.*

Madame Laurent (Granger, 1869): bright rose, fine large globular flower, handsome and distinct; *mod.*

Madame Marie Finger (Rambaux, 1873): flesh, centre deep salmon-pink, well formed; a fine and distinct Rose, very free blooming; *vig.*

Madame Marie Lagrange (Lagrange, 1883): brilliant carmine, large, almost full; *mod.*

Madame Melaine Vigneron (Vigneron, 1883): beautiful lilac-rose, edge of petals silvery, flowers large and very full; *mod.*

Madame Moreau (Gonod, 1864): bright red, shaded violet, very large and full; *rob.*

Madame Montet (Liabaud, 1880): very soft rose, large, almost full, very fine; *vig.*

Madame Nachury (Damaizin, 1873): fine satin-like rose, with a soft lavender shade; a new colour, flowers large, full and cupped, distinct and well formed; *vig.*

Madame Nonan (Guillot père, 1867): pure white with peach centre, exquisite form; one of the best light Roses; *mod.*

Madame Norman Neruda (Paul & Son, 1885): light cherry-carmine, medium size and perfect form; *vig.*

Madame Olympe Terestchenko (Leveque, 1883): rosy white or carmined rose, large, full and well formed: *vig.*

Madame Oswald de Kerchove (Schwartz, 1879): white, shaded pink, centre tinted coppery yellow, medium size, full and very sweet; a splendid button-hole Rose; *vig.*

Madame Prosper Langier (E. Verdier, 1875): bright rose colour, shaded fiery red, very large, full and fragrant; a good Rose; *vig.*

Madame Rambaux (Rambaux, 1883): beautiful rosy carmine, very large and full; *vig.*

Madame Sophie Fropot (Levet, 1876): pale satin-rose, broad smooth even petals, flowers cupped; a beautiful and distinct Rose; *vig.*

Madame Therenot (Jamain, 1869): bright lively red, flowers very large, full and globular; very sweet; *mod.*

Madame Veuve Alexandre Pommery (Leveque, 1883): pink-rose, shaded with bright rose, very large and full; *mod.*

Madame Victor Verdier (E. Verdier, 1863): brilliant rosy crimson, colour very beautiful, flowers large and well formed; a distinct and beautiful Rose; *vig.*

Madame Vidot (Verdier, 1853): palest flesh, most beautifully formed; a most perfect Rose; *mod.*

Mdlle. Bonnaire (Pernet, 1859) : pure white, centre beautifully shaded with clear flesh, flowers of medium size and well formed ; a very beautiful free-blooming Rose ; *mod.*

Mdlle. Catherine Soupert (Lacharme, 1879): white, bordered and shaded with rose, large, full, of perfect form ; a fine Rose ; *vig.*

Mdlle. Eugénie Verdier (Guillot fils, 1869) : centre clear satin-pink, outer petals pale satin, colour clear and beautiful, flowers large, full and cupped ; a superb Rose ; *vig.*

Mdlle. Julia Dymonier (Gonod, 1879): pink, changing to blush, flowers compact, beautifully and evenly formed, large and full ; an improved *Marie Cointet; mod.*

Mdlle. Marie Cointet (Guillot fils, 1872): bright satin-pink, outer petals paler, glossy thick petals; a very beautiful and distinct Rose ; *mod.*

Mdlle. Marie Digat (Levet, 1883) : fine crimson-red, large and globulous ; a free bloomer; *vig.*

Mdlle. Marie Rady (Fontaine, 1865): brilliant red, flowers large, very full and beautifully imbricated ; one of the most perfect ; *vig.*

Mdlle. Marie Verdier (E. Verdier, 1875) : bright rose, good cupped form ; a beautiful Rose ; *vig.*

Mdlle. Marguerite Dombrain (E. Verdier, 1865): satiny rose colour, very large, full and globular ; *vig.*

Mdlle. Marguerite Manoin (Fontaine, 1879): deep carmine-rose, beautiful fresh colour, very large and full ; a fine Rose ; *vig.*

Mdlle. Therese Levet (Levet, 1866): brilliant rose colour, large, full and globular ; one of the best ; *vig.*

Magna Charta (W. Paul & Son, 1876): flowers bright pink, suffused with carmine, very large and full, and of good form ; *vig.*

Marchioness of Exeter (Laxton, 1877): bright rose flushed with carmine, a large cup-shaped and well-built flower; good habit and distinct ; *vig.*

Marechal Vaillant (Jamain, 1861): rosy crimson, colour bright, flowers large, double and well formed ; a fine Rose ; *vig.*

Marguerite Brassac (Brassac, 1875): dark velvety crimson, similar to *Charles Lefebvre*, very smooth and even in form ; *vig.*

Marguerite de Roman (Schwartz, 1883): pink-white, flesh-rose in the centre ; very large and well formed ; *vig.*

Marguerite de St. Amand (Sansal, 1864): glossy satin-rose, a beautiful flesh colour, flowers extra large, globular and well formed; a good distinct Rose; *vig.*

Marie Baumann (Baumann, 1863): rich carmine-crimson, flowers large and of exquisite colour, perfectly formed; one of the best Roses; *vig.*

Marie Louise Pernet (Pernet, 1876): deep rosy red, a fine large globular flower and well formed; a very good and distinct Rose; *vig.*

Marshall P. Wilder (Ellwanger & Barry, 1885): cherry-carmine, large semi-double, full and well formed; an American variety, recommended for its vigour, hardiness, and freedom in blooming; *vig.*

Mary Bennett (Bennett, 1884): very brilliant rosy-cerise, large, full and of fine form; a good Rose; *mod.*

Mary Pochin (Pochin, 1881): rich velvety crimson, flowers moderate size, petals broad, smooth and evenly disposed; a striking and beautiful Rose; *vig.*

Marquise de Castellane (Pernet, 1869): deep cerise, colour clear and good, flowers large, circular, and perfect; one of the finest; *rob.*

Marquise de Gibot (De Sansal, 1868): clear rose colour, large, full and of fine form; a good Rose; *vig.*

Marquise de Mortemart (Liabaud, 1868): blush-white, centre pale flesh, beautiful, rather delicate; *mod.*

Marquis of Salisbury (Paul & Son, 1879): deep rose colour, shaded crimson, large, globular, full and imbricated; *vig.*

Masterpiece (W. Paul & Son, 1880): bright rosy crimson; the flowers are very large, full and of perfect globular shape; habit good, and foliage fine; *vig.*

Maurice Bernardin (Granger, 1861): rich crimson shaded with violet, colour superb, flowers very large and double; a splendid Rose; *vig.*

May Quennell (Postans, 1878): brilliant magenta-carmine shaded with crimson, very large and full, and of perfect globular form; *mod.*

Merveille de Lyon (Pernet, 1883): fine pure exquisite white, slightly rosy, finely cupped and opening freely, very large, 4 to 5 inches in diameter; is a seedling from *Baroness Rothschild*, with the same habit, but larger. This superb variety has been awarded several first prizes, and is undoubtedly the best light Hybrid Perpetual Rose ever raised; *vig.*

Miss Hassard (Turner, 1875): beautiful delicate flesh colour, large, full and fine form, very sweet; a free autumnal bloomer; *rig.*

Monsieur Alfred Dumesnil (Margottin fils): deep rose, bright centre, flowers globular, large, well formed; distinct and very sweet; *rig.*

Monsieur Benoit Comte (Schwartz, 1884): brilliant scarlet-red, shaded with vermilion inside, large, full, globulus and cupped; *rig.*

Monsieur Boncenne (Liabaud, 1864): intensely rich plum, superb, flowers well formed; one of the best dark Roses; *rig.*

Monsieur Etienne Levet (Levet, 1871): carmine-red, with a soft velvety lavender shade, flowers very large and full, petals exquisitely smooth and shell-shaped; superb; *rig.*

Monsieur Eugène Delaire (Vigneron, 1879): velvety, lighted with fire-red, large, full; extra; *rig.*

Monsieur E. Y. Teas (Eugène Verdier fils, 1874): deep red, large, full and of the most perfect form; one of the best Roses grown, and very fragrant; *rig.*

Monsieur Fillion (Gonod, 1876): fine rose, striking colour: a large, full and well formed flower; *rig.*

Monsieur François Michelon (Levet, 1871): fine deep rose, reverse of petals silvery white, large and full; very beautiful; *rig.*

Monsieur Francisque Rives (Schwartz, 1884): bright cherry-red, very large and full, well formed; *mal.*

Monsieur Gabriel Tournier (Levet, 1876): rosy crimson, flowers extra large, fine large petals, globular flower; a distinct and good Rose; *rig.*

Monsieur Noman (Guillot père, 1867): delicate rosy pink, flowers large, deep, and of fine globular form; a superb Rose; *rig.*

Monsieur Thoncenel (Vigneron, 1880): velvety red, large and full; *rig.*

Mrs. Baker (Laxton, 1876): beautiful shaded crimson, large, full and well formed; very beautiful; *rig.*

Mrs. Caroline Swailes (G. Swailes, 1885): beautiful light flesh colour, very bright and clear, the petals broad and of good substance. The growth is strong and vigorous, and it is a true Hybrid Perpetual, one of the first to bloom in summer, and the flowers are produced abundantly till late in the autumn; *rig.*

Mrs. George Dickson (Bennett, 1884): bright satiny pink, flowers large, not too full, opening freely; *rig.*

Mrs. Harry Turner (Turner, 1880): colour intense crimson-scarlet, with rich maroon shading, flowers large, beautifully imbricated, foliage dark and handsome; somewhat resembling *Charles Lefebvre*; *vig.*

Mrs. Jowitt (Cranston): brilliant glowing crimson, shaded with lake, flowers very large and globular; a bold well-built flower of grand form and substance; habit robust; flowers very fragrant; one of the best English Roses ever raised. Four First Class Certificates; *vig.*

Mrs. John Laing (Bennett, 1886): soft pink in colour, in the way of *Madame Gabriel Luizet*; the flowers are large, finely shaped and very fragrant; a constant and abundant bloomer; *vig.*

Mrs. Laxton (Thos. Laxton, 1877): bright rosy crimson, large and perfect, as perfect as a Ranunculus; a first-class Rose; *mod.*

Mrs. Rivers (Guillot père, 1850): pale flesh, nearly white, petals beautifully formed, cupped, large and full; good habit; *vig.*

Nardy Frères (Ducher, 1865): rose, shaded soft lavender, flowers very large, full and well formed; a very distinct and first-rate Rose; *vig.*

Olivier Delhomme (V. Verdier, 1861): brilliant rosy carmine, flowers well formed, of good depth and high centre; *vig.*

Orgueil de Lyon (Besson, 1886): dark velvety crimson, shaded with vermilion, medium size and full; *vig.*

Oxonian (Turner, 1876): shaded rose, large and full, fine globular form; a good exhibition Rose; *vig*

Paul Neron (Levet, 1869): rose colour, very large; fine form and habit; *vig.*

Paul's Single Crimson Perpetual (W. Paul & Son, 1883): large single crimson flowers, with yellow stamens; *vig.*

Paul's Single White Perpetual (W. Paul & Son, 1883): pure white, single flowers, with yellow stamens in centre; distinct, *vig.*

Paul Verdier (C. Verdier, 1866): rich rosy crimson, flowers large, double, and of fine imbricated form; a fine pillar or wall Rose; *vig.*

Peach Blossom (W. Paul & Son, 1874): delicate peach, a new and beautiful colour, large, full and fine shape; *vig.*

Pierre Notting (Portemar, 1863): deep velvety shaded crimson, globular, beautifully formed flower; fine and distinct; *vig.*

Pitord (Lacharme, 1867): crimson-scarlet, with dark plum shade; a really good Rose ; *mod.*

Préfet Limbourg (Margottin fils, 1878): crimson tinged with violet, double or full ; a Rose of fine colour ; *vig.*

President Willermoz (Ducher, 1867): rich brilliant carmine, with a very soft and pleasing violet tint; flowers of moderate size, double and well formed ; *vig.*

Pride of Reigate (Brown, 1885) : crimson, striped with white ; a sport from *Countess of Oxford* ; *vig.*

Pride of Waltham (W. Paul & Son, 1881): delicate flesh colour, superb ; *vig.*

Prince Arthur (B. R. Cant, 1875) : very rich crimson, shaded deeper colour ; a dark form of *General Jacqueminot ;* distinct and good ; *vig.*

Prince Camille de Rohan (E. Verdier, 1861) : rich dark maroon-crimson, flowers moderate size, double; one of the finest dark Roses ; *vig.*

Princess Beatrice (W. Paul & Son, 1872) : foliage large, bright and handsome ; flowers deep pink, with clear blush margin, large, full and globular form ; *vig.*

Princess Mary of Cambridge (Paul & Son, 1866) : pale silvery pink, flowers large, full and high in the centre ; beautiful and desirable Rose ; *vig.*

Princess of Wales (Wm. Paul & Son, 1864) : vivid crimson cupped, large and very double; free, hardy and of good habit *vig.*

Prosper Laugier (E. Verdier, 1884): very bright scarlet-carmine, large, full and very vigorous ; *vig.*

Queen Eleanor (W. Paul & Son, 1876): pure pink, cupped, large and full, very fragrant ; *vig.*

Queen of Queens (W. Paul & Son, 1883): pink with blush edges, large, full, and of perfect form; *vig.*

Queen of Waltham (W. Paul & Son, 1875): beautiful rose-cherry, a very distinct and lovely colour; large, full and double ; *vig.*

Queen Victoria (Fontaine, 1850) : flesh shaded with pink, very large, full and beautiful ; *vig.*

R. C. Sutton (Frettingham, 1882) : deep rose colour, reverse of petals white, sweetly scented; *mod.*

Red Dragon (W. Paul & Son, 1878) : a hybrid climbing Rose, colour brilliant crimson, very bright and striking ; *rob.*

Red Gauntlet (Postans, 1881) : bright scarlety crimson ; *rig.*

Reine Blanche (Damaizin, 1868) : pearly white, centre palish flesh, flowers large, full and cupped ; *mod.*

Reine du Midi (Rolland, 1867): fine satin-pink, flowers large and of a fine globular form ; a fine Rose ; *rob.*

Rev. J. B. M. Camm (Turner, 1875) : rosy pink colour, large, full and globular ; very sweet ; *rig.*

Reynolds Hole (Paul & Son, 1873) : maroon shaded with crimson, flowers of good size, perfectly formed ; a fine Rose of new and distinct colour ; *rig.*

Richard Laxton (Laxton, 1878) : colour reddish crimson, large, full and cupped ; beautiful shell-like petal and a fine Rose ; *rig.*

Robert Marnock (Paul & Son, 1878) : rich brownish crimson, flowers large, imbricated and well formed ; *mod.*

Rosieriste Jacobs (Ducher, 1880) : fine velvety red, shaded with black, large, full, well formed, globulous ; extra fine ; *rig.*

Rosy Morn (W. Paul & Son, 1878) : delicate peach colour, richly shaded with salmon-rose, large and full ; *rig.*

Royal Standard (Turner, 1874): beautiful soft satiny rose, large, very full and exquisitely formed ; *rig.*

St. George (W. Paul & Son, 1874): crimson, shaded with black-purple, large and full ; *rig.*

Secretaire J. Nicolas (Schwartz, 1884): dark purple velvety red, large, full, well formed and globulous ; *rig.*

Senateur Vaisse (Guillot père, 1859): intense glowing scarlet, fine thick petals, flowers perfectly full, large, exquisitely formed and highly fragrant ; a superb Rose ; *rig.*

Silver Queen (W. Paul & Son, 1887) : deep brilliant crimson, shaded with scarlet and black, large, full and of perfect form ; *rig.*

Sultan of Zanzibar (Paul & Son, 1876): blackish maroon, shaded with crimson, flowers globular; *mod.*

The Puritan (Evans, 1887) : flowers white, equal in size to *Merveille de Lyon* ; very free bloomer and sweetly scented ; *rig.*

Thomas Mills (E. Verdier, 1873) : flowers extra large, full and of fine cup shape ; colour dazzling bright rosy carmine with whitish stripes ; a very free bloomer ; *rig.*

Ulrich Brunner Fils (Levet, 1882): carmined rose, very large; a seedling from *Paul Neron*; *vig.*

Vicomte de Vigier (V. Verdier, 1861): intensely rich velvety crimson and lilac, colour superb, large petals; a well-formed globular flower, distinct; *vig.*

Victor Verdier (Lacharme, 1859): deep rose, centre brilliant rose; a charming colour, flowers very large and full; an excellent Rose; *vig.*

Ville de Lyon (Ducher, 1866): dark rose colour, large, full, and globular; *mod.*

Violette Bouyer (Lacharme, 1881): white, shaded with pink, large, full, fine form; *vig.*

White Baroness (Paul & Son, 1882): pure white, large and full; *vig.*

Xavier Olibo: rich velvety crimson, colour superb, distinct and very beautiful; *mod.*

THE BOURBON ROSE.

(Rosa Bourboniana.)

The Bourbon Rose, a native of the Isle of Bourbon, was introduced into this country about the year 1825. These Roses are distinguishable by their large handsome shining foliage and profusion of bloom throughout the autumn. Although they flower early as well as late (with few exceptions), it is rarely that blooms of the natural size, or with characteristic colours, are produced until the cool of autumnal weather sets in, when for brilliancy and tone of colour they are unsurpassed.

Many of the varieties are of moderate growth; others vigorous and robust, forming the best pillar

Roses, and having fine handsome foliage and vigorous growth, they are well adapted for walls. The varieties designated as vigorous and robust, are the only suitable kinds for growing as standards; those of moderate growth should not be grown higher than half-standards, and many are better even as dwarf standards.

Acidalie (Rousseau, 1838): white, in dry weather beautifully tinted; a fine wall Rose; *vig.*

Apolline (V. Verdier, 1848): flowers light pink; a beautiful Rose, and a good creeper, pillar, or wall Rose; *vig.*

Baronne de Noirmont (Granger): fresh rosy pink, petals of good substance, flowers large, full and beautifully formed, possessing a delicious violet scent; *mod.*

Baron Gonella (Guillot, 1859): bright cerise, with fine bronze hue, petals large, smooth and thick; a fine Rose; *vig.*

Catherine Guillot (Guillot, 1860): carmine-rose, flowers large and full; a superb Rose; *vig.*

Jules Jurgensen (Schwartz, 1879): rose-magenta, velvety carmine with slaty reflex in the interior, large, full, well formed: *vig.*

Louis Odier (Margottin, 1861): rosy pink, full and finely formed; a good growing and beautiful Rose; *vig.*

Louise Margottin (Margottin, 1862): satin-rose, large, full and well formed; *mod.*

Madame de Sevigne (Moreau-Robert, 1874): very bright rose in the centre, border of the petals lighter, large and full growth; blooms in clusters; *vig.*

Madame Scipion (Cochet, 1871): very bright rose, large, cupped and finely formed; a fine pillar or wall Rose; *vig.*

Malmaison Rouge (Gonod, 1880): deep velvety red; a sport from *Souvenir de la Malmaison*; valuable; *vig.*

Michael Bonnet (Guillot père, 1864): fresh rose, flowers full and well formed; a fine Rose; *vig.*

Modele de Perfection (Guillot fils, 1861): pale satin-pink, fading off to a beautiful carmine tint; *mod.*

Queen (Manger, 1834): fawn and rose; a desirable kind, blooming freely throughout the season; *mod.*

Queen of Bedders (Noble, 1876): a remarkably free-flowering deep crimson Rose, producing large clusters of buds; *mod.*

Reine Victoria (Labruyere, 1872): soft rose; a pretty Rose of good climbing habit; *vig.*

Sir Joseph Paxton (Laffay, 1852): bright rose; a free-blooming handsome kind for pillars; *vig.*

Souvenir de la Malmaison (Beluze, 1843): blush, centre flesh, fine foliage and habit; one of the finest Roses grown: *vig.*

THE CHINA ROSE

(*Rosa indica.*)

The China Rose, or Rosa indica, is a native of China, and was introduced into this country about the year 1789; from this and the old crimson variety have sprung all the members of this family. They are most abundant autumnal-blooming Roses. Some are most brilliant and attractive in colour, others are of the purest white. Few of the kinds are suited for standards, though most of them succeed well when budded upon low stocks. For small beds grown upon their own **roots** they are well suited, and produce an abundance of flowers through-out the autumn. Perhaps the greatest objection to the China Roses is their having little or no scent. They succeed best in warm dry soil, with a mode-rate dressing of well-decayed manure and leaf-mould once a year.

Archduke Charles (Laffay): rose, changing to rich crimson, very large, full, and fine; *mod.*

Cels Multiflore (Cels, 1838): pale flesh, large and full; *mod.*

Cramoisie Superieure (Plantier, 1834): rich velvety crimson, beautiful, full; *vig.*

Ducher (Ducher, 1869) : white, medium size, fine form, full, free flowering ; promising as a free and continuous white bedding Rose ; *mod.*

Eugène Beauharnais (Moreau, 1865) : amaranth, superb, large and full ; *mod.*

Fabvier (Laffay) : brilliant scarlet, dazzling, semi-double ; *mod.*

Marjolin : rich dark crimson, flowers large and full ; *mod.*

Mrs. Bosanquet (Laffay, 1832) : pale flesh, delicate and waxy in appearance, very free blooming and beautiful ; a vigorous grower and makes a good standard ; *vig.*

Old Blush : The type of the China Rose, still considered a useful Rose for borders, also a good wall Rose ; *vig.*

Old Crimson : brilliant crimson, introduced soon after the preceding : from these two varieties have sprung all our Chinese Roses ; *mod.*

Prince Charles : bright cherry, very double ; *mod.*

Viridiflora (The Green Rose) : petals are completely green, more curious than pretty ; *mod.*

THE MINIATURE CHINA ROSE.

(*Rosa Lawrenceana*)

The Miniature China or Fairy Rose is supposed to be a distinct species introduced from China in 1810. These Roses are of the dwarfest habit possible, growing only a few inches in height, and yet loaded with beautiful flowers of the smallest size. They may truly be called Roses in miniature. There are some fifteen or sixteen varieties, but the most popular and generally cultivated is the Fairy ; flowers rosy pink. If they are planted out, they should have a warm light dry soil, but they seem to be best suited for pot culture.

THE TEA-SCENTED ROSE.

(*Rose indica odorata.*)

The Rosa odorata, one of the most tender, one of the most fragrant of all Roses, was introduced from China in 1810; this, and the old yellow Tea-scented Rose, introduced in 1824, became the parents of all the beautiful varieties in this class. The whole tribe are more or less tender, though many of the varieties possess greater vigour and a more hardy constitution than the parent plants.

These Roses (excepting in the north and colder parts of England) may be grown successfully as low standards, and no Roses are more beautiful, or produce blooms in greater profusion throughout August and September ; for beds upon their own roots they are alike suitable, and very beautiful. In conservatories they grow and bloom in such perfection, and with so little trouble, that here they may be considered to be quite at home. For pot culture, too, they are perhaps the finest of all Roses. Directions for preparing beds for the Tea-scented Roses, protecting, &c., will be found from pages 24 to 39.

Abricoté (F. Dupuis): pale fawn, with deeper centre ; an excellent hardy free Rose ; *mod.*

Adam (Adam, 1833): flesh, centre salmon and fawn, moderately hardy and beautiful ; *mod.*

Adrienne Christophle (Guillot fils, 1868) : yellow centre, and apricot shaded with rosy peach ; sometimes deep yellow ; highly fragrant ; *vig.*

Alba rosea (Guillot père, 1848): white, tinted with rose, distinct and beautiful ; *vig.*

Aline Sisley (Guillot fils, 1874) : varying from deep purple-rose to shaded violet-red, medium size or large ; scent most delicious ; *vig.*

Amazone (Ducher, 1872): deep lemon-yellow, buds long, useful for cutting; *mod.*

Anna Olivier (Ducher, 1872): flesh and buff, shaded with rose, flowers tolerably large, smooth and beautiful; *vig.*

Beauté de l'Europe (Gonod, 1882): deep yellow, with reverse of petals coppered, very large and full, extra fine form; *Gloire de Dijon* type; *vig.*

Belle Fleur d'Anjou (Touvais, 1872): light flesh colour, shaded, large, globular, and double; somewhat like *Souvenir d'un Ami; vig.*

Belle Lyonnaise (Levet, 1869): deep canary-yellow, flowers globular, large and full; a fine wall or pillar Rose; *vig.*

Bougere (Bougere, 1832): very large, full and hardy; *vig.*

Catherine Mermet (Guillot fils, 1869): bright flesh-coloured rose, large, full, and finely formed; a superb Rose; *vig.*

Charles de Legrady (Pernet, 1885): carmine-red, changing to rosy crimson, edges of petals silvery, large and full; *vig.*

Chateau des Bergeries (V. Ledechaux, 1887): pale canary colour, deeper in the centre, large, very full and globular, fine in the bud: a good new Rose; *vig.*

Climbing Devoniensis (Pavitt, 1858): like the *Devoniensis*, but more vigorous in the habit; forms a fine climbing Rose; *vig.*

Clotilde (Rolland, 1867): creamy white, centre bright salmon-pink, flowers of moderate size and full; *mod.*

Comte de Paris (Hardy, 1839): pale flesh, very large and full; a moderately hardy and superb Rose; *vig.*

Comte de Sembui (Neauve Ducher, 1874): salmon-rose, reverse of petals silvery, large, full and well formed; growth very vigorous, very distinct and good; *vig.*

Comtesse de Frigneuse (Guillot, 1886): canary-yellow, striking colour, large and full; *mod.*

Comtesse de Nadaillac (Guillot fils, 1871): orange and copper, centre salmon colour, fine deep petals and handsome bud, highly fragrant; a superb Rose; *vig.*

Comtesse Horace de Choiseul (Leveque, 1886): pale rose colour, shaded with coppery yellow, large, full and finely formed; *vig.*

Comtesse Ouvaroff (Margottin, 1860): delicate cream, suffused with pink, petals of good substance; *mod.*

Comtesse Riza du Parc (Schwartz, 1876): metallic rose, changing to pink, flowers large and well formed; distinct; *mod.*

Dacid Pradel (Pradel, 1851): pale rose and lavender, mottled; a peculiar flower, distinct and pretty; *mod*.

Devoniensis (Foster, 1838): creamy white, centre sometimes blush; a most superb and deliciously-scented Rose: *mod*.

Duc de Magenta (Margottin, 1859): pale flesh, delicately tinted with fawn, petals large and of fine waxy substance, flowers large; *mod*.

Duchesse de Bragance (Dubreuil, 1887): bright canary-yellow, edges paler, very full and opens well; *vig*.

Duchess of Edinburgh (Nabonnand, 1874): deep glowing crimson, very free flowering; distinct and very beautiful; *mod*.

Edouard Gautier (Pernet, 1884): yellowish, with rose reflex, large, full, globulous, well formed; a seedling from *Devoniensis*; *mod*.

Etendard de Jeanne d'Arc (F. Margottin fils, 1884): beautiful cream-white changing to the purest white, flower very large, full, always opening well, much in the form of *Gloire de Dijon*, as also in the foliage; growth very vigorous; extra; a seedling from *Gloire de Dijon*; *vig*.

Etoile de Lyon (Guillot, 1882): fine striking sulphur-yellow, deeper in the centre, very large, full, and very fine form; one of the best yellow Roses ever raised; *vig*.

Exadelphé (Nabonnand, 1886): yellow, large and full, very sweetly scented; a splendid new Rose; *vig*.

Fiancialles de la Princess Stephanie (Levet): salmon-orange yellow, medium size; a seedling from *Gloire de Dijon*; *mod*.

Gloire de Dijon (Jacotot, 1853): buff, with orange centre, very large and double, handsome foliage and vigorous free-blooming habit; the most useful of all the Tea-scented Roses; *vig*.

Goubault (Goubault, 1843): salmon-pink, highly fragrant, most beautiful in the bud; *mod*.

Grace Darling (Bennett, 1884): creamy white, tinted and shaded with peach-colour, distinct, large and full, opening well; *vig*.

Homere (Robert, 1859): blush, with deeper centre, very free and hardy; beautiful in the bud; *vig*.

Hon. Edith Gifford (Guillot, 1883): blush-white, base of petals slightly yellow, centre rosy salmon changing to white; a large, full, and finely shaped Rose; *vig*.

Innocente Pirola (Ducher, 1878): very light fawn, changing to white ; a charmingly formed flower of medium size ; beautiful in bud ; *vig.*

Isabella Sprunt (Sprunt, 1866) : orange-yellow, fine buds for bouquets ; *vig.*

Jaune d'Or (Oger, 1863) : fine golden yellow, flowers full and globular, medium size, beautiful ; *mod.*

Jeanne Abel (Guillot, 1883), pink-white, yellowish in the centre, of medium size, full, and well-formed ; a free bloomer ; *vig.*

Jean Ducher (Ducher, 1874) : salmon-yellow, shaded with rose-peach in the centre, large, full, and globular, growth very vigorous ; distinct and superb ; *vig.*

Jean Pernet (Pernet, 1867) : light orange-yellow, outer petals paler, flowers of moderate size and double ; *vig.*

Jules Finger (Ducher, 1879) : bright red, passing to clear red, shaded outside of flower, large, full, and fine form ; *vig.*

La Boule d'Or (Margottin, 1860), outer petals pale yellow, centre rich nankeen-yellow, flowers globular and very large, with fine broad smooth petals ; *mod.*

La Sylphide (Laffay) : outer petals cream, tinted with pale carmine, centre fawn ; large, full, and well formed, highly fragrant ; *mod.*

L'Elegante (Guillot, 1883) : Chinese rose, copper-yellow in the centre, medium size, fine form : a very select colour, and quite new. First Class Certificate ; *vig.*

Letty Coles (Keynes, 1875) : shaded pink; a sport from *Madame Willermoz ; vig.*

Le Pactole (Pean) : lemon, centre pale-yellow : a good and moderately hardy Rose ; *mod.*

Louis de Savoie (Ducher, 1853) : clear pale yellow, very large and full, good shape, and vigorous habit, very fragrant ; *vig.*

Louis Richard (Ducher, 1877) : copper-rose, changing to deep red in the centre, large, full and well formed ; *vig.*

Luciole (Guillot, 1887), rosy red, tinted with coppery yellow, large, full, and of good shape and habit, deliciously scented ; *vig.*

Ma Capucine (Levet, 1871) : orange-yellow, nasturtium colour, small and semi-double ; *mod.*

Madame A. Etienne (Bernaix, 1887) : rosy claret colour on edges of petals, gradually diminishing to pale rose with white in the centre : petals very large, flowers large, full and cupped ; *mod.*

Madame Angele Jacquier (Guillot fils, 1879): flamed cerise, with coppered yellow at the base, charming bright colour, flowers large, full and well formed ; a distinct and beautiful Rose ; *vig.*

Madame Barillet Deschamps (Bernède, 1855): white, centre cream, large and well formed, very free bloomer and excellent; *mod.*

Madame Berard (Levet, 1870): bright buff or fawn colour, with slight salmon tint, flowers very large, full and well formed ; a superb Rose for pillar or wall ; *vig.*

Madame Bonnet Eymard (Pernet, 1874) : pure white, sometimes yellow in the centre, full and of medium size; blooms freely; *mod.*

Madame Brary (Guillot père, 1848) : see *Alba rosea ; vig.*

Madame Camille (Guillot fils, 1871): delicate rose, violet shade, veined flowers, very large and full ; a fine Rose, free habit ; *vig.*

Madame Caro (Levet, 1880): salmon-yellow, of medium size, fine form, very full ; *vig.*

Madame Célina Noirey (Guillot fils, 1868): salmon-rose, flowers large and full ; *vig.*

Madame Chedane Guinoisseau (Leveque, 1880) : sulphured canary-yellow ; beautiful bud, in the shape of *Madame Falcot :* distinct ; *vig.*

Madame Cusin (Guillot, 1882) : purple-rose, with white centre, tinted with yellow, large, full and well formed ; *vig.*

Madame Denis (Gonod, 1872) : waxy white, centre fawn and flesh, flowers large, full and cupped ; a distinct and very fine Rose, with a peculiar musk scent : *mod.*

Madame de Vatry (Guerin, 1855) : centre bright pink, slightly tinted, outer petals paler, good size, full : *vig.*

Madame de Watteville (Guillot, 1884) : white, lightly salmoned, large, full, well-formed : remarkable for its colour ; extra ; *mod.*

Madame Emile Dupuy (Levet, 1870) : pale fawn, flowers large, full and well formed ; a good Rose for wall or pillar : *vig.*

Madame Eugène Verdier (Levet, 1883) : deep chamois, large and well formed ; a first-class variety, and a good climber; *vig.*

Madame Falcot (Guillot fils, 1858) : deep rich orange-yellow, petals large, flowers double ; rich dark foliage ; a beautiful Rose; *vig.*

Madame François Janin (Levet, 1872) : orange-yellow, centre coppery, medium size, very sweet ; *mod.*

Madame Hippolyte Jamain (Guillot fils, 1869) : pure white, centre coppery-yellow, tipped with light rose, large and full : *vig.*

Madame Honoré Defresne (C. Levet, 1886) : beautiful deep yellow, with coppery reflex, large, full and of good form ; *vig.*

Madame Joseph Halphen (Margottin, 1858) : white, beautifully tinted with carmine ; full and free blooming ; *mod.*

Madame Joseph Schwartz (Schwartz, 1880) : white, tinged with flesh-rose, full, medium size ; a seedling from *Comtesse Labarthe ;* extra fine ; *vig.*

Madame Jules Margottin (Levet, 1871) : copper and rosy cerise, variable, distinct, and very pretty ; *vig.*

Madame Lambard (Lacharme, 1877) : fine, bright red, large, full, and well-formed buds ; beautiful and distinct ; *mod.*

Madame Levet (Levet, 1869) : buff, centre shaded salmon, very much resembling *Gloire de Dijon*, large, cupped and full ; *mod.*

Madame Margottin (Guillot fils, 1866) : rich yellow, with salmon-pink centre, full and of good form ; *vig.*

Madame Maurin (Guillot père, 1853) : cream and fawn, flowers large, full and finely formed ; a beautiful and distinct kind ; *mod.*

Madame Remond (Lambert, 1885) : yellow, outside petals shaded Nasturtium yellow ; specially good for pot culture ; *mod.*

Madame Scipion Cochet (Bernaix, 1887) : canary-yellow, shaded with white, and tipped with rose, large and double ; a striking variety ; *vig.*

Madame Sertot (Pernet) : white, large, full and well formed; *mod.*

Madame Trifle (Levet, 1869) : pale fawn, changing to cream, shape and habit like *Gloire de Dijon*, flowers somewhat paler ; a good Rose; *vig.*

Madame Welche (Ducher, 1878) : flowers very large and double, of the finest form, the outside petals pale yellow, the centre deep orange, often shaded reddish copper ; *mod.*

Madame Willermoz (Lacharme, 1845) : creamy white, centre tinted with fawn, petals very thick and finely formed ; *vig.*

Mdlle. Alexandrine Bruel (Levet, 1885) : white, large and full ; a seedling from *Gloire de Dijon ; mod.*

Mdlle. Annette Murat (Levet, 1885) : lemon-yellow, large and full ; *mod.*

Mdlle. Cecile Berthod (Guillot fils, 1871) : golden yellow, colour clear and beautiful, flowers cupped, tolerably large and full ; distinct ; *vig.*

Mdlle. Clotilde Soupert (Levet, 1884) : fine carmine-rose, large, very full, always opening well ; a seedling from *Gloire de Dijon ; vig.*

Mdlle. Elisabeth de Gramont (Levet, 1887) : bright rose colour, base of the petals coppery yellow, large, full, and of good shape ; a good new variety ; *vig.*

Mdlle. Lazarin Poizeau (Levet, 1876) : deep canary-yellow, small conical-shaped buds ; quite a gem for button-hole flowers; *vig.*

Mdlle. Marie Arnaud (Levet, 1872) : fine canary-yellow, centre deep golden yellow ; *mod.*

Mdlle. Marie Berton (Levet, 1873) : pale yellow, changing to white, very large and fine ; a good wall Rose ; *mod.*

Mdlle. Mathilde Lenaerts (Levet, 1879) : fine bright rose, bordered with white, of medium size or large, full, and very well formed ; climbing variety ; *vig.*

Mdlle. Therese Genevay (Levet, 1874) : fine peach-rose, large, full, and of fine form ; blooms freely, very effective ; *vig.*

Marcelin Roda (Ducher, 1872) : pale yellow, centre canary-yellow, flowers good size, globular and full ; a beautiful Rose ; *vig.*

Maréchal Bugeaud : bright rose, very large and full ; a moderately early and excellent Rose ; *vig.*

Marie de Medicis : centre fawn, outer petals mottled with crimson, highly fragrant ; *mod.*

Marie Ducher (Ducher, 1868) : cream and fawn, flowers large, full and well formed, the shape of the flower and habit of the plant resembling *Gloire de Dijon* ; a good Rose ; *mod.*

Marie Guillot (Guillot fils, 1873) : beautiful white, large, globular, full, of very fine form ; a superb Rose ; *vig.*

Marie Sisley (Guilot fils, 1868) : cream, deeply margined and shaded with rosy salmon, size moderate, full, and very fragrant; *vig.*

Marie Van Houtte (Ducher, 1871) : white, slightly tinted with yellow, border of the petals tipped with rose, flowers quite full and well formed ; a superb Rose; *vig.*

Marquise de Sanima (Ducher, 1875) : copper-rose centre, sometimes light rose, in the way of *Reine de Portugal*, large, full, and fine form ; *vig.*

Miss Ethel Brownlow (A. Dickson & Sons, 1887) : bright salmon-pink, shaded yellow at base of petals, flowers large, of great substance and most perfect form, always opening well ; petals thick, large, round, and very smooth ; *vig.*

K

Miss May Paul (Levet, 1882) : white, lilac in the interior, outside petals red, large, and well formed; of a climbing habit; *vig.*

Monsieur Furtado (Laffay, 1866) : very bright sulphur-yellow, medium size, full, and finely formed ; *mod.*

Niphetos (Bougere, 1844) : white, centre pale straw, long buds, very large thick petals in dry weather ; a superb Rose; *vig.*

Pauline Labonte : outer petals flesh, tinted cream, centre deep salmon-buff, very large, full, and fragrant ; a distinct Rose ; *mod.*

Perfection de Montplaisir (Levet, 1871) : clear lemon, handsome buds; good and distinct ; *mod.*

Perle de Lyon (Ducher, 1872) : deep fawn and apricot, colour of *Madame Falcot*, petals large, flowers globular ; a beautiful yellow Rose ; *mod.*

Perle des Jardins (Levet, 1874) : fine straw-yellow, sometimes deep canary-yellow, very large, full, and fine form; one of the best yellow Roses ; *vig.*

Princess Beatrice (Bennett, 1887) : outer petals pale yellow, centre rich golden yellow, edge of petals slightly laced with bright rose; a distinct and handsome variety, of perfect form and a free bloomer ; *vig.*

Princess Prosper d'Aremberg (Soupert et Notting, 1881) : salmon-red, carmine in centre, reverse of petals clear carmine, of medium size, full ; *vig.*

Princess of Wales (Bennett, 1884) ; outside petals rosy yellow, centre rich deep golden yellow, the colour being exceedingly chaste and very waxy in appearance, quite distinct, opens well, buds long pointed; *vig.*

Reine du Portugal : golden yellow, flowers large, full, and globular ; a distinct and good yellow Rose ; *vig.*

Reine Maria Pia (Schwartz) : deep rose, crimson in the centre, large, full ; a seedling from *Gloire de Dijon ; vig.*

Rubens : white, delicately tinted with rose, flowers large and beautifully formed ; a superb Rose ; *vig.*

Safrano (Beauregard, 1839) : bright apricot, fine dark foliage, moderately hardy ; a most beautiful Rose in the bud; *vig.*

Shirley Hibberd (Levet, 1873) : nankeen-yellow, medium size, cupped and full ; a new colour, blooms freely ; *mod.*

Socrates (Robert, 1858) : deep rose, fawn centre, large and full ; *mod.*

Sombreuil (Robert, 1850): pale straw, large, double and very beautiful; hardy; *vig.*

Souvenir d'Elise (Marest, 1853): creamy white, petals large, flowers full and generally perfect, though occasionally it produces a hard centre; a superb Rose; *vig.*

Souvenir de Paul Neron (Levet, 1871): white, with rose and buff tint, flowers large and full; distinct and good; *vig.*

Souvenir de Therese Levet (Levet, 1883): red, shaded with scarlet, large and full; a new colour, extra; *vig.*

Souvenir d'un Ami (Defougere, 1846): salmon and rose, very large and full, large and handsome foliage: a superb Rose; *vig.*

Souvenir de Madame Pernet (Pernet, 1875): salmon-pink, petals broad, smooth and even; a good Rose; *vig.*

Sunset (P. Henderson & Co, 1884): deep apricot colour, of good size, free blooming and splendid in the bud; foliage of a deep crimson colour, contrasting beautifully with the flowers; *mod.*

The Bride (May, 1886): a white sport from *Catherine Mermet*, but much more free flowering; produces blooms of symmetrical form, large, full and perfect; highly recommended; *vig.*

Triomphe de Milan (Ducher, 1876): pale yellow, deeper in the centre, form and colour of *Triomphe de Rennes;* a good and distinct Rose; *vig.*

Unique (Guillot fils, 1869): white ground, flamed with rose and purple; a distinct Rose, but delicate; *mod.*

Vicomtesse de Cazes (Pradel, 1844): yellow, centre copperish yellow; tender; *vig.*

Yellow (1824): pale yellow, very large and fine petals; beautiful in the bud, but very tender; *mod.*

HYBRID TEA-SCENTED.

Antoine Mermet (Guillot fils, 1883): deep carmine-rose, petals bordered with white, very large, full, well formed, cupped; a seedling from *Madame Falcot; vig.*

Attraction (Dubreuil, 1886): clear carmine, shaded China-rose; a very free-flowering and good variety; *vig.*

Beauty of Stapleford (Bennett, 1878): outer range of petals very pale pinkish rose, gradually shaded to a deep rosy centre; *vig.*

Bedford Belle (Laxton, 1884) : blush-white, tinted rose externally, large, full and expanding well ; raised from *Gloire de Dijon* and *Souvenir du Comte Cavour ; vig.*

Camoens (Schwartz, 1882) : bright China-rose, deep yellow, almost always striped with white, of medium size ; *mod.*

Cheshunt Hybrid (Paul & Son, 1873) : colour cherry-carmine, large full open flowers ; very hardy and distinct ; a very fine pillar or wall Rose ; *vig.*

Countess of Pembroke (Bennett, 1882) : delicate satiny rose, large, full and of perfect shape, sweetly scented ; *vig.*

Distinction (Bennett, 1882) : shaded peach colour, not very full, but well-shaped, and opens freely ; *vig.*

Duchess of Connaught (Bennett, 1878) : pale rose and lavender, dwarf hybrid habit, flowers large and well formed ; *mod.*

Duke of Connaught (Bennett, 1878) : deep velvety crimson, edged with the brightest red ; one of the best of this class ; *mod.*

Gipsy (Laxton, 1884) : dark velvety red, every bloom coming perfect, like a miniature *Charles Lefebvre ; vig.*

Hon. George Bancroft (Bennett, 1878) : flowers very large, colour bright rosy crimson, shaded purple ; *vig.*

Jean Sisley (Bennett, 1878) : flowers very large, very full of petal, colour outside petals rosy lilac, the centre bright pink ; *mod.*

Lady Mary Fitzwilliam (Bennett, 1882) : bright delicate flesh colour, flowers of globular form and rather full ; a good exhibition variety ; *vig.*

Madame Joseph Desbois (Guillot, 1886) : flesh white, centre rosy salmon, very large, full, and of good shape ; raised from *Baroness Rothschild* and *Madame Falcot* ; a good new Rose ; *vig.*

Madame Barthelemy Levet (Levet, 1879) : rich deep clear yellow ; good form ; *mod.*

Michael Saunders (Bennett, 1878) : flowers very large, of good form, colour bronzy pink, very sweet scented ; *vig.*

Nancy Lee (Bennett, 1879) : colour bright rosy pink, dwarf hybrid habit, moderate size ; *mod.*

Pierre Guillot (Guillot, 1879) : bright dazzling red, petals bordered with white, very large, with erect flower, well formed, very free bloomer ; extra fine ; *vig.*

The Meteor (W. Paul & Son, 1887) : rich dark velvety crimson, constant and free bloomer ; a good new Rose ; *vig.*

Viscountess Folkestone (Bennett, 1886): creamy pink, centre salmon-pink, large, full, and very sweet; *vig.*

W. F. Bennett (Bennett, 1885): crimson, large and double, very fragrant; a most valuable variety for forcing for winter blooming, the flowers being produced in great abundance; *vig.*

Ye Primrose Dame (Bennett, 1886): primrose colour, centre apricot, free blooming, full and of good form; *vig.*

THE NOISETTE ROSE.

The Old Blush or original Noisette is of American origin; the characteristic properties are its blooming in large clusters, free habit of growth (producing long vigorous shoots), and a rich perfume, partaking of the fragrance of the Musk and Tea-scented Roses. Many of the varieties raised have been crossed with the Tea-scented, and thereby have become less hardy than the original kind; they are, however, little less valuable on that account, for though not so well suited for standards, they form the finest of Roses for south and west walls; many of them have large handsome flowers, highly fragrant, and of vigorous habit. Maréchal Niel may be instanced as being the finest double yellow perpetual-blooming Rose in cultivation. Some few varieties are of moderate growth, adapted for standards or half-standards.

In pruning the vigorous growers, thin out the small and unripe wood, and shorten the remaining shoots one-third or one-half. Cloth of Gold should either be grown against a south wall, or planted out in the conservatory. It should be encouraged to make all the growth possible, when after the first or second year it will commence to bloom.

Aimée Vibert (Vibert, 1828): pure white, blooming in large clusters; very pretty handsome glossy foliage; a good wall Rose; *vig.*

America (Page, 1859): cream, with salmon and fawn centre, large, and very full; a fine Rose, but suitable only for south wall or the conservatory; does not open freely when grown as a standard: *vig.*

American Banner (Cartwright, 1879): striped rose and white like the *York and Lancaster*; peculiar; *mod.*

Bouquet d'Or (Ducher, 1872): deep yellow, centre copper colour, large and full; a climbing or wall Rose; *vig.*

Celine Forestier (Leroy, 1858): deep canary-yellow, outer petals pale yellow, flowers good size, well formed and highly fragrant; an excellent climbing Rose for south walls or conservatory; *vig.*

Cloth of Gold (Coquereau, 1843): pure yellow, globular, very large and very double; a superb Rose, but a shy bloomer, and very tender: a fine Rose for a south wall; *vig.*

Eclair de Jupiter: light crimson colour, beautiful and attractive; a good pillar Rose; *vig.*

Fellenberg: crimson, very bright and beautiful, clustering; a fine pillar Rose; *vig.*

Jaune Desprez (Desprez, 1838): fawn, pink and fawn centre; vigorous growing, highly scented, superb wall Rose; *vig.*

Lamarque (Maréchal, 1830): sulphur-white, very large and full: a fine wall Rose; *vig.*

Madame Caroline Kuster (Pernet, 1872): centre canary-yellow, outer petals pale lemon, flowers large, globular; a very fine Rose; *vig.*

Madame Miolan Carvalho (Leveque, 1875): deep sulphur-yellow, large, full, and fine form; a seedling from *Cloth of Gold*; *vig.*

Maréchal Niel (Pradel, 1864): rich brilliant yellow, petals large, smooth, and of good substance, flowers very large, full, deep, and exquisitely formed; the most superb of all yellow Roses; *vig.*

Narcisse (Crozy, 1859): beautiful straw-yellow, medium, full and free blooming; *vig.*

Ophirie (Goubault, 1841): bright salmon and fawn, distinct and peculiar; best adapted for a weeping, pillar, or wall Rose; *vig.*

Rêve d'Or (Ducher, 1869): orange-yellow, flowers moderate size and full; a good climbing Rose; *vig.*

Solfaterre (Boyau, 1843): fine sulphur-yellow, superb, large and full; a fine Rose for a wall; *vig.*

Triomphe de Rennes (Lansezeur, 1857): straw, centre pale yellow, highly fragrant, flowers of good size and well formed; an excellent Rose; *vig.*

Unique Jaune (Moreau, 1872): pale fawn, with flesh tint, very pretty colour, clustering in the way of *Jaune Desprez*, and quite as sweet; fine foliage; an excellent wall Rose; *vig.*

William Allan Richardson (Ducher, 1878): beautiful orange yellow; superb in the bud; *vig.*

HYBRID NOISETTE.

Albane d'Arneville (Schwartz, 1885): pure white, slightly tinted flesh colour, medium and full; petals imbricated, free blooming; *vig.*

Madame Alfred Carriere (Schwartz, 1879): flesh-white, with salmon-yellow at the base of the petals, large, full, well-formed; a very vigorous climber; *vig.*

Madame Fanny de Forest (Schwartz, 1883): salmon-white in opening, changing to white, tinted with rose; large; *mod.*

Olga Maris (Schwartz, 1873): flesh-white, medium and full; *mod.*

Perfection des Blanches (Lacharme, 1872): pure white, blooming in clusters, flowers of medium size and full; *mod.*

Perle des Blanches (Lacharme, 1872): pure white, medium size, full and globular, blooming in clusters; *mod.*

A SELECT LIST OF ROSES ADAPTED TO VARIOUS CIRCUMSTANCES, SITUATIONS, &c.

1.—*Selection of about* 100 *hardy Roses, suitable for growing in the neighbourhood of large manufacturing towns, where much smoke prevails.*

For 50 *of the choicest varieties, take those marked thus* (*).
For 24 *only, select those marked thus* (†).

Bourbon.—Apolline, *Baron Gonella, *Baronne de Noirmont, Catherine Guillot, Empress Eugénie, Sir Joseph Paxton, Queen.

China.—Cramoisie Superieure, †*Mrs. Bosanquet, Old Blush.

**Climbing Roses.*—All excepting the Banksian.

Damask.—*La Ville de Bruxelles.

French.—*Boula de Nanteuil, *Kean, Ohl.

Hybrid Bourbon.—†*Charles Lawson, Coupe d'Hébé, †*Madame Isaac Pereire.

Hybrid China.—*Brennus, *Chénédolé, *Fulgens, Leopold de Bauffremont, Madame Riviere.

Hybrid Perpetual.—*Abel Grand, †*Alfred Colomb, *Anna Alexieff, Antoine Mouton, †*Baronne Prevost, Beauty of Waltham, Boieldieu, †Boule de Neige, *Captain Christy, †*Centifolia rosea, †*Charles Lefebvre, *Climbing Jules Margottin, †*Comtesse de Chabrillant, *Comtesse de Serenyi, †*Countess of Oxford, Crimson Bedder, †*Dr. Andry, Duc de Rohan, Duc de Wellington, †Duke of Albany, †*Duchess of Bedford, †Duchesse de Vallombrosa, Edouard Morren, Exposition de Brie, Felix Genero, Fisher Holmes, †*General Jacqueminot, †*Jean Liabaud, †*John Hopper, †*John Stuart Mill, †*Jules Margottin, La Duchesse de Morny, La France, La Reine, *La Rosiere, Leopold I., *Madame Caillat, *Madame Charles Crapelet, *Madame Clemence Joigneaux, *Madame Gabriel Luizet, †Madame Knorr, Mdlle. Marie Rady, Marie Beauman, *Marquise de Castellane, †*Maurice Bernardin, *Merveille de Lyon, Miss Hassard, *Monsieur Boncenne, Monsieur Benoit Comte, †*Monsieur Paul Neron, Mrs. Rivers, Nardy Frères, Paul Verdier, †*Pierre Notting, President Willermoz, *Prince Camille de Rohan,

*Senateur Vaisse, Souvenir d'Arthur Sansal, Sultan of Zanzibar, Victor Verdier.

Noisette.—*Aimée Vibert, *Celine Forestier, Fellenberg, Ophirie, †*William A. Richardson.

**Scotch Roses.*

Sweet Brier.—*Double Scarlet.

Tea-scented.—Belle Lyonnaise, Climbing Devoniensis, *Etendard de Jeanne d'Arc, *Gloire de Dijon, Sombreuil.

Hybrid Tea-scented.—Cheshunt Hybrid, Reine Marie Henriette.

2.—*Selection of about* 100 *hardy Roses, suitable for the North of England and Scotland, also for cold localities.*

For 50 of the choicest varieties, take those marked thus (*).
For 24 only, select those marked thus (†).

Austrian.—*Harrisonii, †*Persian Yellow.

Bourbon.—Baronne de Noirmont, Empress Eugénie, *Michael Bonnett, Sir Joseph Paxton, Queen.

China.—Archduke Charles, Cramoisie Supérieure, Mrs. Bosanquet.

Climbing Roses.—All excepting the Banksian.

Damask.—La Ville de Bruxelles, *Madame Zoutman.

French.—*Boule de Nanteuil, Kean, *Ohl.

Hybrid Bourbon.—*Charles Lawson, Coupe d'Hébé, †Madame Isaac Pereire, *Paul Ricaut.

Hybrid China.—Brennus, *Chénédolé, Double Margined Hip, Fulgens.

Hybrid Perpetual.—†*Abel Carriere, *Abel Grand, †*Alfred Colomb, Antoine Ducher, Antoine Mouton, Baronne de Maynard, Baronne Prevost, †*Boule de Neige, †Centifolia rosea, †*Charles Lefebvre, *Climbing Jules Margottin, †*Comtesse de Chabrillant, *Comtesse de Serenyi, †*Countess of Oxford, †*Crimson Bedder, †*Dr. Andry, Duc de Rohan, Duc de Wellington, †Duchess of Bedford, *Duchesse de Vallombrosa, *Duke of Edinburgh, *Dupuy Jamain, *Edouard Morren, *Exposition de Brie, *Felix Genero, François Lacharme, *Horace Vernet, *Jean Liabaud, †*John

Hopper, John Stuart Mill, †*Jules Margottin, *La Rosiere, Leopold I., Lord Macaulay, Madame Caillat, †*Madame Charles Crapelet, †*Madame Charles Wood, *Madame Knorr, †*Madame la Baronne de Rothschild, *Madame Gabriel Luizet, Madame Victor Verdier, Marie Beauman, †*Mdlle. Marie Rady, *Marquise de Castellane, Maurice Bernardin, *Merveille de Lyon, Miss Hassard, Monsieur Boncenne, *Monsieur Etienne Levet, †*Monsieur Paul Neron, †*Pierre Notting, Prince Camille de Rohan, *Senateur Vaisse, †*Sir Garnet Wolseley, Souvenir de Arthur Sansal, Sultan of Zanzibar, Victor Verdier.

Moss.—Baronne de Wassenaer, †*Crested, *Gloire des Mousseuses, Lanei, *White Bath.

Perpetual Moss.—Blanche Moreau, General Drouot, Madame Edouard Ory, Perpetual White.

Provence.—†*Cabbage, De Meaux, Unique.

Sweet Briar.—Double Scarlet.

Tea-scented.—†*Gloire de Dijon, Gloire de Bordeaux.

Hybrid Tea-scented.—*Reine Marie Henriette.

3.—*Selection of* 100 *of the finest Exhibition Roses.*

For 50 of the choicest varieties, take those marked thus (*).
For 24 only, select those marked thus (†).

Bourbon.—*Souvenir de la Malmaison.

Hybrid Perpetual.—†*Abel Carriere, †*Alfred Colomb, Abel Grand, *A. K. Williams, *Annie Wood, Auguste Rigotard, Avocat Duvivier, Beauty of Waltham, Camille Bernardin, *Captain Christy, Catherine Soupert, Centifolia rosea, Charles Darwin, †*Charles Lefebvre, †*Countess of Oxford, Countess of Rosebery, †*Comtesse de Serenyi, Devienne Lamy, Dr. Andry, *Duc de Rohan, Duc de Wellington, Duchesse de Caylus, †*Duchesse de Vallombrosa, Duke of Connaught, Duke of Edinburgh, †*Dupuy Jamain, *Edouard Morren, *Elie Morel, †*Emilie Hausburg, Exposition de Brie, Fisher Holmes, General Jacqueminot, Harrison Weir, Hippolyte Jamain, †*Horace Vernet, †*Jean Liabaud, John Hopper, John Stuart Mill, Jules Margottin, La Duchesse de Morny, *La France, *La Rosiere, Lady Sheffield, *Lælia, Le Havre, Lord Macaulay, *Louis Van Houtte (Lacharme), *Madame

Charles Crapelet, †*Madame Gabriel Luizet, *Madame Charles Wood, *Madame Georges Schwartz, Madame Lacharme, †*Madame la Baronne de Rothschild, †Madame Victor Verdier, Mdlle. Marie Rady, *Mdlle. Eugénie Verdier, Magna Charta, *Maréchal Vaillant, †*Marguerite de St. Amand, †*Marie Beauman, †*Marquise de Castellane, †Merveille de Lyon, *Monsieur Boncenne, Monsieur Etienne Levet, †*Monsieur E. Y. Teas, *Monsieur François Michelon, *Monsieur Noman, †*Pierre Notting, Pride of Waltham, Prince Arthur, *Prince Camille de Rohan, *Princess Beatrice, Reynolds Hole, Senateur Vaisse, *Sir Garnet Wolseley, Sultan of Zanzibar, Ulrich Brunner fils, Violette Bouyer, *Xavier Olibo.

Noisette.—†*Maréchal Niel.

Tea-scented.—Alba rosea, †*Belle Lyonnaise, Catherine Mermet, Comtesse de Nadaillac, †*Devoniensis, Francisque Kruger, *Gloire de Dijon, Jean Ducher, Madame Lambard, *Madame Willermoz, †*Marie Van Houtte, Niphetos, Perle des Jardins, *Souvenir d'Elise, Souvenir de Paul Neron, *Souvenir d'un Ami, *The Bride.

Hybrid Tea-scented.—†*W. F. Bennett.

4.—*Selection for bedding, grouping, or planting in masses.*

Austrian.—Harrisonii, Persian Yellow.

Bourbon.—Queen, Souvenir de la Malmaison.

China.—Cramoisie Supérieure, Mrs. Bosanquet, Old White.

Damask Perpetual.—Crimson Superb.

Hybrid Bourbon.—Paul Ricaut.

Hybrid China.—Double Margined Hip, Madame Plantier.

Hybrid Perpetual.—Alfred Colomb, Boule de Neige, Centifolia rosea, Charles Lefebvre, Comte Bobinsky, Comtesse d'Oxford, Crimson Bedder, Dr. Andry, Duke of Edinburgh, Dupuy Jamain, Etienne Levet, Fisher Holmes, Général Jacqueminot, John Hopper, Jules Margottin, La France, Louisa Wood, Madame Charles Crapelet, Madame Knorr, Mademoiselle Bonnaire, Marguerite de St. Amand, Marquise de Castellane, Monsieur Noman, Monsieur Paul Neron, Pierre Notting, Prince Camille de Rohan, Senateur Vaisse, Sir Garnet Wolseley, Souvenir de Charles Montault, Victor Verdier.

Moss.—Common, or Old Moss.
Noisette.—Aimée Vibert, Celine Forestier, Triomphe de Rennes.
Provence.—Old Cabbage, Unique or White.
Perpetual Scotch.—Stanwell Perpetual.
Sweet Briar.—Double Scarlet.

5.—*Selection of the best Climbing Roses for a south or east wall.*

Banksian.—White and Yellow.
Bourbon.—Acidalie.
Noisette.—Aimée Vibert, Celine Forestier, Cloth of Gold, Jaune Desprez, Lamarque, Maréchal Niel, Ophirie, Rêve d'Or, Triomphe de Rennes, William A. Richardson.
Tea-scented.—Belle Lyonnaise, Climbing Devoniensis, Gloire de Dijon, Homère, Madame Berard, Madame Falcot, Safrano, Sombreuil.
Hybrid Tea-scented.—Reine Marie Henriette.

For a west or north wall, or for open trellis-work.

Ayrshire.—Bennett's Seedling, Ruga, Multiflora alba.
Bourbon.—Acidalie, Sir Joseph Paxton.
Evergreen.—Banksiæflora.
Hybrid Bourbon.—Charles Lawson, Coupe d'Hébé, Juno.
Hybrid China.—Blairii No. 2, Chénédolé, Double Margined Hip, Fulgens, Leopold de Bauffremont, Madame Plantier, Magna Rosea.
Hybrid Perpetual.—Anna Alexieff, Baronne Prevost, Boule de Neige, Climbing Victor Verdier, Climbing Jules Margottin, Duke of Edinburgh, General Jacqueminot, Jules Margottin, Maréchal Vaillant, Monsieur Boncenne, Monsieur Paul Neron, Paul Verdier, Pierre Notting, Prince Camille de Rohan.
Noisette —Aimée Vibert, Celine Forestier, Fellenberg, Solfaterre.
Tea-scented.—Gloire de Dijon, Madame Levet, Madame Trifle, Marie Van Houtte, Sombreuil.

6.—*Selection of the finest Pillar or Pole Roses.*

Austrian.—Harrisonii, Persian Yellow.

Bourbon.—Acidalie, Appoline, Baronne de Noirmont, Sir Joseph Paxton.

Damask.—La Ville de Bruxelles.

Hybrid Bourbon.—Charles Lawson, Coupe d'Hébé, Juno.

Hybrid China.—Blairii No. 2, Brennus, Chénédolé, Fulgens, Leopold de Bauffremont, Madame Plantier, Magna Rosea.

Hybrid Perpetual.—Anna Alexieff, Baronne Prévost, Boule de Neige, Centifolia rosea, Climbing Charles Lefebvre, Climbing Jules Margottin, Climbing Madame Victor Verdier, Climbing Victor Verdier, Duke of Edinburgh, Edouard Morren, Eugène Appert, General Jacqueminot, Jules Margottin, Lord Raglan, Madame Clemence Joigneaux, Madame Gabriel Luizet, Madame Knorr, Magna Charta, Maréchal Vaillant, Monsieur Boncenne, Monsieur Paul Neron, Paul Verdier, Paul's Single Crimson, Paul's Single White, Pierre Notting, Prince Camille de Rohan.

Moss.—Luxembourg, Lanei.

Noisette.—Aimée Vibert, Celine Forestier, Eclair de Jupiter, Fellenberg, Jaune Desprez, La Biche, Ophirie, Rêve d'Or, Solfaterre, W. A. Richardson.

Hybrid of Noisette.—Madame Alfred Carriere.

Tea-scented.—Gloire de Dijon, Gloire de Bordeaux, Madame Levet, Madame Trifle.

7.—*Selection of the best Weeping Roses.*

Austrian.—Harrisonii.

Ayrshire.—Bennett's Seedling, Ruga.

Bourbon.—Appoline.

Boursault.—Weeping.

Evergreen.—Banksiæflora.

Hybrid China.—Blairii No. 2, Fulgens.

Multiflora.—Félicite Perpetue, The Garland.

Noisette.—La Biche, Ophirie, Solfaterre.

Tea.—Gloire de Dijon.

8.—*Six best Yellow Roses.*

Austrian.—Persian Yellow.
Noisette.—Cloth of Gold, Solfaterre, Maréchal Niel.
Tea-scented.—Etoile de Lyon, Perle des Jardins.

9.—*Six best White Roses.*

Hybrid Perpetual.—Boule de Neige, Merveille de Lyon, Violette Bouyer.
Provence.—Unique.
Tea-scented.—Niphetos, The Bride.

10.—*Six of the best Crimson Roses.*

Hybrid Perpetual.—Alfred Colomb, A. K. Williams, Charles Lefebvre, Duchess of Bedford, Marie Beauman, Senateur Vaisse.

11.—*Six of the finest Dark Roses.*

Hybrid Perpetual.—Abel Carriere, Duke of Connaught, Jean Liabaud, Louis Van Houtte (Lacharme), Monsieur Boncenne, Prince Camille de Rohan.

12.—*Selection of the finest Roses for pot culture.*

Where only a small collection is required, choose those sorts marked thus (*).

Bourbon.—*Souvenir de la Malmaison.
China.—*Mrs Bosanquet.
Hybrid Bourbon.—*Charles Lawson, *Juno.
Hybrid China.—Blairii, Chénédolé, Leopold de Bauffremont.
Hybrid Perpetual.—Abel Carriere, *Alfred Colomb, Alphonse Soupert, A. K. Williams, Baroness Rothschild, *Beauty of Waltham, Captain Christy, *Centifolia rosea, *Charles Lefebvre, Countess of Oxford, Comtesse de Serenyi, Dr. Andry, Duchess of Bedford, *Duke of Edinburgh, Eclair, Edouard Morren, Exposition de Brie, *General Jacqueminot, *Horace Vernet, Jean Liabaud, *John Hopper, *Jules Margottin, La France, Lælia, Louis Van Houtte, Madame Charles Crapelet, Madame Clemence Joigneaux, Madame Georges Schwartz, Madame Knorr, *Madame la Baronne de Rothschild, Madame Marie Finger, *Madame Victor Verdier, *Mdlle.

Marie Rady, Mdlle. Eugénie Verdier, Magna Charta, Marie Beauman, Marquise de Castellane, Merveille de Lyon, *Monsieur Etienne Levet, *Monsieur Noman, Monsieur Paul Neron, *Paul Verdier, *Pierre Notting, Pride of Waltham, *Senateur Vaisse, *Sir Garnet Wolseley, Ulrich Brunner fils, Violette Bouyer.

Moss.—*Common or Old, Gloire des Mousseuses, Lanei.

Noisette.—*Celine Forestier, Lamarque, Madame Caroline Kuster, *Maréchal Niel, Triomphe de Rennes, *William A. Richardson.

Provence.—Cabbage.

Tea-scented.—*Adam, *Alba rosea, Belle Lyonnaise, Climbing Devoniensis, Catherine Mermet, Comtesse de Nadaillac, Comtesse Riza du Parc, *Devoniensis, *Etendard de Jeanne d'Arc, Etoile de Lyon, *Franeisque Kruger, Gloire de Dijon, Innocente Pirola, Jean Ducher, Madame Berard, Madame Falcot, Madame Lambard, *Madame Margottin, *Madame Willermoz, Madame Sertot, Marie Van Houtte, *Marie Ducher, *Niphetos, Perfection de Montplaisir, *Perle des Jardins, Perle de Lyon, *President, Rubens, *Safrano, *Souvenir d'Elise, Souvenir de Paul Neron, *Souvenir d'un Ami, *Sunset, *The Bride.

13.—*Selection of the finest Roses for forcing.*

Bourbon.—Souvenir de la Malmaison.

China.—Cramoisie Superieure.

Damask Perpetual.—Crimson Superb.

Hybrid Bourbon.—Charles Lawson, Juno, Paul Ricaut.

Hybrid Perpetual.—Alfred Colomb, Alphonse Soupert, Beauty of Waltham, Boule de Neige, Charles Lefebvre, Countess of Oxford, Crimson Bedder, Duchess of Bedford, Duke of Edinburgh, Dupuy Jamain, Exposition de Brie, General Jacqueminot, Jean Liabaud, Jules Margottin, La France, La Reine, Madame Knorr, Madame Gabriel Luizet, Madame la Baronne de Rothschild, Marie Beauman, Marquise de Castellane, Maurice Bernardin, Merveille de Lyon, Monsieur Noman, Monsieur Paul Neron, Senateur Vaisse, Victor Verdier.

Moss.—Common, Gloire des Mousseuses, Lanei.

Noisette.—Lamarque, Maréchal Niel.

Provence.—Cabbage.

Tea-scented.—Alba rosea, Belle Lyonnaise, Catherine Mermet,

Comtesse de Nadaillac, Devoniensis, Gloire de Dijon Innocente Pirola, Jean Ducher, Louise de Savoie, Madame Bravy, Madame Camille, Madame Falcot, Madame Margottin, Madame Maurin, Madame Sertot, Madame Willermoz, Marie Guillot, Marie Van Houtte, Niphetos, Perle des Jardins, Souvenir d'Elise, Souvenir d'un Ami, Souvenir de Paul Neron, Sunset.

Hybrid Tea-scented.—W. F. Bennett.

14.—*Thirty-six of the finest Roses for growing as specimens, in pots, for exhibition.*

Bourbon.—Souvenir de la Malmaison.

Hybrid Bourbon.—Charles Lawson, Paul Ricaut.

Hybrid Perpetual.—Alfred Colomb, Charles Lefebvre, Comtesse Chabrillant, Countess of Oxford, Comtesse de Serenyi, Dr. Andry, Duchesse de Caylus, Duke of Edinburgh, Dupuy Jamain, Exposition de Brie, Sir Garnet Wolseley, Jules Margottin, La France, Lælia, Louis Van Houtte, Madame la Baronne de Rothschild, Madame Victor Verdier, Marguerite de St. Amand, Marie Beauman, Merveille de Lyon, Monsieur Paul Neron, Paul Verdier, Pierre Notting, Prince Camille de Rohan.

Noisette.—Celine Forestier, Maréchal Niel.

Tea-scented.—Alba rosea, Devoniensis, Gloire de Dijon, Madame Willermoz, Souvenir d'un Ami, The Bride.

15.—*For beds of Roses of brilliant and decided colours, select from the following kinds :—*

Brilliant Crimson.

Crimson Bedder, Duke of Teck, General Jacqueminot, Madame Victor Verdier, Senateur Vaisse.

Carmine-Crimson.

Alfred Colomb, Countess of Oxford, Dupuy Jamain, Madame C. Wood, Monsieur Etienne Levet, Sir Garnet Wolseley, Ulrich Brunner fils.

Dark Crimson.

A. K. Williams, Charles Lefebvre, Duc de Wellington, Duke of Edinburgh, Fisher Holmes, Monsieur E. Y. Teas.

DARK PURPLE AND CRIMSON.

Abel Carriere, Jean Liabaud, Louis Van Houtte (Lacharme), Monsieur Boncenne, Pierre Notting, Prince Camille de Rohan.

DEEP ROSE.

Annie Laxton, Edouard Morren, Mdlle. Marie Rady, Magna Charta, Marquise de Castellane, Marie Beauman, Marguerite de St. Amand.

PALE ROSE.

Alphonse Soupert, Comtesse Cecille de Chabrillant, Countess of Rosebery, La France, Madame Cusin, Madame Gabriel Luizet, Mdlle. Marie Finger.

PURE WHITE.

Aimée Vibert, Boule de Neige, Clara Sylvain, Mrs. Bosanquet, White China, Niphetos.

BLUSH WHITE.

Captain Christy, Madame Lacharme, Mdlle. Bonnaire, Marquise de Mortemart, Merveille de Lyon, Reine Blanche, Souvenir de la Malmaison, Souvenir de Paul Neron, Violette Bouyer.

PALE FLESH.

Baroness Rothschild, Devoniensis, Innocente Pirola, Mdlle. Eugène Verdier.

DEEP YELLOW.

Etoile de Lyon, Madame Falcot, Maréchal Niel, Perle des Jardins, Persian Yellow, Reine du Portugal.

PALE YELLOW.

Belle Lyonnaise, Celine Forestier, Gloire de Dijon, La Boule d'Or, Louise de Savoie, Narcisse, Rêve d'Or, Solfaterre, Triomphe de Rennes.

16.—*Very highly Scented Roses.*

Hybrid Perpetual.—Abel Grand, Alice Dureau, Beauty of Beeston, Beauty of Waltham, Boule de Neige, Camille Bernardin, Charles Lefebvre, Comtesse Cecille de Chabrillant, Constantine Fretiakoff, Dr. Sewell, Felix Genero, Géant des Batailles, La France, L'Esperance, Louis Van Houtte, Madame Furtado, Madame Gabriel

Luizet, Madame Knorr, Madame Thevenot, Marie Beauman, Monsieur Alfred Dumesnil, Monsieur E. Y. Teas, Mrs. Jowitt, Mrs. John Laing, R. C. Sutton, Senateur Vaisse, Souvenir de Charles Montault, The Puritan.

Bourbon.—Baronne de Noirmont, Madame Isaac Pereire.

Tea-scented.—Adrienne Christophle, Aline Sisley, Devoniensis, Goubault, La Sylphide, Louis de Savoie, Luciole, Madame Eugénie Verdier, Madame Margottin, Marie de Medicis, Marie Sisley, Socrates, Sombreuil, Souvenir d'un Ami, Viscountess Folkestone.

Hybrid Tea-scented.—Countess of Pembroke, Waltham Climber No. 2.

Noisette.—Celine Forestier, Jaune Desprez, Marechal Niel, Ophirie, Triomphe de Rennes, Unique Jaune.

Moss.—Common, or Old.

CALENDAR OF OPERATIONS.

JANUARY.—Presuming the necessary protection has been properly applied to all the tender varieties, there will be little to fear now from the effects of frost. It is requisite that every Rose plant should receive a good dressing of manure at least once a year; advantage should, therefore, be taken of hard frost to have it wheeled on and spread over the surface, and during open weather let it be forked in. I usually prepare for this purpose (a month or two before it is required) a large heap, consisting of horse dung and pig dung, to this is added a few hundredweight of half-inch bones, burnt earth, and any decayed vegetable matter at hand. About four or five spadefuls of this are put to each plant; and for the Rose beds it is spread about an inch thick over the surface. Any spare time may be advantageously employed in preparing labels and going over the stock, and renewing such as are obliterated.

FEBRUARY.—Proceed with pruning all the most hardy summer-blooming kinds, commencing with the French, Moss, Alba, and Provence, and finishing with the Hybrid China and Hybrid Bourbon. Let all planting be completed whenever the weather is favourable; it should never be delayed beyond the middle of March, for no plant suffers more than the Rose from late planting. Fork in manure, and take off close to the stem every root sucker as this operation proceeds. Where any plant is observed to be in an unhealthy condition, let it be taken up, the old soil removed, and replace with fresh loam and manure. Examine and trim the roots, and carefully remove all the suckers before re-planting.

MARCH.—If the summer-blooming Roses have been pruned as directed last month, proceed at once with the Hybrid Perpetuals, Bourbons, and the hardiest of the Noisettes. The moderate, and even free-growing Hybrid Perpetuals will require rather close pruning, and the dwarf varieties in this class must be cut down hard, the closer the better, provided a good eye is secured. There are many varieties in this class which have an erect habit of growth, the shoots being crowded together, and the blooms only seen at the top of the plant. A little assistance by tying out the branches will be necessary to make such assume a more branching appearance, and by this means handsomely formed heads of a good size may be obtained of all the compact-growing kinds. Pillar Roses should be pruned into a pyramidal form. Commence by training up one strong shoot, and keep the side branches well pruned in. Attend to plants in pots, and have them trained to the form desired as they are growing. Look well after grubs, and fumigate to destroy green-fly.

APRIL.—Tea-scented and China Roses may now be pruned: let the whole of this work be dispatched as soon as possible. See that the beds are properly forked and dressed. Mulch newly planted Roses; a little short straw, hay, or manure put upon the surface of the soil will effect this object. Evaporation during hot and dry weather being thus prevented, the growth of the plant is encouraged, and possibly the loss of those not well rooted prevented. Should the weather be dry, give a good watering; this, if done effectually where the plants are mulched, will not soon require repeating. Bear in mind, one thorough good watering is more beneficial than frequent small doses. Beds may now be prepared for planting the Tea-scented, China, and Bourbon Roses, grown upon their own roots. Choose for these a warm, dry situation: let the soil be prepared at least eighteen inches deep; it should consist of one half good rotten turfy loam, the other half equal proportions of leaf-mould, rotten manure, and sharp sand. Plant, when the weather is suitable, towards the middle or end of the month, but let the plants be previously well hardened under a north border; protect them also for a week or two after planting, by placing a few branches of evergreens amongst them.

MAY.—The plants will now be making considerable progress, and every opportunity should be embraced to examine and regulate the shoots, as well as to search for and destroy insects. The advantage of planting in open and dry situations will now be apparent. In such places the plants will be nearly free, or suffer very little from the attacks of green-fly, whereas those in confined situations will require almost daily attention to keep them free from this pest. Disbudding is an important operation, and can be performed whilst examining the plants for insects. Remove the small shoots where the heads are too much crowded, leaving the strong and vigorous shoots which are growing in a proper direction. By attending carefully to this point, additional strength is given to the plants, and the size and quality of the blooms are much improved, besides which the necessity of "thinning" at the time of pruning is lessened. Fumigate plants in greenhouses and frames to keep down green-fly, and where mildew appears apply flour of sulphur. If this proves ineffectual, try Fowler's Insecticide, using from two to two and a half ounces to the gallon; let the plant be syringed or otherwise well wetted with the mixture, and in a few hours afterwards syringe the plants over with clear water. Where the least sign of insect is observed upon the trees against walls, syringe frequently at night or morning. In favourable situations, towards the end of the month, many of the wall plants will be gay with flowers. Remove all suckers from the wild stock as they appear.

JUNE.—The directions given last month for the destruction of insects must be strictly attended to throughout the present month. The neglect of these precautions for only a few days may lead to the injury of many of the finest blooms. See that each plant is properly disbudded as previously directed ; also tie out the shoots of the compact and upright-growing varieties, where they are too much crowded. Where large blooms are desired, a few of the smaller buds should be thinned out with a pair of sharp-pointed scissors. Tie standard plants firmly to their stakes ; a high wind at this time would do injury to any not properly secured. Water recently planted beds of the Tea-scented and Chinese varieties, and all late planted Roses, should the weather be dry. Manure-water may be applied to established plants with good effect, particularly to those from which blooms are required for exhibition. Plants which were budded last summer will now be making vigorous shoots ; these must be carefully tied up as they grow, otherwise the first gust of wind will blow them out. Suckers will be numerous ; always take them off close to the stock.

JULY.—The greater portion of the plants will now be in full bloom, and if the needful attention has been given to pruning a few of the hardiest varieties in the autumn, and others again early and late in the spring, a succession of bloom will be kept up until the Perpetuals commence their second flowering, by which means a continuous bloom may be had from June till November. A stroll through the Rose garden at this season is delightful in the extreme, more especially early in the morning, when every bloom is fresh with dew and untarnished by the sun's rays. Those who have devoted time, labour, and attention to their plants will now derive the greater pleasure, and more fully appreciate their beauty. Now is the time to take notes, describing not only the flowers, but the habit and character of all new varieties. This will be found most useful at pruning time. If any plants are observed with insufficient bloom, try to ascertain the cause : with some sorts this may occur through improper pruning.

Note down the result produced by different manures, where applied by way of experiment. Many of the high-coloured and dwarf-growing Bourbon Roses bloom very indifferently during the hot summer months, the colours being faint and the quality of the bloom inferior, but towards the latter part of the summer and in early autumn these are most beautiful. It is well, therefore, to deprive them, or at least a part of them, of their summer bloom; the plants will then be strong, and produce an earlier and finer autumnal bloom. Gather the faded flowers daily, and whilst doing so observe if any of them are infested with insects. Where it is desired to save seed, leave the earliest blooms for that purpose. Give a top-dressing of manure to the Perpetuals when the first bloom is over, and water occasionally with weak liquid manure.

AUGUST.—This is the best month for budding; commence with those sorts which have made the earliest growth and have well matured shoots. Let the stocks be kept in a healthy growing state; never bud from a scion that is not firm and well ripened; tie with cotton, and let the ligature be loosened in about three weeks after budding.

SEPTEMBER.—Let all budding be completed as soon as possible. Loosen the ligature of those already done before it cuts into the bark, and attend to the removal of suckers, etc. This is the best month for budding upon the Manetti stock. Towards the end of the month, cuttings of all hardy Roses may be put in under hand-glasses. Choose a north border under a hedge or wall; let the cuttings be put in about four inches deep, and the soil pressed firmly round them. Water once or twice with clear lime water, which will keep the worms from disturbing the cuttings. Tender Roses in pots should now be put into the greenhouse, or otherwise protected from heavy rains. Continue to apply sulphur or Fowler's Insecticide where mildew is observed, or it will very soon destroy the foliage and bloom.

OCTOBER.—Examine the stock of plants, and note those to be replaced or removed for others next month. What purchases are intended to be made, either in new or old varieties, should be determined as soon as possible, as the strongest plants are always sold out early in the season ; and unless good robust plants are procured, there is little chance of having fine blooms the first season of planting. Have in readiness a quantity of loam, rotten manure, burnt weeds and sand. When alterations are contemplated, or a new Rosery is to be formed, let the ground be prepared this month ; if at all wet it must in the first place be drained, and afterwards trenched to the depth of eighteen inches or two feet, throwing the soil into ridges. Select and take up from the open ground, for potting, a few well-formed dwarf plants of good varieties ; cut them back rather hard, then place them in a cold frame, where they may remain, giving air and water as required. These plants without being forced will come into bloom towards May and the early part of June.

NOVEMBER.—Having made the selection required, proceed with planting whenever the soil is sufficiently dry, but by no means let it be done when the soil is wet or heavy ; it is better to let the plants remain in by the heels for a month or two than do this. See to the directions given for soil and planting. Remove any plant that is sickly or that does not appear to thrive properly ; examine the roots and trim them : take out all the old soil and replant in fresh soil and a small quantity of manure. Ill health may arise from various causes, such as deep planting, sour soil, too much manure, or unhealthy stock : in the latter case it would be better to throw the plant away and replace it with another. Briars for budding next season may be procured and planted this month.

DECEMBER.—Let the necessary materials for protecting the tender varieties be prepared and had in readiness to apply the moment that frost has fairly set in. The severe winter of 1861 proved so destructive to the tender Roses where no protection was applied, that every precaution should in future be taken to avoid a similar occurrence. If the weather continues open and dry, finish planting if possible, otherwise let it be deferred until February. Have the standards which are planted properly staked, that they may not be moved by the wind. Mulching should also be applied to newly planted Roses. It is better to put it on the surface now than in the spring.

A COMPLETE
CATALOGUE OF ROSES.

—◆—

IT would be next to impossible for such a list to attain absolute perfection. With the assistance of lists already issued and information derived from private sources, I have endeavoured to make it the most comprehensive register of Roses yet published.

Explanation of divisions of Catalogue, and of abbreviations used :—

First column : Name of Rose. Second column : Class or family to which it belongs, viz., A., Alba ; A.B., Austrian Briar ; Ayr., Ayrshire ; BK., Banksian ; Ben., Bengal ; B., Bourbon ; Bour., Boursault ; C., China ; D., Damask ; D.P., Damask Perpetual ; E., Evergreen ; Fr., French ; G., Gallica ; H.A., Hybrid Ayrshire ; H.C., Hybrid China ; H.N., Hybrid Noisette ; H.P., Hybrid Perpetual ; H.R., Hybrid Rugosa ; H.T., Hybrid Tea-scented ; Mac., Macartney ; Mic., Microphylla ; M., Moss ; Mult., Multiflora ; P.M., Perpetual Moss ; P.S., Perpetual Scotch ; N., Noisette ; P., Polyantha ; Pra., Prairie ; Prov., Provence, Rug., Rugosa ; S., Scotch ; T., Tea-scented. Third column : Name of the raiser. Fourth column : Year of introduction. Fifth column : Colour of flower. Sixth column : Relative size of flower. Seventh column : Habit of growth, viz., mod., moderate ; rob., robust ; vig., vigorous.

Name.	Class.	Raiser.	Year.	Colour.	Size.	Habit.
Abbé Berlèze	H.P.	Guillot fils	1864	cerise-red	2	vig.
Abbé Bramerel	H.P.	Guillot fils	1871	deep crimson	1	vig.
Abbé Fetel	H.P.	Ducher	1857	rose	2	mod.
Abbé Girardin	B.	Bernaix	1882	rose	1	vig.
Abbé Giraudier	H.P.	Levet	1869	bright rose	2	vig.
Abbé Lauray	H.P.	Trouillard	1864	bright rose	2	mod.
Abbé Reynaud	H.C.	Guillot fils	1863	carmine	1	vig.
Abbé Venière	H.P.	Guillot père	1867	clear rose	2	vig.
Abd-el-Kader	H.P.	Verdier	1860	bright crimson	2	mod.
Abel Carrière	H.P.	E. Verdier	1875	maroon-cmson	1	vig.
Abel Grand	H.P.	Damaizin	1865	light rose	1	vig.
Abraham Zimmermann	H.P.	Lévêque	1879	purple-red	1	vig.
Abricoté	T.	Dupuis	..	apricot-yellow	2	mod.
A Bouquets	T.	Cherpin	1872	yellow-white	2	mod.
Achille Gonod	H.P.	Gonod	1864	carmine-red	1	vig.
Acidalie	B.	Rousseau	1838	blush-white	1	vig.
Adam	T.	Adam	1833	rose-salmon	1	mod.
Adanson	H.P.	Schwartz	1874	red-amaranth	2	vig.
Adélaide Fontaine	H.P.	Fontaine	1856	light rose	2	mod.
Adelaide de Meynot	H.P.	Gonod	1883	rose-cerise	2	mod.
Adélaïde de Savoie	H.P.	Moreau	1864	satiny rose	2	vig.
Adèle Bécar	H.C.	Laffay	1847	bright rose	1	mod.
Adèle Bourdeau	B.	Vigneron	1873	light rose	1	vig.

Name.	Class.	Raiser.	Year.	Colour.	Size.	Habit.
Adèle Dufresnoy	H. P.	Robert	1876	rosy flesh	2	vig.
Adèle Jougand	T.	Ledechaux	...	yellow	3	mod.
Adelina Patti	H. P.	Fontaine	...	carmine-rose	2	mod.
Admiral Coubert	H. P.	Dubreuil	1885	carmine-red	2	mod.
Admiral Gravina	H. P.	Mor. et Rob.	..	purple	2	mod.
Admiral Nelson	H. P.	Ducher	1859	bright red	1	vig.
Admiral Seymour	H P.	Liabaud	1883	purple-red	1	vig.
Adolphe Bronguiart	H. P.	Margottin	1868	carmine-red	2	vig.
Adolphe Noblet	H. P.	Ledechaux	1861	bright red	2	vig.
Adolphe Poulain	H. P.	E. Verdier	...	red	2	vig.
Adrian Marx	H. P.	Bernardin	1866	cerise	1	vig.
Adrienne de Cardoville	B.	Guillot fils	1864	delicate rose	2	vig.
Adrienne Christophle	T.	Guillot fils	1868	apricot-yellow	1	vig.
Adrienne de Montebello	H. P.	Margottin	1868	satiny rose	1	mod.
A. Geoffroy St. Hilaire	H. P.	E. Verdier	1878	red-crimson	2	mod.
Aimée Vibert	N.	Vibert	1828	white	2	vig.
Aimée Vibert scandens	N.	Curtis	1841	white	2	rob.
Aimée Vibert variegata	N.	Schwartz	1878	white	2	vig.
Alba	BK.	...	1807	white	3	vig.
Alba carnea	H. P.	Touvais	1866	blush-white	2	vig.
Alba floribunda	H. P.	Touvais	1868	flesh	2	vig.
Alba mutabilis	H. P.	E. Verdier	1865	rose tinted	1	mod.
Alba odorata	Mac.	Levet	1876	yellow	3	vig.
Alba rosea	T.	Guillot père	1848	flesh-white	1	vig.
Albane d'Arneville	H. N.	Schwartz	1885	white	2	vig.
Albert la Blotais	H. P.	Mor. et Rob.	1882	purple-red	2	mod.
Albert Dureau	M.	E. Verdier	1869	bright red	2	mod.
Albert Payne	H. P.	Touvais	1873	flesh-pink	1	vig.
Albert de Stella	H. P.	Guillot	1858	cherry-red	2	mod.
Albion	H. P.	Liabaud	1869	cerise-red	1	vig.
Alcindor	H. P.	Lartey		rose	2	vig.
Alexander Chomer	H. P.	Liabaud	1874	deep red	1	vig.
Alexander Dickson	H. P.	Dickson	1873	rose	1	mod
Alexandre Dumas	H. P.	Margottin	1860	dark crimson	2	vig.
Alexandre Dupont	H. P.	Liabaud	1883	red-crimson	1	vig.
Alexandre Dutitre	H. P.	Lévêque	1842	rose	2	mod.
Alexandre de Humboldt	H. P.	C. Verdier	1860	bright rose	1	mod
Alexandrine Bachmeteff	H. P.	Margottin	1853	bright carmine	1	vig.
Alexandrine Belfroy	H. P.	Fontaine	1859	rose-pink	2	mod.
Alexina	Ben.	Beluze	1841	rose	2	mod.
Alexis Lepère	H. P.	Vigneron	1875	clear red	1	vig.
Alfred Colomb	H. P.	Lacharme	1865	rich red	1	vig.
Alfred de Dalmas	P. M.	Laffay	1855	flesh-pink	2	rob.
Alfred de Rougemont	H. P.	Lacharme	1862	fiery crimson	1	vig.
Alfred K. Williams	H. P.	Schwartz	1877	carmine-red	1	vig.
Alice Dureau	H. P.	Vigneron	1867	bright rose	1	vig.
Alice Leroy	M.	Trouillard	1842	pink	3	mod.
Aline Pierron	B.	Guillot	1858	red	2	mod.
Aline Rozey	H. N.	Schwartz	1885	flesh	3	mod.
Aline Sisley	T.	Guillot fils	1874	rose-red	1	vig.
Alpaide de Rotalier	H. P.	Campy	1863	velvety red	1	rob.
Alphonse Berlin	H. P.	Gautreau	1863	red-cerise	2	mod.

Name.	Class.	Raiser.	Year.	Colour.	Size.	Habit.
Alphonse Damaizin	H.P.	Damaizin	1861	bright crimson	2	mod.
Alphonse Fontaine	H.P.	Fontaine pè.	1868	red-carmine	1	vig.
Alphonse Karr	T.	Nabonnand	1878	deep red	1	vig.
Alphonse Karr	H.P.	Portemer	1845	flesh	2	mod.
Alphonse Karr	H.P.	Feuillet	1855	rose	3	mod.
Alphonse Lamartine	H.P.	Ducher	1853	rose	2	mod.
Alphonse Mortelmans	T.	Md. Ducher	1875	rose-lilac	2	vig.
Alphonse Soupert...........	H.P.	Lacharme	1884	rose	1	vig.
Alsace-Lorraine	H.P.	Duval	1879	deep crimson	1	vig.
Amadis	Bour.	Laffay	1829	crimson	2	vig.
A. M. Ampére	H.P.	Liabaud	1882	purple	2	mod.
Amazone	T.	Ducher	1872	deep yellow	2	mod.
Ambrogio Maggi	H.P.	Pernet	1879	bright rose	1	vig.
Amédée Langlois	B.	E. Verdier	1871	red-purple	1	vig.
Amédée Philibert	H.P.	Lévêque	1879	purple and red	1	vig.
Amélie Hoste	H.P.	Gonod	1874	light pink	1	vig.
America......................	N.	Page	1859	cream	2	vig.
American Banner............	N.	Cartwright	1879	carmine	3	mod.
American Beauty	H.P.	Bancroft	1885	rose-pink	1	vig.
Amœna	H.P.	Soup. et Not.	1877	rose-carmine	1	mod.
Anacréon	H.P.	Schwartz	1875			
André Dunand..............	H.P.	Schwartz	1871	tender rose	1	vig.
André Fresnoy	H.P.	Pernet	1868	deep red	1	mod.
André Gill	H.P.	R. Barrault	1883	red-carmine	1	vig.
André Leroy................	H.P.	Pradel	...	light rose	2	mod.
André Leroy d'Angers	H.P.	Trouillard	1862	maroon-crmsn.	1	vig.
André Nabonnand	T.	Nabonnand	1878	carmine-red	1	mod.
André Schwartz	T.	Schwartz	1884	crimson	2	vig.
Angèle Fontaine	H.B.	Fontaine	1877	red-carmine	2	mod.
Angélina Granger...........	H.P.	Granger	1852	rose-pink	2	mod.
Anicet Bourgeois	H.P.	Mor. et Rob.	1880	cherry-red	2	vig.
Anna Alexieff	H.P.	Margottin	1858	clear rose	1	vig.
Anne Beluze............ ...	B.	Beluze	1842			
Anna Blanchon..............	H.P.	Liabaud	1874	bright rose	1	rob.
Anna de Diesbach	H.P.	Lacharme	1858	bright rose	1	vig.
Anna Maria	Pra.	Feast	1843	pink	3	mod.
Anna Olivier	T.	Ducher	1872	flesh-rose	1	vig.
Anne Marie Cote	H.N.	Guillot fils	1875	white	2	mod.
Anne Marie de Montravel.	P.	Rambaux	1879	white	3	vig.
Annette Séant	T.	Levet	1869	sulphur	2	mod.
Annie Laxton	H.P.	Laxton	1871	rose-crimson	1	mod.
Annie Wood..................	H.P.	E. Verdier	1866	bright red	1	vig.
Anisette.......................	T.	Guillot	1852			
Antoine Alleon..............	H.P.	Margotn. fils	1872	cerise-red	1	vig.
Antoine Castel..............	H.P.	E. Verdier	1873	rose-red	1	mod.
Antoine Chantin	H.P.	E. Verdier	1883	rose	1	vig.
Antoine Devert..............	T.	Gonod	1880	sulphur-white	1	vig.
Antoine Ducher	H.P.	Ducher	1866	purple-red	1	rob.
Antoine Mermet	H.T.	Guillot fils	1884	carmine	2	mod.
Antoine Mouton	H.P.	Levet	1874	rich rose	1	vig.
Antoine Quihou	H.P.	E. Verdier	1879	purple-maroon	1	vig.
Antoine Wintzer	H.P.	E. Verdier	1884	red-carmine	1	vig.

Name.	Class.	Raiser.	Year.	Colour.	Size.	Habit.
Antonia Decarli	T.	Levet	1873	yellow	2	mod.
Antoinette Bouvague	T.	Beluze	1842			
Antonine Verdier	H.P.	Jamain	1871	rose-carmine	1	rob.
Apolline	D.	V. Verdier	1848	rosy pink	1	vig.
Arch. Elizabeth d'Autriche	H.P.	Mor. et Rob.	1882	rose	1	vig.
Archduc Charles	C.	Laffay	..	crimson	2	mod.
Archevêque de Cambrai	B.	Guillot	1851			
Archevêque de Paris	H.P.	Touvais	1861	purple & violet	2	vig.
Archimide	T.	Robert	1856	fawn	2	mod.
Ardoisé de Lyon	H.P.	Plantier	1865	violet-rose	2	vig.
Argo	S.		...	blush	3	vig.
Aristide Dupuis	H.P.	Trouillard	1867	ruby-red	1	rob.
Arles Dufour	H.P.	Liabaud	1862	crimson-purple	1	vig.
Armosa	B.	Marcheseau	1840	pink	2	mod.
Arténise	H.P.	Mor. et Rob.	1876	rose-carmine	1	vig.
Arthur Oger	H.P.	Oger	1874	red-purple	1	vig.
Arthur de Sansal	H.P.	Cochet	1855	crimson-purple	2	mod.
Arthur's Seat	S.		...	pale blush	3	mod.
Aspasie	H.P.	Touvais	1866	clear red	2	mod.
Attraction	H.T.	Dubreuil	1886	carmine	1	vig.
Audubon	H.P.		1856	bright rose	2	mod.
Augusta	N.	(American)	1853	deep sulphur	2	mod.
Auguste Buchner	H.P.	Lévêque	1880	red-scarlet	1	vig.
Auguste Mie	H.P.	Laffay	1850	glossy pink	1	vig.
Auguste Neumann	H.P.	E. Verdier	1869	bright red	1	mod.
Auguste Oger	T.	Oger	1856	coppery	2	mod.
Auguste Rigotard	H.P.	Schwartz	1871	bright red	1	vig.
Auguste Rivière	H.P.	E. Verdier	1864	red-carmine	1	mod.
Auguste Vacher	T.	Lacharme	1853	deep yellow	1	mod.
Aureus	T.	Ducher	1873	coppery yellow	2	mod.
Aurore	H.P.	Touvais	1861	rose, copper	1	mod.
Aurore Boréale	H.P.	Oger	1865	brilliant red	1	rob.
Aurore du Guide	B.		1850	violet-crimson	2	mod.
Aurore du Matin	H.P.	Robert	1867	bright rose	1	vig.
Avocat Duvivier	H.P.	Lévêque fils	1875	purple-red	1	vig.
Avocat Lambert	H.P.	Besson	1884	satiny rose	1	vig.
Bacchus	H.P.	Paul & Son	1855	crimson	2	mod.
Baltimore Belle	Pra.	Feast	1843	blush	3	vig.
Baptistes Desportes	H.P.	Trouillard	1864	bright red	2	mod.
Barillet Deschamps	H.P.	Vigneron	1867	brilliant rose	1	vig.
Baron de Bonstetten	H.P.	Liabaud	1871	velvety crimson	1	vig.
Baron Chaurand	H.P.	Liabaud	1869	purple-red	2	mod.
Baron L. de St.-Genies	H.	Granger	1867	rosy red	1	rob.
Baron Gonella	B.	Guillot père	1859	rosy pink	1	vig.
Baron Haussmann	H.P.	Lévêque fils	1867	poppy-red	1	vig.
Baron de Houlley	H.P.	Vigneron	1867	purple-red	1	vig
Baron Larray	H.P.		1854	pink	2	mod.
Baron A. de Rothschild	H.P.	Lacharme	1862	bright red	1	vig.
Baron de Rothschild	H.P.	Guillot fils	1862	carmine-red	1	vig.
Baron Nath. de Rothschild	H.P.	Lévêque	1883	rose	1	vig.
Baron Taylor	H.P.	Dugat	1879	pale rose	2	mod.

Name.	Class.	Raiser.	Year.	Colour.	Size.	Habit.
Baron A. de Vrints	T.	Gonod	1880	red-pink	2	vig.
Baron de Wassenaër	P.M.	V. Verdier	1854	rose	1	vig.
Baron Wolseley	H.P.	E. Verdier	1883	crimson	1	vig.
Baroness Rothschild	H.P.	Pernet	1869	pale flesh	1	vig.
Baronne de Beauverger	H.P.	Gautreau	...	rose	2	vig.
Baronne Blochausen	H.P.	Ketten fr.	1885	flesh	2	mod.
Baronne L. de St. Genies	H.P.	Granger	1862	purple-red	1	mod.
Brune. Maurice des Graviers	H.P.	E. Verdier	1866	red-cerise	1	vig.
Baronne Haussmann	H.P.	E. Verdier	1866	carmine-red	1	vig.
Baronne Hallez	H.P.	...	1850	dark red	2	mod.
Brune. Pelletin de Kinkelin	H.P.	Granger	1863	deep red	2	mod.
Baronne de Maynard	H.P.	Lacharme	1865	white	2	mod.
Baronne de Medem	H.P.	E. Verdier	...	cerise	1	vig.
Baronne de Noirmont	B.	Granger	...	rose	3	mod.
Baronne J. Panvilliers	H.P.	Duval	1879	bright rose	1	vig.
Baronne de Prailly	H.P.	Liabaud	1871	bright red	1	vig.
Baronne Prevost	H.P.	Desprez	1843	bright rose	1	vig.
Baronne A. de Rothschild	H.P.	Pernet	...	tender rose	2	vig.
Brune. Nath. de Rothschild	H.P.	Pernet	1885	rose	2	mod.
Baronne de Sinety	T.	Gonod	1884	yellow	2	vig.
Baronne Travot	H.P.	Ch. Verdier	1885	rose	2	mod.
Baronne Louise Uxkull	H.P.	Guillot fils	1871	rose-carmine	1	mod
Baronne Vittat	H.P.	Liabaud	1873	flesh-rose	1	mod.
Baronne M. Werner	T.	Nabonnand	1885	white-salmon	2	vig.
Barthélemy Joubert	H.P.	Mor. et Rob.	1877	cherry-red	1	vig.
Barthélemy Levet	H.P.	Levet	1878	bright rose	2	mod.
Béatrix	H.P.	Cherpin	1865	rose-carmine	2	mod.
Béatrix	B.	Cherpin	1865			
Beauté de l'Europe	T.	Gonod	1882	yellow	2	vig
Beauté Français	H.P.	Lartey	...	red	2	mod.
Beauté Lyonnaise	H.P.	Guillot	1851	rose	2	mod.
Beauté Séduisante	B.	Touvais	1861	red-maroon	1	vig.
Beauty of Beeston	H.P.	Frettingham	1872	crimson	2	mod.
Beauty of Greenmount	N.	Pentland	1854	rosy red	3	vig.
Beauty of Stapleford	H.T.	Bennett	1878	rose-pink	1	vig.
Beauty of Thane	H.P.	Walker	1873	maroon-crmsn.	1	vig.
Beauty of Waltham	H.P.	W. Paul	1862	rose-carmine	1	vig.
Beauty of Westerham	H.P.	Cattell	1864	red-crimson	2	vig.
Bedford Belle	H.T.	Laxton	1884	blush-white	2	vig.
Belle Allemande	T.	Beluze	1840	pink	2	mod.
Belle Américaine	H.P.	Boll	1837	pink	3	mod.
Belle Anglaise	H.P.	Ducher	1856	rose-flesh	3	mod.
Belle Fleur d'Anjou	T.	Touvais	1872	rosy white	1	vig.
Belle Brune	H.P.	Lartey	1861	violet	2	mod.
Belle Chartronnaise	T.	Lartey	1861	crimson & cerise	1	mod.
Belle Cuivrée	T.	Pernet	1866	yellow	2	mod.
Belle Jardinière	H.P.	Crozy	1853	rose	2	vig.
Belle des Jardins	G.	Guillot fils	1872	red str. white	2	mod.
Belle Lyonnaise	T.	Levet	1869	salmon-yellow	1	mod.
Belle Lyonnaise	H.P.	Ducher	1854	blush-pink	2	vig.
Belle Maçônnaise	T.	Ducher	1870	salmon-rose	1	mod.
Belle des Massifs	H.P.	Ducher	1862			

Name.	Class.	Raiser.	Year.	Colour.	Size.	Habit.
Belle Normande	H.P.	Oger	1864	silvery rose	2	vig.
Belle du Printemps	H.P.	Damaizin	1862	rose and red	2	vig.
Belle Fille du Printemps .	H.P.	Touvais	1862	pale rose	1	mod.
Belle de Bourg-la-Reine ...	H.P.	Margottin	1859	satiny rose	1	vig.
Belle Rose	H.P.	Touvais	1864	clear rose	1	vig.
Belle de Segur	A.	...	...	rose-flesh	3	mod.
Belzunce	H.P.	Mor. et Rob.	1885	vermilion	1	vig.
Benjamin Drouet	H.P.	E. Verdier	1878	purple-red	1	vig.
Bennett's Seedling	Ayr.	Bennett	1840	white	2	rob.
Benoît Broyer	H.P.	Gonod	1874	rich red	2	vig.
Benoit Comte	H.P.	Schwartz	1884	red	2	mod.
Benoit Cornet	H.P.	Cornet	1863	rose	1	mod.
Béranger	H.P.	...	1851	rose-crimson	1	mod.
Berberifolea Hardii	Mac.	...	...	yellow	3	mod.
Berceau Impérial	H.P.	...	1856	delicate rose	2	vig.
Bernard Palissy	H.P.	Margottin	1864	carmine-red	1	vig.
Bernard Verlot	H.P.	Margottin	1874	red-scarlet	1	mod.
Berthe Baron...............	H.P.	Veillard	1869	silvery rose	1	vig.
Berthe Lévêque	H.P.	Cochet	1866	rose	2	mod.
Bessie Johnson	H.P.	Curtis	1872	blush	1	vig.
Bicolor Incomparable	H.P.	Touvais	1861	dark rose	2	vig.
Bignonia	T.	Levet	1872	red	2	mod.
Bijou de Lyon	P.	Schwartz	1883	white	3	mod.
Bijou des Prairies............	Pra.	Schwartz	1878	bright rose	2	vig.
Black Prince	H.P.	W. Paul	1866	dark crimson	1	vig.
Blairi No. 2	H.C.	Blair	1845	rose blush	1	vig.
Blanche de Beaulieu	H.P.	Margottin	1851	pink	1	vig.
Blanchfleur	Fr.	Vibert	1846	blush	2	mod.
Blanche Lafitte	B.	Pradel	1851	blush	2	mod.
Blanche de Méru	H.P.	C. Verdier	1869	bright rose	2	vig.
Blanche Moreau	P.M.	Mor. et Rob.	1880	pure white	3	vig.
Blanche Portemer............	H.P.	Portemer	1851	pure white	2	mod.
Boccace	H.P.	Mor. et Rob.	...	crimson	2	vig.
Boieldieu	H.P.	Margottin	1877	cherry-red	1	vig.
Boileau	H.P.	Mor. et Rob.	1884	rose	1	vig.
Bon Silène..................	T.	Hardy	1839	rose-salmon	2	vig
Bougère	T.	Bougère	1832	deep salmon	1	vig.
Boule de Nanteuil	G.	...	...	crimson	3	mod.
Boule de Neige	H.P.	Lacharme	1867	pure white	2	mod.
Boule d'Or..................	T.	Margottin	1860	yellow	2	vig.
Bouquet de Marie	H.P.	Damaizin	1858	flesh	3	mod.
Bouquet d'Or...................	N.	Ducher	1872	coppery yellow	1	vig.
Bouquet Rose	H.P.	Touvais	...	cerise	2	mod.
Bouquet da la Vierge	B.	Soup. et Not.	1873	rose-white	3	mod.
Bourbon Queen	B.	Manger	1834	rose	2	vig.
Bouton d'Or	T.	Guillot fils	1866	deep yellow	2	vig.
Brennus	H.C.	Laffay	1830	light carmine	1	vig.
Brightness of Cheshunt ...	H.P.	Paul & Son	1881	vivid red	2	vig.
Brilliant...................	H.P.	W. Paul	1886	crimson	2	vig.
Buffon	H.P.	Guillot Père	1859	crimson	2	mod.
Burgmester Karl Muller ...	H.P.	Soup. et Not.	...	red	2	mod.

Name.	Class	Raiser.	Year.	Colour.	Size.	Habit.
Calliope	H.P.	Mor. et Rob.	1879	satiny rose	1	vig.
Camille Bernardin	H.P.	Gautreau	1865	bright red	1	vig.
Camoëns	H.T.	Schwartz	1882	rose-yellow	2	mod.
Canary	T.	Guillot père	1852	yellow	2	mod.
Candide	H.P.	Touvais		blush	3	mod.
Cannes la Coquette	H.T.	Nabonnand	1877	salmon	2	mod.
Captain Cherpin	H.P.	Guillot	1851			
Captain Christy	H.P.	Lacharme	1873	flesh colour	1	mod.
Captain Louis Frère	H.P.	Vigneron	1884	rose	2	mod.
Captain Ingram	M.	Laffay	1856	velvety purple	2	vig.
Captain Lamure	H.P.	Levet	1870	deep red	2	mod.
Captain Paul	H.P.	Boyan	1866	bright red	2	mod.
Captain Rognat	H.P.	Guillot père	1864	brilliant red	1	mod.
Capucine Liabaud	H.P.	Liabaud	1882	red	2	mod.
Cardinal Patrizzi	H P.	Trouillard	1857	purplish crmsn.	2	mod.
Carl Coers	H.P.	Granger	1865	crimson-purple	1	vig.
Caroline	T.	...	...	pink	1	vig.
Caroline Cook	T.	A. Cook	1871	yellow	3	mod.
Caroline Marniesse	N.	Roeser	1848	creamy white	3	mod.
Caroline Milson	H.P.	Guillot	1853	flesh	2	mod.
Caroline Riquet	B.	...	1858	white	2	vig.
Caroline de Sausal	H.P.	Desprez	1850	flesh-pink	1	vig.
Caroline Schmitt	N.	Schmitt	1881	yellow	2	mod.
Casimir Perrier	H.P.	Schwartz	1874	ruby-red	1	vig.
Catherine Bell	H.P.	Bell & Son	1877	rose	2	mod.
Catherine Bonnard	H.B.	E. Verdier	1871	carmine-rose	1	vig.
Catherine Guillot	B.	Guillot père	1860	rosy purple	1	vig.
Catherine Mermet	T.	Guillot fils	1869	flesh-rose	1	vig.
Catherine Soupert	H.P.	Lacharme	1879	peach	2	mod.
Catinat	H.P.	Oger	1873	bright rose	2	vig.
Cecile Brunner	P.	Ducher	1880	bright rose	2	mod.
Celestial	A.	...	...	flesh	3	mod.
Celine	M.	Robert	1855	crimson	3	mod.
Céline Dubois	D.P.	...	1850	French-white	2	mod.
Céline Forestier	N.	A. Leroy	1858	pale yellow	2	vig.
Celine Gonod	B.	Gonod	1863	rose	2	mod.
Célestine Pourreaux	H.P.	Fontaine	1873	bright cerise	1	vig.
Cels's multiflora	C.	Cels	1838	flesh	3	mod.
Cendres Napoleon	B.	Beluze	1841			
Centifolia rosea	H.P.	Touvais	1863	bright pink	1	vig.
Chamois	T.	Ducher	1869	chamois	2	mod.
Charlemagne	H.P.	Oger	1863	red-cerise	1	mod.
Charlemagne	B.	Dorisy	1846	blush-pink	1	mod.
Charles Baltet	H.P.	E. Verdier	1877	carmine-red	1	vig.
Charles Bosierre	H.P.	...	1849	carmine	2	mod.
Charles Darwin	H.P.	Laxton	1879	dark crimson	1	vig.
Charles Dickens	H.P.	W. Paul&Son	1886	rose	1	vig.
Charles Duval	H.P.	E. Verdier	1877	bright red	2	mod.
Charles Fauquet	H.P.	Lévéque	1884	red	1	mod.
Charles Fontaine	H.P.	Fontaine	1868	crimson	2	mod.
Charles Getz	B.	Cook	1871	rose-pink	2	vig.
Charles Lamb	H.P.	W. Paul&Son	1884	red	2	vig.

Name.	Class.	Raiser.	Year.	Colour.	Size.	Habit.
Charles Lawson	H.B.	Lawson	1853	rose-carmine	1	vig.
Charles Lee	H.P.	Gautreau	1868	red	2	mod.
Charles Lefebvre	H.P.	Lacharme	1861	velvety crimson	1	vig.
Charles Legrady	T.	Pernet	1885	rose	2	vig.
Charles Lévêque	T	Nabonnand	1885	red	2	mod.
Charles Margottin	H.P.	Margottin	1864	carmine-red	1	vig.
Charles Martel	B.	Guillot	1842			
Charles Ravolli	T.	Pernet	1875	rose	3	mod.
Charles Rouillard	H.P.	E. Verdier	1865	bright rose	1	rob.
Charles Turner	H.P.	E. Verdier	1865	bright red	1	vig.
Charles Turner	H.P.	Margottin	1869	brilliant rose	1	vig.
Charles Verdier	H.P.	Guillot père	1866	silvery rose	1	rob.
Charles Wood	H.P.	Portemer	1864	dark red	1	vig.
Charlotte Corday	H.P.	Joubert	1864	purple-red	1	mod
Chateau des Bergeries	T.	Ledechaux	1887	pale yellow	1	vig.
Chateau de Jeanne d'Arc	B.	Beluze	1842			
Châteaubriand	H.P.	Portemer	1852	light pink	2	mod.
Chenedolé	H.C.	...	...	crimson	3	vig.
Cheshunt Hybrid	H.T.	Paul & Son	1873	red-carmine	1	vig.
Chevalier de Colquhoun	T.	Nabonnand	1878	bright red	2	mod.
Chevalier Nigra	H.P.	C. Verdier	1865	dark crimson	1	vig.
Christine Nilsson	H.P.	Lévêque fils	1867	deep rose	1	vig.
Christian Puttner	H.C.	Oger	1861	rose	2	mod.
Ciceron	H.P.	Ducher	1854			
Cimabue	H.B.	...	1858	rich crimson	1	vig.
Citoyen des Deux Mondes.	Ben.	Lacharme	1850			
Claire Carnot	N.	Guillot fils	1873	rich yellow	2	mod.
Claire Jacquier	P.	Bernaix	1888	yellow	3	vig.
Claire Renard	H.P.	Oger	1866	bright rose	1	vig.
Claire Thierry	H.P.	Oger	1874	rosy cerise	2	mod.
Clara Cochet	H.P.	Lacharme	1886	rose	1	vig.
Claude Bernard	H.P.	Liabaud	1878	deep rose	1	vig.
Claude Levet	H.P.	Levet	1872	deep red	1	rob.
Claude Millou	H.P.	E. Verdier	1863	velvety red	2	vig.
Claudia Augustin	N.	Damaizin	1868	white & yellow	2	rob.
Clemence Delarue	H.P.	Fontaine	...	rose	3	mod.
Clémence Raoux	H.P.	Granger	1869	satiny-rose	2	vig.
Clémence Thierry	H.P.	Oger	1879	rose-lilac	2	vig.
Clement Nabonnand	T.	Nabonnand	1877	salmon-yellow	2	mod.
Clémentine Serenye	H.P.	Poncet	1842			
Climbing Bessie Johnson	H.P.	Paul & Son	1873	pink	2	vig.
Climbing Captain Christy.	H.P.	Ducher	1881	pink	2	vig.
Climbing Charles Lefebvre	H.P.	Cranston	1876	crimson	1	mod.
Climbing Devoniensis	T.	Pavitt	1858	creamy white	1	vig.
Climbing Jules Margottin.	H.P.	Cranston	1875	carmine-rose	1	rob.
Climbing Edouard Morren.	H.P.	Paul & Son	1879	rose	1	vig.
Climbing Cmtsse. d'Oxford	H.P.	Smith	1875	red-carmine	1	rob.
Climbing Mdlle. Eugènie Verdier	H.P.	Paul & Son	1877	rose-pink	2	vig.
Climbing Victor Verdier	H.P.	Paul & Son	1871	rose-carmine	1	rob.
Clothilde	T.	Rolland	1867	creamy white	2	mod.
Cloth of Gold	N.	Coquereau	1843	deep yellow	1	rob.

Name.	Class.	Raiser.	Year.	Colour.	Size.	Habit.
Clotilde Rolland	H.P.	Rolland	1867	cerise-rose	1	mod.
Clovis	H.P.	Ledechaux	1868	rose-purple	1	vig.
Cœur de Lion	H.P.	W. Paul	1867	bright rose	1	vig.
Colonel Felix Breton	H.P.	Schwartz	1884	red	1	vig.
Colonel de Cambriel........	H.P.	Rob. et Mor.	...	red	2	mod.
Colonel Robert Lefort	M.	E. Verdier	1884	purple	2	mod.
Colonel de Rougemont......	H.P.	Lacharme	1854	clear carmine	1	vig.
Colonel de Sansal	H.P.	Jamain	1874	carmine-red	2	mod.
Commandant Beaurepaire .	G.	Mor. Robert	1875	bright rose	2	rob.
Commandant Fournier ...	H.P.	Laffay	1846	crimson	2	mod.
Commandant Fournier ...	H.P.	Mor. et Rob.	1885	fiery red	1	vig.
Commandant Mausuy	H.P.	Vigneron	1868	bright red	1	mod.
Comice de Tarn et Garonne	E.	Pradel	1852	carmine-red	2	mod.
Comice de Marseille........	H.P.	Dupont	1847			
Comice de Seine et Marne.	D.	Pradel	1842	deep red	2	mod.
Comte de Beaufort	H.P.	...	1858	deep crimson	2	mod.
Comte de Bourmont,...... ..	H.P.	...	1851	pale rose	1	vig.
Comte Florimonde de Bergeyck	H.P.	Soup. et Not.	1879	rosy red	1	vig.
Comte Bobinsky	H.P.	...	1850	carmine	2	mod.
Comte Cavour	H.P.	Liabaud	1856	bright rose	2	mod.
Comte Horace de Choiseul.	H.P.	Lévêque	1879	vermilion	1	vig.
Comte d'Epremesnil........	Rug.	Nabonnand	1882	lilac	2	mod.
Comte d'Eu	B.	Lacharme	1884	crimson	2	mod.
Comte de Flandres	H.P.	Lévêque	1882	purple-red	2	mod.
Comte de Falloux	H.P.	Trouillard	1860	rich crimson	2	mod.
Comte Adrien de Germiny.	H.P.	Lévêque ·	1882	rose	2	mod.
Comte de Grivel	T.	Levet	1871	pale yellow	1	vig.
Comte Litta	H.P.	E. Verdier	1866	velvety red	1	vig.
Comte de Montijo	E.	...	1855	dark crimson	2	mod.
Comte de Mortemart	H.P.	Margottin	1881	rose	2	mod.
Comte de Nanteuil	H.P.	Quietier	1852	lilac-rose	1	vig.
Comte Odart	H.P.	...	1851	deep red	2	mod.
Comte de Paris.............	T.	Mad. Pean	1844	flesh	2	mod.
Comte de Paris.............	H.P.	Laffay	1839	lilac	1	mod.
Comte de Paris.............	H.P.	E. Verdier	1864	rose-red	2	vig.
Comte de Paris.............	T.	Hardy	1839	flesh colour	1	vig.
Comte de Paris.............	H.P.	Lévêque	1887	poppy-red	2	vig.
Comte Raimbaud	H.P.	Rolland	1867	cerise-red	1	rob.
Comte de Ribaucourt.......	H.P.	Jemean	...	red	2	mod.
Comte de Sembui............	T.	Mad. Ducher	1874	salmon-pink	1	vig.
Comte Alphonse Serenye ..	H.P.	Touvais	1865	purple-red	1	rob.
Comte de Taverna	T.	Ducher	1871	yellow	1	vig.
Comte de Thun-Hohenstein	H.P.	Lévêque	1881	crimson	2	mod.
Comtesse Cahen d'Anvers..	H.P.	Ledechaux	1885	rose	1	vig.
Comtesse d'Arnim	H.P.	Soup. et Not.	...	carmine	2	vig.
Comtesse de Barbantanne..	B.	Guillot père	1858	flesh-white	2	vig.
Comtesse de Bearn	H.P.	Lévêque	1885	red	1	mod.
Comtesse de Bessequier ...	B.	Beluze	1842			
Comtesse de Bresson	H.P.	Guinoiseau	1873	lilac-rose	1	vig.
Comtesse de Brossard	T.	Oger	...	yellow	3	mod.
Comtesse de Camondo	H.P.	Lévêque	1880	deep rose	1	vig.

Name.	Class.	Raiser.	Year.	Colour.	Size.	Habit.
Comtesse de Casserta	T.	Nabonnand	1877	copper-red	2	mod.
Comtesse de Casteja	H. P.	Margottin	1883	crimson	1	vig.
Comtesse de Chabrillant	H. P.	Marest	1858	deep pink	2	mod.
Comtesse H. de Choiseul	H. P.	Moreau	1878	cherry-red	1	vig.
Comtesse H. de Choiseul	H. P.	Motteau	1878	bright red	2	vig.
Comtesse Henriette Combbs	H. P.	Schwartz	1881	satin-rose	2	mod.
Comtesse Doria	H. P.	...	1853	crimson	2	mod.
Comtesse Duchatel	H. P.	Laffay	1844	rose-purple	2	vig.
Comtesse de Falloux	H. P.	Trouillard	1867	purple-rose	1	rob.
Comtesse de Flandres	H. P.	E. Verdier	1877	satin-rose	2	mod.
Comtesse de Frigneuse	T.	Guillot	1885	yellow	2	vig.
Comtesse F. de Thurn Hohenstein	H. P.	Lévêque	1880	carmine-crimsn.	1	vig.
Comtesse d'Indre	H. P.	E. Verdier	1879	carmine-red	1	vig.
Comtesse Jaubert	H. B.	Laffay	1847	rose	2	mod.
Comtesse de Jaucort	H. P.	Cochet	1866	rose-flesh	1	vig.
Cmtsse. Louise de Kergolay	H. P.	Touvais	...	purple	2	mod.
Cmtsse. Nathalie de Kleist	H. P.	Soup. et Not.	1880	coppery red	1	vig.
Comtesse de Labarthe	T.	Bernède	1857	pink	2	mod.
Comtesse de Lacepede	H. C.	...	...	blush	2	vig.
Comtesse de Leuse	T.	Nabonnand	1878	salmon-rose	2	mod.
Comtesse de Ludre	T.	E. Verdier	1879	carmine-red	2	mod.
Comtesse de Mailly Nesle	H. P.	Lévêque	1883	bright rose	1	vig.
Comtesse de Maussac	H. P.	Vigneron	1873	clear rose	1	vig.
Comtesse Hélène Mier	H. P.	Soup. et Not.	1876	clear rose	1	rob.
Comtesse F. Morgues	H. P.	Pernet	1866	bright red	1	mod.
Comtesse de Mosbourg	B.	Pradel	1861	satiny rose	1	mod.
Comtesse de Murinais	M.	Vibert	1843	flesh-white	1	rob.
Comtesse de Nadaillac	T.	Guillot fils	1871	delicate rose	1	vig.
Comtesse Ouvaroff	T.	Margottin	1860	creamy rose	1	mod.
Comtesse de Palikao	H. P.	E. Verdier	1865	delicate rose	2	mod.
Comtesse Riza du Parc	T.	Schwartz	1876	delicate rose	2	mod.
Comtesse de Paris	H. P.	E. Verdier	1864	lively rose	1	mod.
Comtesse de Paris	H. P.	Lévêque	1883	rose	2	mod.
Comtesse de Polignac	H. P.	Granger	...	red	2	mod.
Comtesse de Rocqnigny	H. P.	Vaurin	...	salmon-red	2	mod.
Comtesse de Seguier	H. P.	Lévêque fils	1861	dark red	1	mod.
Comtesse de Serenye	H. P.	Lacharme	1874	silvery pink	2	vig.
Comtesse Vally de Serenye	H. P.	Fontaine	1875	amaranth	1	vig.
Comtesse de Serincourt	T.	Pradel	...	salmon	2	mod.
Comtesse Anna Thun	T.	Soup. et Not.	1887	yellow	2	vig.
Comtesse de Turenne	H. P.	E. Verdier	1866	bright flesh	1	vig.
Comtesse de Vallier	H. P.	Damaizin	1866	purple-violet	2	vig.
Ctsse. Alban de Villeneuve	T.	Nabonnand	1882	yellow-rose	2	mod.
Constant Lusseau	H. P.	Trouillard	1864	clear red	2	mod.
Constantin Fretiakoff	T.	Jamain	1877	rose-crimson	1	vig.
Copper Austrian	A. B.	...	...	reddish copper	3	mod.
Coquette des Alpes	H. P.	Lacharme	1867	blush-white	2	mod.
Coquette des Blanches	H. P.	Lacharme	1871	pure white	2	vig.
Coquette de Lyon	T.	Ducher	1870	canary-yellow	2	vig.
Cornelia Koch	T.	Koch	1855	creamy white	1	mod.
Countess of Oxford	H. P.	Guillot père	1869	carmine-red	1	vig.

Name.	Class.	Raiser.	Year.	Colour.	Size.	Habit.
Countess of Pembroke	H.T.	Bennett	1882	satin-rose	2	vig.
Countess of Rosebery	H.P.	Postans	1879	bright car.-rose	1	vig.
Coupe de Cynthée	B.	Guillot	1846			
Coupe d'Hébé	H.B.	Laffay	1840	deep pink	1	rob.
Coquette de Normande	H.P.	Oger	...	white	2	mod.
Couronne de Parterre	H.P.	Touvais	1861	velvety-crimsn.	1	vig.
Cramoisi-superieur	C.	Plantier	1834	crimson	2	vig.
Crested, or Cristata	Prov.	Vibert	1827	rose-pink	2	mod.
Crimson Bedder	H.P.	Cranston	1874	crimson	1	mod.
Crown Prince	H.P.	W. Paul	1880	deep crimson	1	vig.
Curé de Charentay	H.P.	Ducher	1867	rose-purple	2	vig.
Cürt Schultheis	T.	Nabonnand	1882	rose-yellow	2	mod.
Cymédor	H.B.	Guillot	1846			
D'Aguesseau	G.	...	...	crimson	2	mod.
Dames Ptruesses. d'Orleans	H.P.	Vigneron	1877	crimson	1	vig.
Danaë	H.P.	Touvais	1865	cerise-rose	1	vig.
Darzens	H.P.	Ducher	1860	yellowish rose	1	vig.
David Pradel	T.	Pradel	1851	lilac-rose	1	mod.
Dean of Windsor	H.P.	Turner	1878	vermilion	1	vig.
De la Grifferæ	Mult.	...	...	deep rose	3	vig.
Delille	P.M.	Robert	1852	red	2	mod.
Delphine Gaudot	T.	Beluze	1840			
De Meaux	M.	Or. Taunton	1825	pink	3	mod.
Dennis Hélye	H.P.	Gautreau	1864	rosy carmine	1	vig.
Desgaches	H.B.	Plantier	1850	carmine	2	mod.
Desprez	N.	Desprez	1838	red-buff	1	vig.
Deuil de Dunois	H.P.	Vigneron	...	crimson	2	mod.
Deuil de Paul Fontaine	M.	Fontaine	1873	red	2	mod.
Deuil de l'Empereur du Mexique	H.P.	Cordier	1867	red	1	mod.
Deuil du Prince Albert	H.P.	Gonod	1862	dark crimson	1	vig.
Deuil du Col. Denfert	H.P.	Margottin	1878	maroon-purple	1	vig.
Deuil du Prince Jerome	H.P.	Lartay	...	velvet-crimson	2	mod.
Deuil du Mad. Willermoz	H.P.	Lacharme	1853	dark crimson	2	mod.
Devienne-Lamy	H.P.	Lévêque fils	1868	carmine-red	1	mod.
Devoniensis	T.	Foster	1838	creamy white	1	mod.
Diana	H.P.	W. Paul	1874	deep pink	1	vig.
Dingee Conard	H.P.	E. Verdier	1875	crimson	2	mod.
Directeur Alphand	H.P.	Lévêque	1884	scarlet	1	mod.
Directeur N. Jensen	H.P.	E. Verdier	1884	red-carmine	2	mod.
Distinction	H.T.	Bennett	1882	peach	2	vig.
Domingo Aldrufeu	H.P.	Pernet	...	rose	2	mod.
Donna Maria	E.	...	...	white	3	vig.
Double Margined Hip	H.C.	...	...	white	3	vig.
Douglas	B.	V. Verdier	1848	crimson	2	mod.
Dr. Andry	H.P.	E. Verdier	1864	dark red	1	vig.
Dr. Antoine Carlès	T.	Nabonnand	1885	yellow	2	mod.
Dr. Arnal	H.P.	Roeser	1848	crimson	3	mod.
Dr. Auguste Krell	H.P.	E. Verdier	1877	cherry-red	1	mod.
Dr. Baillon	H.P.	Margottin	1878	crimson-purple	1	rob.
Dr. Berthet	B.	Damaizin	1858	cherry-red	1	mod.

Name.	Class.	Raiser.	Year.	Colour.	Size.	Habit.
Dr. Berthet	T.	Pernet	1878	pale rose	1	vig.
Dr. Brechemier	H. P.	Vigneron	1873	crimson	2	vig.
Dr. Bretonneau	H. P.	Trouillard	1858	deep red	1	mod.
Dr. de Chalus	H. P.	Touvais	1871	brilliant red	1	vig.
Dr. Dor	H P.	Liabaud	1885	red	2	mod.
Dr. Garnier	H. P.	Mor. et Rob.	1883	cerise-red	1	vig.
Dr. Guepin	H. P.	Mor. et Rob.	1872	velvety red	2	mod.
Dr. Henon	H. P.	Léon Lille	1853	white	2	mod.
Dr. Hogg	H. P.	Laxton	1880	violet-purple	1	vig.
Dr. Hooker	H. P.	Paul & Son	1876	bright crimson	2	mod.
Dr. Hurta	H. P.	Soup. et Not.	1867	rosy purple	1	rob.
Dr. Jenner	H. P.	Margottin	1878	carmine-red	1	vig.
Dr. Julliard	H. P.	...	1850	rose	2	mod.
Dr. Kane	N.	Pentland	1856	sulph-yellow	1	mod.
Dr. Larray	H. P.	Mor. et Rob.	1866	vinous red	1	vig.
Dr. Lemée	H. P.	Touvais	1871	velvety purple	1	vig.
Dr. Lindley	H. P.	W. Paul	1866	dark crimson	1	mod.
Dr. Marjolin	H. P.	Laffay	1842	rose-crimson	3	dwf.
Dr. Marx	H. P.	Laffay	1842	crimson	1	mod.
Dr. Marx	H. P.	Laffay	1858	carmine	1	vig.
Dr. Pasteur	H. T.	Mor. et Rob.	1888	carmine	2	vig.
Dr. Rushpler	H. P.	...	1856	clear rose	1	rob.
Dr. Sewell	H. P.	Turner	1879	crimson-scarlet	1	vig.
Dr. Vingtrinier	H. P.	Fontaine	1863	red-carmine	2	mod.
Dr. Wilhelm Neubert	H. P.	Soup et Not	1873	cherry-red	1	vig.
Du Guesclin	H. P.	Mor. et Rob.	1875	rich rose	2	vig.
Duarte de Oliviera	N.	Brassac	1879	rose-salmon	2	vig.
Duc d'Aumale	H. P.	E. Verdier	1875	dark cerise	1	vig.
Duc de Cazès	H. P.	Touvais	1860	dark purple	1	mod.
Duc de Chartres	H. P.	E. Verdier	1876	red-purple	1	vig.
Duc d'Harcourt	H. P.	Mor. et Rob.	...	carmine	2	mod.
Duc de Magenta	T.	Margottin	1859	coppery rose	1	mod.
Duc de Malakoff	H. P.	Plantier	1856	red	1	mod.
Duc de Montpensier	H. P.	Lévêque fils	1875	red-crimson	1	vig.
Duc de Nassau	H. P.	Pradel	1873	red-purple	2	mod.
Duc de Rohan	H. P.	Lévêque fils	1861	bright red	1	mod.
Duc de Wellington	H. P.	Granger	1864	crimson	1	mod.
Ducher	C.	Ducher	1869	pure white	2	mod.
Duchess of Bedford	H. P.	W. Paul & Son	1879	scarlet-crimson	1	vig.
Duchess of Buccleuch	G.	...	...	dark rose	2	vig.
Duchess of Connaught	H. P.	Bennett	1878	silvery rose	1	mod.
Duchess of Connaught	H. P.	Noble	1883	crimson	1	vig.
Duchess of Edinburgh	T.	Nabonnand	1874	bright red	1	mod.
Duchess of Edinburgh	H. P.	Bennett	1874	pink	1	vig.
Duchess of Norfolk	H. P.	Margottin	1853	deep crimson	1	rob.
Duchess of Sutherland	H. P.	Laffay	1839	flesh-pink	2	mod.
Duchess of Westminster	H. T.	Bennett	1878	bright cerise	2	mod.
Duchesse d'Alencon	H. P.	Mor. et Rob.	1861	rose	2	mod.
Duchesse d'Aoste	H. P.	Margottin	1867	glossy rose	1	vig.
Duchesse de Bragance	T.	Dubreuil	1887	yellow	1	vig.
Duchesse de Medina Cœli	H. P.	Marest	1864	red-purple	2	vig.
Duchesse de Cambacérès	H. P.	Fontaine	1854	rich rose	1	vig.

Name.	Class.	Raiser.	Year.	Colour.	Size.	Habit.
Duchesse de Caylus	H.P.	E. Verdier	1864	bright carmine	1	mod.
Duchesse de Chartres	H.P.	E. Verdier	1875	bright rose	2	mod.
Duchesse d'Harcourt	H.P.	Oger	1873	rose-lilac	2	mod.
Duchesse d'Istrie	M.	Portemer	1857	rose	2	mod.
Duchesse de Magenta	H.P.	Guillot père	1859	white	2	mod.
Duchesse d'Orleans	H.P.	Quetier	1852	blush	1	mod.
Duchesse d'Ossuna	H.P.	Jamain	1876	rosy red	1	vig.
Duchesse de Thuringe	B.	Guillot père	1847	blush-white	2	vig.
Duchesse Antonine d'Ursel	H.P.	Soup. et Not.	1884	red	1	vig.
Duchesse de Valombrosa	T.	Nabonnand	1879	red-yellow	1	vig.
Duchesse de Valombrosa	H.P.	Schwartz	1875	flesh-pink	1	vig.
Duhamel du Monceau	H.P.	Hugues	1872	brilliant red	1	vig.
Duke of Albeny	H.P.	W Paul&Son	1883	crimson	1	vig.
Duke of Cambridge	H.P.	Margottin	1857	bright rose	1	mod.
Duke of Connaught	H.T.	Bennett	1878	deep crimson	1	mod.
Duke of Connaught	H.P.	Paul & Son	1876	bright crimson	2	vig.
Duke of Edinburgh	H.P.	Paul & Son	1868	scarlet-crimson	1	vig.
Duke of Marlborough	H.P.	Lévêque	1885	crimson	1	vig.
Duke of Teck	H.P.	Paul & Son	1880	scarlet	1	vig.
Dumnacus	H.P.	Mor. et Rob.	1880	carmine-red	1	vig.
Dundee Rambler	Ayr.	Martin	...	pink	2	rob.
Dupetit Thouars	B.	Portemer	1844	red	2	vig.
Dupuy Jamain	H.P.	Jamain	1868	cerise-red	1	vig.
Earl of Beaconsfield	H.P.	Christy	1880	carmine	2	mod.
Earl of Beaconsfield	H P.	Schwartz	1878	rosy crimson	1	vig.
Earl of Dufferin	H.P.	Dickson&Sn.	1887	crimson	1	vig.
Earl of Pembroke	H.P.	Bennett	1882	crimson	1	vig.
Ecæ	Afgh.	In.fr. Afghn.	1884	yellow	3	mod.
Eclaire	H.P.	Lacharme	1884	fiery red	2	vig.
Eclair de Jupiter	N.	...	...	crimson	2	vig.
Edgar Jolibos	H P.	E. Verdier	1884	scarlet	2	mod.
Edith de Murat	B.	Ducher	1858	flesh	2	mod.
Edmund Wood	H.P.	E. Verdier	1875	dark cerise	1	vig.
Edouard André	H.P.	E. Verdier	1879	rich red	1	vig.
Edouard Desfosses	B.	Renard	1840	carmine-rose	2	mod.
Edouard Dufour	H.P.	Lévêque fils	1877	rich crimson	1	vig.
Edouard Fontaine	H.P.	Fontaine	1878	silvery rose	1	mod.
Edouard Gautier	T.	Ducher	1884	white	3	mod.
Edouard Hervé	H.P.	E. Verdier	1885	crimson	2	mod.
Edouard Morren	H.P.	Granger	1868	bright rose	1	vig.
Edouard Pynaert	H.P.	Schwartz	1877	rich red	1	vig.
Egeria	H.P.	Schwartz	1878	rose-pink	2	vig.
Ella Gordon	H.P.	W.Paul&Son	1884	cherry-red	1	vig.
Elie Morel	H.P.	Boucharlet	1867	rosy lilac	1	vig.
Elise Boëlle	H.P.	Guillot père	1869	pale rose	2	vig.
Elise Flory	Ben.	Guillot père	1851	rose	2	mod.
Elise Sauvage	T.	Miellez	1818	yellow	2	mod.
Elizabeth de la Rocheterie.	H.P.	Vigneron	1882	rose	2	mod.
Elizabeth Vigneron	H.P.	Vigneron	1865	rose-pink	1	vig.
Emilie Dulac	H.P.	Guillot	1861	rose	1	mod.
Emilie Dupuy	T.	Levet	...	salmon	2	vig.

Name.	Class.	Raiser.	Year.	Colour.	Size.	Habit.
Emilie de Girardin	P.M.	...	1854	rose	2	mod.
Emilie Hausburg	H.P.	Lévêque fils	1869	satiny rose	1	vig.
Emilie Plantier	H.N.	Schwartz	1878	bright yellow	1	vig.
Emily Laxton	H.P.	Laxton	1877	red-rose	1	vig.
Emma Combey	H.P.	Gonod	1872			
Emotion	B.	Guillot père	1862	flesh-white	2	mod.
Empéréur Alexandre III	H.P.	Soup. et Not	1885	carmine	1	vig.
Empereur de Brésil	H.P.	Soup. et Not	1880	blackish red	2	vig.
Empereur de Maroc	H.P.	Guinoisseau	1858	maroon-crimsn	2	vig.
Emperor	H.P.	W.Paul&Son	1884	crimson	3	vig.
Emperor Napoleon	H.P.	...	1854	crimson	2	mod.
Empress	H.P.	W.Paul&Son	1884	pink	3	vig.
Empress of India	H.P.	Laxton	1876	dark crimson	1	vig.
Enfant d'Ameuguy	H.P.	Ducher	1867	rose	1	vig.
Enfant du Mont Carmel	H.P.	Cherpin	1851	rose	1	vig.
Enfants de Lyon	N.	Crozy	1858			
Ennemond Boule	H.P.	Liabaud	1879	bright red	2	vig.
Ernest Boncenne	H.P.	Cherpin	1867	brilliant rose	2	vig.
Ernest Herger	H.P.	E. Verdier	1873	bright purple	1	vig.
Ernest Prince	H.P.	Ducher	1882	rose	2	vig.
Etendard de Jeanne d'Arc	T.	Margottin	1884	white	2	vig.
Etendard de Lyon	H.P.	Gonod	1885	red	2	mod
Etendard de Sébastopol	H.P.	Ducher	1856	purple-crimson	2	mod.
Etienne Dubois	H.P.	Damaizin	1873	silvery rose	1	vig.
Etienne Dupuy	H.P.	Levet	1873	silvery rose	1	vig.
Etienne Furst	H.P.	Soup. et Not.	...	crimson	2	vig.
Etienne Lecrosnier	H.P.	Oger	1861	amaranth	2	mod.
Etna	M.	Laffay	1845	crimson	2	mod.
Etoile de Lyon	T.	Guillot	1882	yellow	1	vig.
Eugène Appert	H.P.	V. Trouillard	1869	velvety crimson	1	vig.
Eugène Beauharnais	Ben.	Moreau	1865	crimson	2	mod.
Eugène Boucier	H.P.	E. Verdier	1861	purplish red	1	vig.
Eugène Petit	H.P.	Touvais	...	carmine	2	mod.
Eugène Trauson	H.P.	Vigneron	1882	rose	2	mod.
Eugène Verdier	H.P.	Guillot	1863	red	2	vig.
Eugène de Savoie	P.M.	Mor. et Rob.	1861	bright red	2	vig.
Eugène Savary	T.	Gonod	1872	rosy yellow	2	mod.
Eugène Scribe	H.P.	Gautreau	1866	fiery red	1	vig.
Eugène Sue	H.P.	Ducher	1852	satiny rose	1	mod.
Eugénie Bréon	B.	Berlet	1847	flesh	3	mod.
Eugénie Desgaches	T.	Plantier	1835	clear rose	1	vig.
Eugénie Dubus	H.P.	Fontaine	1861	red	2	vig.
Eugénie Guinoisseau	M.	Guinoisseau	1865	red	2	mod.
Euphrasie Rousseau	H.P.	Rousseau	...	rose	2	mod.
Euryanthe	H.P.	Peters	1866	dark red	2	mod.
Evelyn Turner	H.P.	E. Verdier	...	rose	2	mod.
Evêque de Luxembourg	H.P.	Soup. et Not.	1877	velvety crimson	2	vig.
Evêque de Nimes	H.P.	Plantier	1857	scarlet-crimson	1	mod.
Exadelphé	T.	Nabonnand	1886	yellow	1	vig.
Exposition de Brie	H.P.	Granger	1865	bright red	1	vig.
Exposition du Havre	H.P.	Gautreau	1869	rose-carmine	2	mod.

Name.	Class.	Raiser.	Year.	Colour.	Size.	Habit.
Fabvier	C.	Laffay	...	crimson	2	mod.
Fanny Petzold	H.P.	Fontaine	1865	satiny rose	1	vig.
Felicie de Morges	H.P.	Pernet	1866			
Félicien David	H.P.	E. Verdier	1872	carmine-red	2	mod.
Félicité Parmentier	Ayr.	...	...	blush	1	mod.
Félicité Perpétué	E.	Jacques	1828	flesh colour	2	rob.
Félicité Rigaud	H.P.	Fontaine	1824	satin-rose	2	mod.
Félix Genero	H.P.	Damaizin	1866	purple-rose	1	vig.
Felix Mousset	H.P.	E. Verdier	1885	rose-purple	2	mod.
Fellenberg	N.	...	...	crimson	2	vig.
Ferdinand Chaffolte	H.P.	Pernet	1879	bright red	1	vig.
Ferdinand de Lesseps	H.P.	E. Verdier	1869	deep crimson	1	vig.
Fiançailles de la Princesse Stephanie	T.	Levet	1880	orange-yellow	2	mod.
Fimbriata	H.C.	Jacques	1831	red	2	mod.
Firebrand	H.P.	Labruyère	1873	brilliant crmsn.	1	rob.
Fisher Holmes	H.P.	E. Verdier	1865	red-scarlet	1	rob.
Flavescens	T.	In. fr. China	1824	yellow	2	mod.
Flora	S.	...	...	deep rose	3	vig.
Florence de Colquhoun	T.	Nabonnand	1879	red-lilac	2	vig.
Flora Nabonnand	T.	Nabonnand	1877	yellow	2	mod.
Florent Pauwels	H.P.	Soup. et Not.	1879	rose-lilac	1	vig.
Fontenelle	M.	Vibert	1849	rose	3	mod.
Fontenelle	M.P.	Mor. et Rob.	1877	carmine-red	1	vig.
Fortunei	Bk.	In. fr. China	1850	white	2	vig.
Fortune's Yellow	Bk.	In. fr. China	1845	yellow	2	vig.
Fourville	B.	Guillot	1846			
Francis the First	H.P.	Trouillard	1859	deep crimson	2	mod.
Francisque Barillet	H.P.	Damaizin	1873	cherry-red	1	vig.
Francisque Kruger	T.	Nabonnand	1880	flesh	1	vig.
Francisque Rive	H.P.	Schwartz	1884	cerise	1	vig.
François Arago	H.P.	Trouillard	1858	purple-crimson	2	mod.
François Courtin	H.P.	E. Verdier	1873	rich cerise	1	vig.
François Dubois	H.P.	Damaizin	1866	crimson-red	1	vig.
François Dugommier	B.	Mor. et Rob.	1873	purple-red	1	vig.
François Fontaine	H.P.	Fontaine	1867	rose-crimson	2	vig.
François Gaulain	H.P.	Schwartz	1878	deep purple	1	vig.
François Goeschke	H.P.	Soup. et Not.	1865	rose-lilac	1	vig.
François Herincq	H.P.	E. Verdier	1878	poppy-red	2	mod.
François I.	H.P.	Trouillard	1858	amaranth	2	mod.
François Lacharme	H.P.	V. Verdier	1861	carmine-red	2	mod.
François Levet	H.P.	Levet	1880	rose-pink	2	vig.
François Louvat	H.P.	Touvais	1861	lilac-red	1	vig.
François Olin	H.P.	Ducher	1882	red-cerise	2	vig.
François J. Pfister	H.P.	E. Verdier	1876	red-cerise	2	vig.
François Premier	H.P.	Trouillard	1858	red	2	mod.
François Treyve	H.P.	Liabaud	1866	red-scarlet	1	vig.
F. M. Dos Santos Vianna	T.	Nabonnand	1882	rose-lilac	2	mod
Frederick Wood	H.P.	E. Verdier	...	cherry-red	2	vig.
Fringed	Musk.	...	...	white	2	vig.
Froissart	H.P.	Miellez	...	carmine	3	mod.
Fulgens	H.C.	Malton	...	crimson	2	vig.

Name.	Class.	Raiser.	Year.	Colour.	Size.	Habit.
Furstin Johanna Auersperg	H.P.	Soup. et Not.	1884	rose	2	mod.
Gabrielle Martel	T.	Levet	1873	coppery yellow	1	vig.
Garden Favourite	H.P.	W. Paul	1884	pink	1	vig.
Garibaldi	H.P.	Damaizin	1859	rosy lilac	2	mod.
Gaspard Monge	H.P.	Mor. et Rob.	1874	bright red	1	vig.
Gaston Chandon	T.	Schwartz	1885	rose-yellow	2	mod.
Gaston Lévêque	H.P.	Lévêque	1878	bright crimson	1	vig.
Géant des Batailles	H.P.	Nerard	1846	rich red	2	mod.
Gem of the Prairies	Pra.	Burgess	1865	red-white	3	vig.
General Appert	H.P.	Schwartz	1885	red-purple	2	vig.
Général Barral	H.P.	Damaizin	1867	violet-rose	2	mod.
Général Bedeau	H.P.	Margottin	1851	carmine	2	mod.
Général Championnet	H.P.	Mor. et Rob.	1866	rose-red	1	mod.
Général Castellane	H.P.	Guillot père	1851	crimson	1	mod.
Général Cavaignac	H.P.	...	1851	light carmine	1	mod.
Général Chargarnier	H.C.	Laffay	1847	purple-red	1	mod.
Général de Cissey	H.P.	E. Verdier	1875	bright scarlet	1	vig.
Général Dessaix	H.P.	Mor. et Rob.	1867	fiery red	1	vig.
General Dumouriez	H.P.	Moreau	...	cerise	2	mod.
General Grant	H.P.	E. Verdier	1869	crimson-scarlet	1	vig.
Général d'Hautpoul	H.P.	E. Verdier	1864	red-scarlet	1	mod.
Général Jacqueminot	H.P.	Roussel	1853	brilliant red	1	vig.
Général Jacqueminot	H.C.	Laffay	1846	shaded lake	1	mod.
Général Lamartinière	H.P.	Jamain	1869	rose-carmine	1	vig.
Général MacMahon	H.P.	...	1858	rose-carmine	1	mod.
Général Milordowitch	H.P.	Lévêque fils	1869	red-carmine	1	vig.
Général Mirandol	H.P.	Oger	1864	deep red	2	mod.
General von Moltke	H.P.	Bell	1873	red	2	mod.
Général Negzier	H.P.	...	1851	peach-rose	2	mod.
Général Pelissier	H.P.	Ducher	1855	light rose	1	vig.
Général Schlablikine	T.	Nabonnand	1878	bright rose	2	mod.
General Simpson	H.P.	Lacharme	1854	carmine	1	vig.
Général Terwauge	H.P.	Gautreau	1874	brilliant rose	1	vig.
General Washington	H.P.	Granger	1860	red-crimson	1	mod.
General Sir E. Wood	H.P.	Cant	1882	rose	1	mod.
General Zacharzewky	H.P.	Ducher	1860			
George Baker	H.P.	Paul & Son	1881	cerise-lake	2	mod.
George Moreau	H.P.	Mor. Rob.	1881	red	1	vig.
George Patinot	H.P.	Gautreau	1879	cerise	2	vig.
George Paul	H.P.	E. Verdier	1863	bright rose	2	mod.
George Peabody	B.	Peutland	1857	crimson	3	mod.
George Pernet	e.	Pernet fils— Ducher	1887	bright rose	3	vig.
George Prince	H.P.	E. Verdier	1863	rose-red	2	vig.
George Simon	H.P.	Oger	1863	bright red	2	vig.
George Vibert	Prov.	Roberts	1853	purple	2	mod.
Gigantèsque	T.	Odier	1845	rose	2	mod.
Gipsy	H.T.	Laxton	1884	dark red	2	vig.
Gloire d'Angiers	H.P.	Boyau	1846	bright rose	1	mod.
Gloire de Bordeaux	T.	Lartey	1861	lilac-rose	1	vig.
Gloire de Chatillon	H.P.	Fontaine	1861	red	2	mod.

Name.	Class.	Raiser.	Year.	Colour.	Size.	Habit.
Gloire de Dijon	T.	Jacotot	1853	salmon-buff	1	vig.
Gloire de Ducher	H.P.	Ducher	1865	crimson-purple	1	vig.
Gloire de France	H.P.	Margottin	1854	crimson shaded	1	vig.
Gloire de Lyon	H.P.	Ducher	1857	purplish red	2	vig.
Gloire Lyonnais	H.T.	Guilot	1885	white	2	vig.
Gloire de Margottin	H.P.	Margottin	1888	rosy cerise	1	vig.
Gloire de Montplaisir	H.P.	Gonod	1866	bright rose	1	vig.
Gloire des Mousseuses	M.	Laffay	1852	blush	1	vig.
Gloire d'Orient	M.	Beluze	1855			
Gloire d'Orléans	H.P.	Vigneron	1879	carmine-red	1	vig.
Gloire de Polyantha	P.	Guillot et fils	1888	bright rose	3	vig.
Gloire de Bourg-la-Reine	H.P.	Margottin	1879	brilliant red	1	vig.
Gloire de Rosomène	H.P.	Vibert	...	crimson	1	rob.
Gloire de Santenay	H.P.	Ducher	1859	purple-red	2	mod.
Gloire de Thelwitz	H.P.	Peters	1866	rose-lake	2	mod.
Gloire de Vitry	H.P.	Masson	1854	rose-carmine	1	vig.
Gloire du Sacré-Cœur	H.P.	Moreau	1863			
Gloriosa	H.P.	Touvais	...	tender rose	3	mod.
Glory of Cheshunt	H.P.	Paul & Son	1880	rich crimson	1	vig.
Glory of Waltham	H.P.	Vigneron	1865	rich crimson	1	rob
Gonsoli Gaelano	H.P.	Pernet	1874	satiny rose	2	mod.
Goubalt	T.	Goubalt	1843	bright pink	2	mod.
Goliath	H.P.	Trouillard	1861	rose edge white	1	vig.
Grace Darling	T.	Bennett	1884	tinted white	2	vig.
Gracilis	Bour.	Shailler	1796	pink	2	rob.
Grandeur of Cheshunt	H.P.	Paul & Son	1883	crimson	1	vig
Grand Duke Nicholas	H.P.	Lévêque fils	1877	brilliant red	1	mod.
Grand Mogul	H.P.	W.Paul&Son	1887	crimson	1	vig.
Great Western	H.P.	Laffay	1840	crimson-scarlet	1	vig.
Guillaume Guillemot	H.P.	Schwartz	1880	carmine rose	1	vig.
Gustave Courax	H.P.	Duval	...	purple	2	mod.
Gustave Persin	H.P.	Fontaine	1865	fiery red	1	mod.
Gustave Revilliod	H.P.	Schwartz	1875	bright rose	1	mod.
Gustave Rousseau	H.P.	Fargeton	1862	violet-red	2	vig.
Gustave Thierry	H.P.	Oger	1881	cherry-red	2	mod.
Hans Makart	H.P.	E. Verdier	1885	scarlet	2	vig.
Harrison Weir	H.P.	Turner	1879	velvety crimson	1	vig.
Harrison's Yellow	A.B.	Harrison	1830	golden yellow	3	mod.
Hebe	H.P.	Mor. et Rob.	1884	rose	2	mod.
Heinrich Schultheis	H.P.	Bennett	1882	rose	1	mod.
Helen	H.P.	Paul	1854	rosy blush	2	mod.
Helen Paul	H.P.	Lacharme	1882	blush-pink	1	vig.
Héliogable	H.P.	Guinoisseau	...	red	1	vig.
Helvetia	T.	Ducher	1873	rose-salmon	1	vig.
Henri Lecoq	T.	Ducher	1871	shaded rose	2	vig.
Henri Meynadier	T.	Nabonnand	1885	rose	2	mod.
Henriette Laval	H.P.	Guillot	1852			
Henriette Petite	H.P.	Margottin	1879	amaranth-rose	1	vig.
H. W. Beecher	H.P.	E. Verdier	1874	purple-red	1	vig.
Henry Bennett	H.P.	Lacharme	1875	rosy carmine	1	vig.
Henry Bennett	T.	Levet	1872	rosy sulphur	2	mod.

Name.	Class.	Raiser.	Year.	Colour.	Size.	Habit.
Henry IV.	H.P.	C. Verdier	...	purple	2	mod.
Henry Ledechaux	H.P.	Ledechaux	1868	rosy carmine	1	mod.
Henri Martin	M.	Portemer	1862	red	3	mod.
Henry Pagès	H.P.	Levet	1870	bright rose	1	rob.
Henry Vilmorin	H.P.	Lévêque fils	1878	rich red	1	vig.
Her Majesty	H.P.	Bennett	1882	pink	1	rob.
Hermosa	B.	Marcheseau	1840	bright rose	2	vig.
Heroine de Vaucluse	N.	Guillot	1846			
Hippolyte Flandrin	H.P.	Damaizin	1865	soft rose	1	mod.
Hippolyte Jamain	H.P.	Faudon	1869	rose	1	mod.
Hippolyte Jamain	H.P.	Lacharme	1874	carmine-rose	1	vig.
Hippolyte Marchand	H.P.	Vigneron	1882	rose	1	vig.
Homer	T.	Robert	1859	salmon-rose	2	vig.
Hon. George Bancroft	H.T.	Bennett	1878	rose	1	vig.
Hon. Edith Gifford	T.	Guillot	1883	flesh	2	vig.
Horace Vernet	H.P.	Guillot fils	1866	purple-red	2	mod.
Hortense Blachette	H.P.	Damaizin	1862			
Hortense Mignard	H.P.	Baltet	1873	cherry-red	2	mod.
Hortense Vernet	P.M.	Rob. et Mor.	1861	pink	3	mod.
Hortensia	T.	Ducher	1870	rose-salmon	1	vig.
Ida	T.	Mad. Ducher	1875	pale yellow	2	mod.
Imbricata	M.	Ducher	1869	light rose	2	mod.
Impératrice Charlotte	H.P.	E. Verdier	1867	tender rose	1	rob.
Impératrice Eugénie	B.	Beluze	1855	rose	2	mod.
Impératrice Eugénie	P.M.	Guillot	1855			
Impératrice des Français...	H.P.	Oger	1855	flesh	1	vig.
Impératrice Maria Alexandra	H.P.	Damaizin	1862			
Inermis	H.P.	Lacharme	1850	pink	3	mod.
Inigo Jones	H.P.	W. Paul & Son	1886	dark rose	2	vig.
Innocente Pirola	T.	Mad. Ducher	1878	white	1	vig.
Intendant Perrier...	H.P.	Vigneron	1882	cerise-red	1	mod.
Isabella	T.	Cels	1838	white	3	mod.
Isabella Gray	N.	Gray	1855	yellow	2	rob.
Isabella Sprunt	T.	Sprunt	1866	pale yellow	1	vig.
Isocrate	H.P.	...	1851	salmon-rose	1	
Jacob Pereire	H.P.	Moreau	...	purple-red	2	mod.
Jacques Cartier	H.P.	Mor. et Rob.	1868	clear rose	1	vig.
Jacques Lafitte	H.P.	Vibert	1846	bright rose	1	mod.
Jacques Plantier	H.P.	Damaizin	1871	flesh-rose	2	mod.
James Dickson	H.P.	E. Verdier	1861	purplish crimsn.	1	mod.
James Mitchell	P.M.	E. Verdier	1861	lilac-rose	2	mod.
James Sprunt	B.	Sprunt	1856	velvety crimsn.	2	vig.
James Veitch	P.M.	E. Verdier	1864	rosy purple	2	vig.
James Watt	H.P.	Mor. et Rob.	1873	lake	1	vig.
Jane Mossop	T.	Nabonnand	1879	flesh-white	2	mod.
Jaune Desprez	N.	Desprez	1838	fawn and pink	2	vig.
Jaune d'Or	T.	Oger	1863	deep yellow	2	mod.
Jean Bart	H.P.	Margottin	1860	reddish violet	2	vig.
Jean Bodin	M.	Vibert	1847	rose	2	mod.

Name.	Class.	Raiser.	Year.	Colour.	Size.	Habit.
Jean Brosse	H. P.	Ducher	1867	clear rose	2	vig.
Jean Cherpin	H. P.	Liabaud	1865	velvety red	1	mod.
Jean Dalmais	H. P.	Ducher	1873	cerise-red	1	vig.
Jean Ducher	T.	Mad. Ducher	1874	salmon-yellow	1	vig.
Jean France	H. P.	Levet	1866	dark purple	2	mod.
Jean Goujon	H. P.	Margottin	1862	deep rose	1	vig.
Jean B. Guillot	H. P.	E. Verdier	1861	purple-red	2	mod.
Jean Hardy	N.	Hardy	1859	yellow	2	mod.
Jean Lambert	H. P.	E. Verdier	1865	dark red	1	vig.
Jean Lelièvre	H. P.	Oger	1879	red-crimson	1	vig.
Jean Liabaud	H. P.	Liabaud	1875	velvety crimsn.	1	vig.
Jean Lorthois	T.	Ducher	1879	rose	2	vig.
Jean Monford	M.	Robert	1852	rose	3	mod.
Jean Pernet	T.	Pernet	1867	clear yellow	1	vig.
Jean Rosenkrantz	H. P.	Portemer fils	1864	rich red	1	vig.
Jean Sisley	H. T.	Bennett	1878	rose-lilac	2	mod.
Jean Soupert	H. P.	Lacharme	1875	velvety purple	1	mod.
Jean Touvais	H. P.	Touvais	1863	purple-red	2	vig.
Jeanne Abel	T.	Guillot	1883	rose	2	vig.
Jeanne d'Arc	N.	V. Verdier	1848	white	2	vig.
Jeanne d'Arc	N.	Ducher	1869	light yellow	2	mod.
Jeanne Chevalier	H. P.	Rambaux	1879	bright red	2	vig.
Jeanne Drivon	P.	Schwartz	1884	tinted white	3	mod.
Jeanne Guillot	H. P.	Liabaud	1869	satiny rose	1	vig.
Jeanne Hachette	H. P.	Oger	...	carmine	2	mod.
Jeanne Renou	H. P.	Oger	...	rose	2	vig.
Jeanne Sury	H. P.	Faudon	1868	claret-crimson	1	mod.
Jenny Lind	H. M.	...	1845	crimson	2	mod.
Joachim du Bellay	H P.	Mor. et Rob.	1883	vermilion	2	vig.
John Bright	H. P.	Paul & Son	1878	scarlet	1	vig.
John Cranston	P. M.	E. Verdier	1861	violet-red	2	vig.
John Fraser	H. P.	E. Verdier	1876	red-crimson	1	vig.
John Fraser	P. M.	Lévêque	1861	red & carmine	2	vig.
John Grier	H. P.	E. Verdier	1865	bright-red	1	vig.
John Harrison	H. P.	E. Verdier	1873	purple-crimson	1	vig.
John Hopper	H. P.	Ward	1862	rosy crimson	1	vig.
John Keynes	H. P.	E. Verdier	1864	bright red	1	vig.
John Laing	H. P.	E. Verdier	1872	bright crimson	3	mod.
John Stuart Mill	H. P.	Turner	1874	clear red	1	vig.
John Saul	H. P.	Mad. Ducher	1878	carmine-red	2	vig.
John Gould Veitch	H. P.	Lévêque fils	1864	rosy purple	1	mod.
Joseph Bernacchi	N.	Ducher	1878	pale yellow	2	vig.
Joseph Chappaz	H. P.	Schmidt	1883	lilac	2	mod.
Joseph Decaisne	H. P.	...	1852	bright rose	2	mod.
Joseph Metral	H. P.	Liabaud	1884	garnet-red	2	mod.
Joseph Tasson	H. P.	Soup. et Not.	1883	purple	2	vig.
Josephine Beauharnais	H. P.	Guillot fils	1865	pale rose	1	vig.
Josephine Clement	B.	Guillot	1858	pink	2	mod.
Jules Bourgeois	H. P.	Ledechaux	1867	velvety red	2	mod.
Jules Calot	H. P.	E. Verdier	1866	red-carmine	1	vig.
Jules César	B.	E. Verdier	1865	rose-cerise	1	vig.
Jules Chrétien	H. P.	Damaizin	1869	satiny rose	1	vig.

Name.	Class.	Raiser.	Year.	Colour.	Size.	Habit.
Jules Chrétien	H.P.	Schwartz	1877	purple-crimson	1	vig.
Jules Finger	T.	Mad. Ducher	1879	blush-white	1	vig.
Jules Jurgensen	B.	Schwartz	1879	purple-crimson	1	vig.
Jules Lavay	H.P.	Damaizin	1864	rosy flesh	1	vig.
Jules Marquinant	H.P.	Vigneron	1883	red	1	mod.
Jules Margottin	H.P.	Margottin	1853	rosy red	1	vig.
Jules Mongès	H.P.	Guillot	1882	carmine	1	vig.
Jules Seurre	H.P.	Liabaud	1869	carmine-red	2	vig.
Julie de Mersant	M.		...	rose	2	vig.
Julie Fontaine	H.P.	Fontaine	1878	salmon-rose	1	vig.
Julie Touvais	H.P.	Touvais	1868	rose-flesh	1	vig.
Julie Treyve	H.P.	Liabaud	1868	pale rose	1	vig.
Julius Finger	H.P.	Lacharme	1879	rosy red	1	vig.
Juno	H.C.	Laffay	1847	light rose	1	vig.
Jury	B.	Guillot	1885	cherry-red	2	mod.
Karl Müller	H.P.	Soup. et Not.	...	amaranth	2	mod.
Kate Hausburg	H.P.	Granger	1863	rose-pink	1	vig.
Katkoff	H.P.	Mor. et Rob.	1888	carmine	1	vig.
Kean	G.	...	...	purple	2	vig.
King of the Prairies	Pra	Feast	1843	rose	3	vig.
King's Acre	H.P.	Cranston	1864	vermilion	1	mod.
Kleber	H.P	Boyau	1872	crimson-red	2	mod.
Kronprinzessin Victoria	B.	Spath	1888	white	1	vig.
L'Abondance	H.P.	E. Verdier	1864	bright red	2	vig.
L'Abondance	N.	Mor. et Rob.	1888	pure white	3	vig.
L'Ideal	N.	Nabonnand	1888	yellow	2	vig.
La Lisette de Béranger	H.P	Moreau	1867	flesh	2	mod.
La Tour d'Auvergne	G.		...	rose	2	vig.
La Vaillante Bergère	H.P.	Cherpin	1847			
La Boule d'Or	T.	Margottin	1860	yellow	1	mod.
La Bouquetière	B.	Laffay	1843	rose	2	mod.
La Brillante	H.P.	E. Verdier	1861	bright carmine	2	mod.
La Ville de Bruxelles	D.	Vibert	1836	rose	2	mod.
La Ville de St. Denis	H.P.	Thomas	...	rosy carmine	1	mod.
L'Etincelante	H.P.	E. Verdier	1875	bright red	1	vig.
La Favorite	H.P.	Guillot	1871	tender rose	2	mod.
La Fontaine	H.C.	Guinoisseau	1855	red	2	mod.
La France	H.P.	Guillot fils	1867	bright pink	1	vig.
La Grandeur	T.	Nabonnand	1877	rose	1	vig.
La Jonquille	T.	Ducher	1871	deep yellow	2	mod.
La Lune	T.	Nabonnand	1878	creamy yellow	1	vig.
La Madeleine	H.P.	Nabonnand	1882	ruby-red	2	mod.
La Duchesse de Morny	H.P.	E. Verdier	1863	bright rose	1	vig.
La Motte Sanguine	H.P.	Vigneron	1869	crimson	1	rob.
La Nuance	T.	Guillot fils	1875	rosy white	1	vig.
La Princesse Véra	T.	Nabonnand	1878	creamy white	2	mod.
La Quintinie	H.P.	...	1853	deep crimson	1	mod.
La Reine	H.P.	Laffay	1843	rosy pink	1	mod.
La Rosière	H.P.	Damaizin	1874	dark crimson	2	mod.
La Saumonée	H.P.	Margottin	1877	salmon-rose	1	mod.

Name.	Class.	Raiser.	Year.	Colour.	Size.	Habit.
La Séduisante	H.P.	Lacharme	1850	carmine	2	mod.
La Sirène	H.P.	Soup. et Not.	1867	amaranth-purp.	3	vig.
La Souveraine	H.P.	E. Verdier	1874	magenta-rose	1	rob.
La Sylphide	T.	Laffay	...	cream	1	mod.
La Toulousaine	H.N.	Brassac	1877	rose-white	3	mod.
La Tulipe	T.	Ducher	1868	white-rose	2	mod.
Lacépède	H.P.	C. Verdier	1865	clear red	2	mod.
Lady Mary Fitzwilliam	H.T.	Bennett	1882	flesh	1	vig.
Lady Fordwick	H.C.	Laffay	1838	rose	2	mod.
Lady of the Lake	H.P.	Paul & Son	1884	peach	1	vig.
Lady Emily Peel	H.N.	Lacharme	1862	carmine	2	vig.
Lady Sheffield	H.P.	Postans	1881	rosy cerise	1	vig.
Lady Shelley	H.P.	Mitchell	1853	shaded crimson	1	vig.
Lady Helen Stewart	H.P.	Dickson&Sn.	1886	scarlet	1	vig.
Lady Stuart	H.C.	Portemer	1852	pink	2	mod.
Lady Suffield	H.P.	W. Paul	1866	purple-crimson	1	vig.
Lælia	H.P.	Crozy	1857	rose-pink	1	vig.
Lælia	H.P.	Laffay	1844	rose-lilac	1	mod.
Laïs	T.	Damaizin	1863	yellow	2	mod.
Lamarque	N.	Maréchal	1830	sulphur-white	2	vig.
Lamarque à Fleurs Jaunes.	N.	Ducher	1869	golden yellow	2	mod.
Lamartine	H.B.	Guillot	1842			
Lanei	M.	Laffay	1845	rose-crimson	1	vig.
Laura Davoust	Mult.	...	...	pink	3	vig.
Laure Remond	H.P.	Lacharme	1850	blush	2	mod.
Laure Fontaine .. ,	T.	Fontaine	1867	creamy white	2	mod.
Laurent de Rillé	H.P.	Lévêque	1885	cerise	2	mod.
Laurente Descours	H.P.	Liabaud	1862	velvet-purple	2	mod.
Lays	N.	Guillot	1848			
Le Blanqui	T.	Ducher	1871	white	1	vig.
Le Bignonia	T.	Levet	1873	orange-yellow	2	mod.
L'Eblouissante	H.P.	Touvais	1861	crimson	1	mod.
Le Camée	B.	Beluze	1845			
L'Elegante	T.	Guillot	1883	yellow-pink	2	vig.
L'Enfant du Mont-Carmel.	H.P.	Cherpin	1851	rose	1	vig.
Le Royal Epoux	H.P.	Damaizin	...	pink	2	mod.
L'Esperance	H.P.	Fontaine	1871	cherry-red	1	mod.
L'Esperance	H.P.	Lartay	...	rose	2	vig.
Le Florifère	T.	Ducher	1870	salmon-white	2	mod.
Le Havre	H.P.	Eude	1870	vermilion	1	vig.
Le Khedive	H.P.	Barrault	1883	crimson	2	mod.
Le Loiret	H.P.	Ribault	1883	carmine	1	vig.
Le Mont Blanc	T.	Ducher	1869	white-yellow	1	vig.
Le Nankin	T.	Ducher	1871	white-rose	1	vig.
Le Pactole	T.	Pean	...	cream	1	mod.
Le Rhône	H.P.	Guillot fils	1862	scarlet-crimson	1	mod.
Le Roitelet	B.	Soup. et Not.	1868	satiny rose	3	mod.
Lecocq-Dumesnil	H.P.	E. Verdier	1883	red	1	vig.
Lena Turner	H.P.	E. Verdier	1869	cerise-red	1	vig.
Léonce Giessen	H.P.	Lacharme	1875			
Léon Duval	H.P.	Lévêque	1879	red-carmine	2	vig.
Léon Renault	H.P.	Ledechaux	1878	cherry-red	2	vig.

Name.	Class.	Raiser.	Year.	Colour.	Size.	Habit.
Leon Say	H.P.	Lévêque	1883	red-lilac	1	vig.
Léopold I.	H.P.	Vanasche	1863	deep red	1	vig.
Léopold II.	H.P.	Margottin	1868	rosy red	1	rob.
Léopold de Bauffremont	H.C.	...	...	pink	2	vig.
Léopold Hausburg	H.P.	Granger	1864	bright carmine	1	vig.
Letty Coles	T.	Keynes	1875	rose-carmine	1	vig.
Leveson Gower	H.T.	Beluze	1846	rose-salmon	2	mod.
Lichas	B.	Guillot	1845			
Lion des Combats	H.P.	Lartay	1853	carmine	1	vig.
Lisette de Béranger	H.P.	Guillot fils	1867	rosy flesh	1	vig.
Little Gem	M.	W. Paul	1880	crimson	3	vig.
Loch Ness	S.	...	...	pale rose	3	vig.
Longfellow	H.P.	Paul & Son	1885	crimson	1	vig.
Longworth Rambler	E.	Liabaud	1880	crimson	2	rob.
Lord Bacon	H.P.	W.Paul&Son	1883	crimson	1	vig.
Lord Beaconsfield	H.P.	Bennett	1878	dark crimson	1	vig.
Lord F. Cavendish	H.P.	Frettingham	1883	scarlet	2	vig.
Lord Clyde	H.P.	Paul & Son	1863	red-crimson	1	vig.
Lord Eldon	T.	Coppin	1872	saffron-yellow	1	mod.
Lord Elgin,	H.P.	Guillot père	1858	dark purple	2	mod.
Lord Herbert	H.P.	W. Paul	1862	deep carmine	2	mod.
Lord Macaulay	H.P.	W. Paul	1863	deep crimson	1	rob.
Lord Palmerston	H.P.	Margottin	1857	carmine-rose	2	mod.
Lord Raglan	H.P.	Guillot père	1854	deep crimson	2	mod.
Louis d'Arzens	H.N.	Lacharme	1861	blush	2	mod.
Louis d'Autriche	H.P.	...	1858	violet-red	1	vig.
Louis Barlet	T.	Mad. Ducher	1875	salmon-white	2	mod.
Louis Brassac	H.P.	Brassac	...	satiny rose	1	mod.
Louis Builliat	H.P.	Gonod	1867	red-crimson	1	vig.
Louis Chaix	B.	Lacharme	1857	deep crimson	2	mod
Louis Charlin	H.P.	Damaizin	1871			
Louis Donadine	H.P.	J. M. Gonod	1887	dark maroon	1	vig
Louis Dore	H.P.	Fontaine	1878	red	2	mod.
Louis XIV.	H.P.	Guillot fils	1859	velvety red	1	wk.
Louis Galline	H.P.	Guillot	1859			
Louis Gigot	T.	Ducher	1871	white-rose	2	mod.
Louis Gimard	M.	Pernet	1877	bright red	2	mod.
Louis van Houtte	H.P.	Granger	1863	rich carmine	1	vig.
Louis van Houtte	H.P.	Lacharme	1869	red-crimson	1	mod.
Louis Lille	H.P.	Dubreuil	1887	bright red	1	vig.
Louis Margottin	H.B.	Margottin	1862	pale rose	2	mod
Louis Noisette	H.P.	Ducher	1865			
Louis Odier	B.	Margottin	1861	rich rose	1	vig.
Louis Philippe Albert d'Orleans	H.P.	E. Verdier	1885	cerise	2	vig.
Louis Richard	T.	Mad. Ducher	1877	rosy yellow	2	vig.
Louis Spath	H.P.	Soup. et Not.	1876	rose-pink	1	mod.
Louisa Gretton	H.P.	Cranston	1882	crimson	2	vig.
Louisa Wood	H.P.	E. Verdier	1869	bright rose	1	vig.
Louise Damaizin	H.P.	Damaizin	1863	rosy red	1	vig.
Louise Darzens	H.N.	Lacharme	1861	pure white	2	vig.
Louise Odier	H.P.	Margottin	1850	bright rose	2	mod.

Name.	Class.	Raiser.	Year.	Colour.	Size.	Habit.
Louise Peyronny	H.P.	Lacharme	1844	rose-pink	1	vig.
Louise de Savoie	T.	Ducher	1853	pale yellow	1	vig.
Luciole	T.	Guillot	1887	rosy red	1	vig.
Lucrèce	T.	Oger	1866	salmon-rose	2	mod.
Ludovic Letand	H.P.	Cherpin	1852			
Lusidas	T.	De Costo	1885	yellow	2	vig.
Lutea	Bk.	...	1827	yellow	3	vig.
Luxembourg	M.	...		crimson	2	vig.
Lyonnais	H.P.	Lacharme	1871	bright pink	1	vig.
Ma Capucin	T.	Levet	1871	bright yellow	2	mod.
Ma Frisée	H.P.	Vignerou	...	red	1	mod.
Ma Pivoine	H.P.	Levet	1866	purple-violet	1	vig
Ma Ponctuée	P.M.	Guillot père	1858	spotted rose	2	mod.
Ma Surprise	Mic.	Guillot fils	1872	salmon-pink	2	mod.
Ma Surprise	H.P.	Levet	1884	red	2	mod.
Mabel Morrison	H.P.	Broughton	1878	white	1	vig.
MacMahon	H.P.	E. Verdier	1872	rose	1	mod.
Mad. Albani	H.P.	E. Verdier	1877	brilliant red	2	vig.
Mad. Alboni	M.	V. Verdier	1850	pink	2	mod.
Mad. Caradori Allan	P.	Feast	1843	pink	2	mod.
Mad. Amadieu	T.	Pernet	1881	rose	2	mod.
Mad. Eugène Appert	H.P.	Trouillard	1865	rosy salmon	2	vig.
Mad. d'Arblay	Musk.	...	...	white	3	vig.
Mad. Arntzenius	H.P.	Soup. et Not	1874	deep carmine	1	vig.
Mad. Alphonse Aubert	H.P.	Fontaine	1875	carmine-red	1	vig.
Mad. Amélie Baltet	H.P.	E. Verdier	1878	satiny rose	1	vig.
Mad. Charles Baltet	H.P.	E. Verdier	1865	tender rose	3	mod.
Mad. Lauriol de Barny	H.	Trouillard	1868	deep rose	1	vig.
Mad. Barriot	H.P.	Damaizin	1867	carmine-rose	2	vig.
Mad. Bellon	H.P.	Pernet	1871	tender rose	2	mod.
Mad. Bérard	T.	Levet	1870	salmon-rose	1	vig.
Mad. Alexandre Bernaix	H.T.	Guillot fils	1877	bright rose	1	vig.
Mad. Bernard	T.	Levet	1875	creamy rose	2	mod.
Mad. Lefebvre Bernard	H.P.	Levet	1871	bright rose	1	vig.
Mad. Beruntz	H.P.	Jamain	1874	satin-rose	1	mod.
Mad. Anna de Besobrassoff	H.P.	Gonod	1877	carmine-rose	2	mod.
Mad. Martin de Bessé	H.P.	Granger	1866	tinted rose	2	mod.
Mad. F. Besson	H.P.	Besson	1882	flesh-pink	1	vig.
Mad. Marie Bianchi	H.P.	Guillot	1882	lilac	1	vig.
Mad. Alfred Bleu	H.P.	E. Verdier	1885	rose-crimson	2	mod.
Mad. Boll	H.P.	Boll	1859	carmine-rose	1	vig.
Mad. Gustave Bonnet	H.P.	Lacharme	1860	carmine-pink	2	mod.
Mad. Gustave Bonnet	N.	Lacharme	1864	rose-white	3	vig.
Mad. Maxime Bonnet	B.	Pradel	1861	cerise-red	1	vig.
Mad. Jeanne Bouger	H.P.	Gonod	1877			
Mad. Arsène Bouneau	H.P.	Bouneau	...	rose	2	vig.
Mad. Boutin	H.P.	Jamain	1861	crimson-red	1	vig.
Mad. Jean Bouyer	H.P.	Gonod	1877	rose-pink	1	mod.
Mad. Emilie Boyau	H.P.	Boyau	1861	rose-flesh	1	vig.
Mad. Bravy	T.	Guillot père	1848	creamy white	1	mod.
Mad. Bremond	T.	Guillot fils	1866	deep red	2	mod.

N

Name.	Class.	Raiser.	Year.	Colour.	Size.	Habit.
Mad. G. Bruant	H.R.	Bruant	1888	white	1	vig.
Mad. Bruel	H.P.	Levet	1882	rose-carmine	1	mod.
Mad. Bruny	H.P.	Plantier	1858	rose	3	mod.
Mad. F. Buchner	H.P.	Lévêque	1885	rose	2	mod.
Mad. Anna Bugnet	B.	Gonod	1866	flesh-white	2	mod.
Mad. William Bull	H.P.	E. Verdier	1876	bright rose	2	vig.
Mad. Jules Caboche	H.P.	Vigneron	...	rose	2	vig.
Mad. Caillat	H.P.	E. Verdier	1861	bright cerise	1	vig.
Mad. Camille	T.	Guillot fils.	1871	salmon-rose	1	vig.
Mad. Canrobert	H.P.	Gonichon	1868	lively carmine	2	vig.
Mad. Canrobert	H.P.	Liabaud	1862	pale lilac	2	mod.
Mad. Carl	H.T.	Bernaix	1887	red	2	vig.
Mad. Louis Carique	H.P.	Fontaine	1859	crimson	1	vig.
Mad. Caro	T.	Levet	1880	salmon	1	vig.
Mad. Alfred Carrière	N.	Schwartz	1879	flesh colour	1	vig.
Mad. Miolan Carvalho	N.	Lévêque	1875	sulphur	1	vig.
Mad. Eugène Chambeyran.	H.P.	Gonod	1878	pale rose	1	vig.
Mad. Raoul Chandon	H.P.	C. Verdier	1885	rose	3	mod.
Mad. Charles	T.	Damaizin	1864	apricot-yellow	2	vig.
Mad. Rose Charmeux	H.P.	Gautreau	1874	purple-red	2	mod.
Mad. Chaté	H.P.	Fontaine	1871	cherry-red	2	mod.
Mad. L Chaure	H.P.	Vigneron	1885	red-cerise	1	vig.
Mad. Chaveret	T.	Levet	1872	apricot-yellow	1	vig.
Mad. Elize de Chenier	B.	...	1858	bright pink	2	mod
Mad. Chicrot	H.P.	Pernet	1877	bright rose	1	vig.
Mad. Chignard	H.P.	Vigneron	1877	clear red	1	vig.
Mad. Chirard	H.P.	Pernet	1867	fresh rose	1	vig.
Mad. Marie Cirodde	H.P.	C. Verdier	1867	rose-pink	1	vig.
Mad. Clavel	H.P.	Lacharme	1856			
Mad. Clert	H.P.	Gonod	1868	rosy salmon	1	vig.
Mad. Scipion Cochet	H.P.	Desmazures	1871	cherry-red	1	vig.
Mad. Scipion Cochet	T.	...	1887	yellow	1	vig.
Mad. Collet	B.	Liabaud	1864	rosy white	2	vig.
Mad. Emma Combey	H.P.	Gonod	1872	bright carmine	1	vig.
Mad. Contesse	B.	...	1858	peach	2	vig.
Mad. Adeline Cote	H.P.	Schmidt	1882	red-crimson	1	vig.
Mad. Marcus Cote	H.P.	Guillot fils.	1872	rosy red	1	vig.
Mad. Coulombier	H.P.	Lévêque	1884	rose-red	2	mod.
Mad. Charles Crapelet	H.P.	Fontaine	1859	rose-red	1	vig.
Mad. Creyton	H.P.	Gonod	1868	bright carmine	1	rob.
Mad. Crozy	H.P.	Levet	1882	pink	2	mod.
Mad. Cuzin	T.	Guillot	1882	rose-yellow	2	vig.
Mad. Damaizin	T.	Damaizin	1858	salmon	1	vig.
Mad. Julie Daran	H.P.	Touvais	1861	rosy crimson	1	vig.
Mad. Debelfort	H.P.	Beluze	1847			
Mad. Debray	H.P.	T. Ribault	1885	rose	2	vig.
Mad. Decour	H.P.	Pernet	1863	rich rose	1	rob.
Mad. Th. Delacour	H.P.	E. Verdier	1885	rose-carmine	2	mod.
Mad. Lelievre Delaplace	H.P.	E. Verdier	1883	deep red	1	vig.
Mad. Delaville	T.	Oger	1873	sulphur-yellow	2	mod.
Mad. Dellevaux	H.P.	Besson	1884	satin-rose	1	vig.
Mad. Denis	T.	Gonod	1872	sulphur-white	2	mod.

Name.	Class.	Raiser.	Year.	Colour.	Size.	Habit.
Mad. Desbordeaux	H.P.	Oger	1873	satiny rose	2	mod.
Mad. Joseph Desbois	H.T.	Guillot	1886	flesh	1	vig.
Mad. Barillet Deschamps..	T.	Bernède	1855	yellow	2	mod.
Mad. Honoré Defresne ...	T.	Levet	1888	deep yellow	1	vig.
Mad. Desir	H.P.	Pernet	1886	bright rose	1	vig.
Mad. Baptiste Desportes...	H.P.	Trouillard	1865	bright rose	2	mod.
Mad. Just Detry	B.	Detry	1869	red-carmine	1	mod.
Mad. Devaucoux	T.	Md. Ducher	1874	canary-yellow	2	mod.
Mad. Devert...	H.P.	Pernet	1876	rose-pink	2	mod.
Mad. Angèle Dispott	H.P.	Dauvesse	1869	fiery red	2	mod.
Mad. Domage	H.P.	Margottin	1854	rosy crimson	1	vig.
Mad. Louis Donadine	H.P.	Gonod	1877	bright pink	1	mod.
Mad. Doré	B.	Fontaine	1863	rose-purple	2	mod.
Mad. Dorlia	H.P.	Fontaine	1877	bright cerise	2	vig.
Mad. Derreux Douville ...	H.P.	Lévêque	1863	tender rose	1	vig.
Mad. E. Dreol	H.P.	Dreol	1861	rose-lilac	2	mod.
Mad. Dubuisson	H.P.	Baudry	1861	carmine	2	mod.
Mad. Dubois	H.P.	Fontaine	1866	vermilion-red	2	mod.
Mad. Ducamp	H.P.	Fontaine	1863	purple-red	2	mod.
Mad. Ducher............... ...	T.	Ducher	1869	clear yellow	2	mod.
Mad. Ducher.............	H.P.	Levet	1879	cerise-red	1	mod.
Mad. Emilie Dunau......	N.	Nabonnand	1879	tender rose	1	mod.
Mad. Michel Dupré........	H.P.	Gonod	1876	brilliant red	1	vig.
Mad. Emilie Dupuy........	T.	Levet	1870	yellow	2	vig.
Mad. Alice Dureau	H.P.	Vigneron	1869	rose	2	mod.
Mad. André Duron	H.T.	Bonnaire	1887	clear red	1	vig.
Mad. Dustour	H.P.	Pernet	1869	carmine-red	1	vig.
Mad. Emain	H.P.	Pernet	1872	purple-red	1	vig.
Mad. Bonnet Eymard	T.	Pernet	1874	yellow	2	mod.
Mad. Falcot	T.	Guillot fils	1858	apricot-yellow	2	vig.
Mad. Farfouillon...........	H.P.	Liabaud	1868	satiny rose	1	vig.
Mad. Fauvennier	H.P.	Fontaine	1878	silvery-rose	2	mod.
Mad. Fillion.................	H.P.	Gonod	1865	flesh-rose	2	vig.
Mad. Marie Finger	H.P.	Rambaux	1873	flesh-rose	1	vig.
Mad. A. Fitler	H.P.	Faudon	1873	salmon-rose	1	vig.
Mad. Fanny de Forest......	H.N.	Schwartz	1883	salmon	2	mod.
Mad. Appoline Foulon ...	H.P.	Vigneron	1883	rose-salmon	2	vig.
Mad. Freeman	H.N.	Guillot père	1862	white	2	mod.
Mad. Frémion	H.P.	Margottin	1850	rose-carmine	2	mod.
Mad. Eugène Frèmy	H.P.	E. Verdier	1885	rose	1	vig.
Mad. Fresnoy	H.P.	Pernet	1864	lively rose	2	vig
Mad. Sophia Fropot...	H.P.	Levet	1876	rosy pink	1	vig.
Mad. Furtado	H.P.	V. Verdier	1860	bright rose	1	mod.
Mad. Gadel	H.P.	Perdet	1872	lilac-rose	1	mod.
Mad. Gaillard	T.	Ducher	1870	salmon-yellow	2	mod.
Mad. Marie Garnier	H.P.	Gonod	1882	flesh-pink	1	vig.
Mad. Alice Van Geert......	H.P.	Lévêque	1884	red-rose	2	mod.
Mad. de St. Genêt	H.P.	Lartay	...	violet-red	1	mod.
Mad. Anna Gerold	H.P.	Soup. et Not.	1882	rose	2	mod.
Mad. D. Giraud	H.P.	Haussy	1854	striped	2	mod.
Mad. Fanny Giron	H.P.	Schmidt	1883	satin-rose	2	mod.
Mad. Joseph Godier.........	T.	Pernet	1887	rose	1	vig.

Name.	Class.	Raiser.	Year.	Colour.	Size.	Habit.
Mad. Gonod	H.P.	Mor. et Rob.	1867	satiny rose	1	mod.
Mad. J. M. Gonod	H.P.	Gonod	1875	red-crimson	1	vig.
Mad. Grawitz	H.P.	Soup.et Not.	1878	delicate rose	2	mod.
Mad. Jules Grèvy	H.P.	Schwartz	1882	salmon-pink	2	mod.
Mad. Grondier	H.P.	Gonod	1867	salmon-rose	1	vig.
Mad. James Gros	H.P.	Baumann	1864	bright carmine	2	mod.
Mad. Guillot	H.P.	Guillot	1851	rose-pink	1	vig.
Mad. Chedane Guinoisseau	T.	Lévêque	1880	sulphur-yellow	1	vig.
Mad. Emma Hall	H.P.	Liabaud	1876	rose-carmine	1	vig.
Mad. Marthé d'Halloy	H.P.	Lévêque	1882	rose-carmine	2	mod.
Mad. Joseph Halphen	T.	Margottin	1858	blush	2	mod.
Mad. Hardy	D.	Hardy	1832	white	1	vig.
Mad. Helody	H.P.	...	1856	silvery rose	2	mod.
Mad. James Hennessy	H.P.	Duval	1879	satiny rose	1	vig.
Mad. Henon	H.P.	Plantier	1852			
Mad. Louis Henry	N.	Ducher	1879	pale yellow	3	vig.
Mad. la Marquise d'Hervey	H.P.	Vigneron	1877	velvety red	1	vig.
Mad. Herivaux	H.P.	Jamain	1875	rich red	1	vig.
Mad. Hilaire	H.P.	...	1850	blush	2	mod.
Mad. Hoche	M.	Mor. et Rob.	1859	white	3	mod.
Mad. Hoste	H.P.	Gonod	1865	rosy flesh	1	mod.
Mad. Hoste	T	Guillot fils	1887	white	1	vig.
Mad. Van Houtte	H.P.	Margottin	1857	rosy pink	2	mod.
Mad. Hovart	H.P.	Vigneron	1883	vermilion	1	mod.
Mad. Hunnebelle	H.P.	Fontaine	1873	carmine-rose	1	vig.
Mad. Adèle Huzard	H.P.	C. Verdier	1867	lively rose	1	mod.
Mad. Azélie Imbert	T.	Levet	1870	salmon-yellow	1	vig.
Mad. Jacquier	H.P.	Guillot fils	1868	deep purple	1	vig.
Mad. Angèle Jacquier	T.	Guillot fils	1879	yellow	1	vig.
Mad. E. Jaenisch	H.P.	Soup.et Not.	1869	white-red	2	mod.
Mad. Ferdinand Jamain	H.P.	Ledechaux	1875	rose-carmine	1	vig.
Mad. H. Jamain	T.	Guillot fils	1869	white-yellow	1	vig.
Mad. H. Jamain	H.P.	Garçon	1871	light-pink	2	mod.
Mad. François Jamain	T.	Levet	1872	orange-yellow	2	mod.
Mad. Jard	B.	Guillot père	1858	cherry	1	vig.
Mad. Léon de St.-Jean	T.	Levet	1875	rosy salmon	1	vig.
Mad. Morane Jeune	H.P.	Jamain	1878	silvery rose	1	vig.
Mad. Clémence Joigneaux	H.P.	Liabaud	1861	red-lilac	1	vig.
Mad. Jolibos	H.P.	E. Verdier	1879	rose-carmine	2	vig.
Mad. de St. Joseph	T.	...		salmon-pink	1	vig.
Mad. Jean Joubert	B.	Margottin	1877	carmine-red	2	mod.
Mad. Alex. Jullien	H.P.	Vigneron	1883	rose	1	vig.
Mad. Lacourt Jury	H.P.	Guillot	1854	yellow	2	vig.
Mad. Dr. Jutte	T.	Levet	1872	white	2	mod.
Mad. Bellenden Ker	H.P.	Guillot père	1866			
Mad. Oswald de Kerchove	H.P.	Schwartz	1879	salmon-rose	1	vig.
Mad. Knorr	H.P.	V. Verdier	1855	blush-rose	2	mod.
Mad. Maurice Kuppenheim	T.	Md. Ducher	1877	salmon-yellow	2	mod.
Mad. Caroline Kuster	N.	Pernet	1872	orange-yellow	1	vig.
Mad. de Laboulaye	H.P.	Liabaud	1877	pale rose	2	mod.
Mad. Pauline Labonte	T.	Pradel	1852	salmon	1	mod.
Mad. Eugène Labruyere	H.P.	Gonod	1883	salmon	2	vig.

Name.	Class.	Raiser.	Year.	Colour.	Size.	Habit.
Mad. Lacharme	H.P.	Lacharme	1873	blush	1	vig.
Mad. Lacroix	H.P.	Guillot	1853	pale rose	2	mod.
Mad. Laffay	H.P.	Laffay	1839	purple-rose	2	vig.
Mad. Marie Lagrange	H.P.	Lagrange	1883	carmine	1	mod.
Mad. Lambard	T.	Lacharme	1877	rosy red	1	mod.
Mad. Lamon	H.P.	Lartey	1861	cerise-red	1	vig.
Mad. Lamoricère	H.P.	Mor. et Rob.	1852	bright pink	2	mod.
Mad. Landeau	M.	Mor. et Rob	1873	light red	2	mod.
Mad. Julie Lasseu	N.	Nabonnand	1882	rose	2	mod.
Mad. Prosper Laugier	H.P.	E. Verdier	1875	bright rose	1	vig.
Mad. Laurent	H.P.	Granger	1869	rose-cerise	2	mod.
Mad. Alphonse Lavallée	H.P.	E. Verdier	1878	cherry-red	1	vig.
Mad. Marie Lavalley	H.T.	Nabonnand	1882	rose	1	vig.
Mad. Charles Lavot	H.P.	Vigneron	1882	clear rose	2	mod.
Mad. Clorinde Leblond	H.P.	Dauvesse	1869	velvety red	2	mod.
Mad. Lefrançois	H.P.	Oger	1869	flesh-rose	2	mod.
Mad. Legrand	P.M.	Fontaine	1863	rose-carmine	2	mod.
Mad. Legras	A.	...	...	cream	2	mod.
Mad. André Leroy	H.P.	Trouillard	1864	salmon-rose	2	mod.
Mad. Louis Lévèque	H.P.	Lévèque	1873	bright rose	1	mod.
Mad. Levet	T.	Levet	1869	salmon-yellow	1	mod.
Mad. Barthélemy Levet	T.	Levet	1879	clear yellow	2	mod.
Mad. Etienne Levet	H.T.	Levet	1878	cerise-yellow	1	vig.
Mad. Liabaud	H.P.	Gonod	1869	flesh-white	1	vig.
Mad. Saison Lierval	H.P.	E. Verdier	1873	rose-carmine	2	vig.
Mad. Lilienthal	H.P.	Liabaud	1878	bright rose	1	vig.
Mad. Léonard Lille	H.T.	Nabonnand	1879	fiery red	2	mod.
Mad. H. de Luesmans	H.P.	Soup. et Not	1884	carmine	1	vig.
Mad. Luizet	B.	Liabaud	1867	bright rose	2	mod.
Mad. Gabriel Luizet	H.P.	Liabaud	1877	delicate pink	1	vig.
Mad. B. Mackart	H.P.	E. Verdier	1884	rose	1	vig.
Mad. Maeker	H.P.	Damaizin	1863	deep blush	2	mod.
Mad. Mancel	H.P.	Lacharme	1852			
Mad. Chabaud de St. Mandrier	N.	Nabonnand	1882	salmon	2	mod.
Mad. Maninier	H.P.	Liabaud	1875			
Mad. Pierre Margery	H.P.	Liabaud	1882	red-rose	2	mod.
Mad. Margottin	T.	Guillot fils	1866	citron-yellow	1	vig.
Mad. Jules Margottin	T.	Levet	1871	rose-yellow	1	vig.
Mad. Galli-Marie	H.	E. Verdier	1876	rich rose	1	vig.
Mad. Theodore Martel	H.P.	Ducher	1854	flesh	3	mod.
Mad. Masset	B.	Lacharme	1853	rose	2	mod.
Mad. Masset	N.	Lacharme	1857	rose tinted wht.	3	vig.
Mad. Massicault	H.P.	Schwartz	1885	rose	2	mod.
Mad. Clement Massier	N.	Nabonnand	1885	rose	2	vig.
Mad. Masson	H.P.	Masson	1854	reddish crimsn	1	vig.
Mad. Claire Mathieu	H.P.	Vigneron	1874	soft rose	1	vig.
Mad. Maurin	T.	Guillot père	1853	white-salmon	3	mod.
Mad. Gabrielle Meritte	H.P.	Vigneron	1882	rose-lilac	2	mod.
Mad. Charles Meurice	H.P.	Lévèque fils	1878	velvety purple	1	vig.
Mad. B. du M. de Montchauveau	H.P.	Jamain	1876	rose-pink	1	vig.

Name.	Class.	Raiser.	Year.	Colour.	Size.	Habit.
Mad. Montet	H.P.	Liabaud	1880	soft rose	1	vig.
Mad. Guillot de Montfavet	H.P.	Gonod	1871	pale rose	2	mod.
Mad. de Monseignat	B.	Pradel	1861	purplish cerise	1	mod.
Mad. Grandin Monville ...	H.P.	E. Verdier	1875	bright cerise	2	vig.
Mad. Moreau	H.P.	Gonod	1864	deep crimson	1	rob.
Mad. Moreau	P.M.	Mor. et Rob.	1872	vermilion-red	1	vig.
Mad. Anna Moreau	H.P.	Mor. et Rob.	1884	rose	1	vig.
Mad. Leopold Moreau	H.P.	Vigneron	1883	rose	1	vig.
Mad. Viviand-Morel	H.P.	Schwartz	1883	carmine	3	mod.
Mad. Nachury	H.P.	Damaizin	1873	delicate rose	1	vig.
Mad. Norman Neruda	H.P.	Paul & Son	1885	carmine	2	vig.
Mad. de Nerval	B.	Gonod	1867			
Mad. Céline Noirey	T.	Guillot fils	1868	tender rose	1	vig
Mad. Noman	H.P.	Guillot père	1867	white	2	mod.
Mad. Pierre Oger	B.	Oger	1878	blush	2	vig.
Mad. Hersilie Ortgies	B.	Mor. et Rob.	1868	salmon-white	2	vig.
Mad. Edouard Ory	P.M.	Robert	1854	rose-crimson	2	mod.
Mad. Louis Paillet	H.P.	E. Verdier	...	rose	1	vig.
Mad. Thérèse de Parrieu	H.P.	Gautreau	...	rose	1	vig.
Mad. George Paul	H.P.	E. Verdier	1866	flesh-rose	1	vig.
Mad. Marmy Paul	T.	Marmy	1885	yellow	2	mod.
Mad. W. Paul	H.P.	V. Verdier	1863	purple-crimson	2	mod.
Mad. W. Paul	P.M.	Mor. et Rob.	1869	bright rose	1	vig.
Mad. Pauvert	B.	Rambaux	1876	pale pink	1	mod.
Mad. Pauwells	T.	Soup. et Not.	1885	yellow	3	mod.
Mad. Isaac Pereire	H.B.	Margottin	1880	vivid carmine	1	vig
Mad. P. Pernet	T.	Nabonnand	1879	canary-yellow	2	vig.
Mad. Auguste Perrin	H.N.	Schwartz	1878	pearly rose	2	mod.
Mad. Ernest Piard	H.T.	Bonnaire	1887	bright red	1	vig.
Mad. François Pettit	H.N.	Lacharme	1877	white	3	vig.
Mad. Gustave Pierret	H.P.	Vigneron	1885	rose-lilac	2	mod.
Mad. Pitaval	H.B.	Liabaud	1885	red	1	mod.
Mad. Place	H.P.	Margottin	1854	rose-pink	2	mod.
Mad. Platz	P.M.	Moreau	1864	rose-lilac	2	mod.
Mad. Plantier	H.B.	Plantier	1835	white	1	vig.
Mad. Vve. A. Pommery	H.P.	Lévêque	1885	rose	2	mod.
Mad. Fey Pranard	H.P.	Cherpin	1869	pale rose	1	mod
Mad. Prud'homme	H.P.	Mor. et Rob.	1872	cerise-red	1	vig
Mad. de St. Pulgent	H.P.	Gautreau	1871	vermilion	1	mod.
Mad. Pulliat	H.P.	Ducher	1866	deep rose	2	vig.
Mad. Puissant	H.P.	Mor. et Rob.	1868	rose-red	1	rob.
Mad. Rambaux	H.P.	Rambaux	1883	carmine	1	vig.
Mad. Récamier	H.P.	Lacharme	1853	flesh-white	2	mod.
Mad. Remond	T.	Lambert	1883	yellow	2	mod.
Mad. Renard	H.P.	Mor. et Rob.	1864	deep rose	2	mod.
Mad. Retornap	T.	Guillot père	1865	coppery yellow	2	mod.
Mad. Richer	H.P.	Faudon	1869			
Mad. de Ridder	H.P.	Margottin	1871	amaranth	2	mod.
Mad. Adélaïde Ristori	B.	Pradel	1861	cerise & fawn	2	mod.
Mad. Rival	H.P.	Gonod	1866	tender rose	2	vig.
Mad. Rivière	H.C.	E. Verdier	1874	light rose	1	vig.
Mad. Maurice Rivoir	H.P.	Gonod	1876			

Name.	Class.	Raiser.	Year.	Colour.	Size.	Habit.
Mad. Maurice Rivoire	H.P.	Gonod	1878	rose-flesh	1	mod.
Mad. Rochet	H.P.	Liabaud	1883	rose	2	mod.
Mad. Mxme. de la Rocheterie	H.P.	Granger	1881	rose	1	mod.
Mad. Marie Roederer	H.P.	Lévêque	1882	rose-cerise	2	mod.
Mad. Roger	H.P.	Mor. et Rob.	1877	pale rose	2	vig.
Mad. Rolland	H.P.	Mor. et Rob.	1867	rosy flesh	1	vig.
Mad. Rollet	H.P.	Gonod	1875	rosy salmon	1	mod.
Mad. de Forçade la Roquette	H.P.	Gautreau	1869	red	2	mod.
Mad. la Bnne. de Rothschild	H.P.	Pernet	1867	pale rose	1	vig.
Mad. A. de Rougemont .	H.N.	Lacharme	1862	white-pink	2	vig.
Mad. Rougier	H.P.	Jamain	1874	clear red	2	vig.
Mad. Rousset	H.P.	Guillot fils	1864	tender rose	1	vig.
Mad. Charles Salleron	P.M.	Fontaine	1867	red-crimson	1	mod.
Mad. Schmitt	H.P.	Schmitt	1855	rose-lilac	2	mod.
Mad. Schultz	N.	Beluze	1856	pale yellow	3	vig.
Mad. George Schwartz	H.P.	Schwartz	1871	glossy rose	1	vig.
Mad. Joseph Schwartz	T.	Schwartz	1880	flesh-rose	2	vig.
Mad. Scipion...	H.P.	Cochet	1871	cerise-rose	1	vig.
Mad. de Loeben Sels	H P.	Soup. et Not.	1879	salmon-pink	1	mod.
Mad. Charles Séguret	B.	Pradel	1861	crimson	2	mod.
Mad. Théobald Sernin......	H.P.	Brassac	1877	carmine-red	2	mod.
Mad. Sertot	T.	Pernet	1848	white	2	mod.
Mad. de Sévigné	B.	Mor. et Rob.	1874	soft rose	1	vig
Mad. Louis Seydoux	H.P.	Fontaine	1867	clear rose	1	mod.
Mad. Nathalie Simon	H.P.	Vigneron	1883	red	2	mod.
Mad. Max Singer	T.	Soup. et Not	1887	yellow	2	vig.
Mad. J. Sisley	Ben.	Dubreuil	1885	white	3	mod.
Mad. Raphael de Smet ...	T.	Nabonnand	1885	rose	3	mod.
Mad. Soubeyron	H.P.	Gonod	1872	bright rose	3	mod.
Mad. Soupert	P.M.	Soup et Not.	1871	cerise-red	2	vig.
Mad. de Staël	P.M.	...	1858	rosy flesh	2	mod.
Mad. Standish	H.P.	Trouillard	1860	satiny rose	1	vig.
Mad. E. Stchegoleff...	T.	Nabonnand	1882	rose	2	mod.
Mad. de Stella	B.	Guillot père	1863	bright rose	2	vig.
Mad. Hermann Stenger ...	H.P.	Gonod	1864	bright rose	1	mod.
Mad. Stingue	H.P.	Liabaud	1885	red	2	mod.
Mad. Stoltz	D.	...	...	pale lemon	2	vig.
Mad. de Tartas	T.	Bernède	..	rose	3	mod.
Mad. Elise Tasson	H.P.	Lévêque	1879	cerise	1	vig
Mad. John Taylor	T.	Nabonnand	......	sulphur	2	mod.
Mad. Olympe Terestchenko	H.P.	Lévêque	1883	tinted white	1	vig.
Mad. Thevenot	H.P.	Jamain	1869	red	2	mod.
Mad. Thiers	B.	Pradel	...	rose	2	mod.
Mad. Trifle	T.	Levet	1869	salmon-yellow	1	vig.
Mad. Charles Truffaut ...	H.P.	E. Verdier	1878	satiny rose	1	vig.
Mad. Ambroise Truillet ..	H.P.	Moreau	1869	rose-salmon	2	mod.
Mad. John Twombly	H.P.	Schwartz	1882	bright red	1	vig.
Mad. Trotter	H.C.	Granger	1855	red	3	vig.
Mad. Trudeau	H.P.	Boll	1850	rose-lilac	2	mod.
Mad. Vachez	B.	Ducher	1864	rosy white	3	mod.
Mad. Valembourg...........	H.P.	Oger	...	purple	2	mod.
Mad. Valton	D.	Nabonnand	...	pink	2	vig.

Name.	Class.	Raiser.	Year.	Colour.	Size.	Habit.
Mad. Henriette Vapereau..	H.P.	Pradel	...	cerise	1	mod.
Mad. de Vatry	T.	Guerin	1855	pink	1	vig.
Mad. Dos Santos Vianna ..	H.P.	Soup. et Not.	1883	rose-carmine	1	mod.
Mad. Guyot de Villeneuve	H.P.	Gautreau	...	tender rose	1	vig.
Mad. Charles Verdier	H.P.	Lacharme	1864	bright rose	1	vig.
Mad. Eugène Verdier	H.P.	V. Verdier	1859	flesh colour	2	mod.
Mad. Eugène Verdier	H.P.	E. Verdier	1878	silvery rose	1	rob.
Mad. Eugène Verdier	T.	Levet	1883	chamois	1	vig.
Mad. Victor Verdier	H.P.	E. Verdier	1863	bright red	1	vig.
Mad. Verlot	H.P.	E. Verdier	1876	bright cerise	1	vig.
Mad. Rival Verne	H.P.	Liabaud	1873	salmon-rose	2	vig.
Mad. Ambroise Verschaffelt	H.P.	E. Verdier	1864	pale rose	2	mod.
Mad. George Vibert	H.P.	Mor. et Rob.	1879	carmine-rose	1	vig.
Mad. Vidot	H.P.	Couturier	1854	flesh-white	2	mod.
Mad. Vigneron	H.P.	Vigneron	1858	peach	1	vig.
Mad. Louis Vigneron	H.P.	Vigneron	1883	rose	2	mod.
Mad. Melanie Vigneron ...	H.P.	Vigneron	1883	rose-lilac	2	mod.
Mad. de Villars	P.M.	Beluze	1885			
Mad. Elise Vilmorin	H.P.	Levêque	1864	rose-carmine	2	vig.
Mad. Henri Vilmorin	T.	Nabonnand	1882	yellow	2	mod.
Mad. Watteville	T.	Guillot	1884	tinted white	2	mod.
Mad. Julie Weidman	H.P.	Soup. et Not.	1881	salmon-rose	2	vig.
Mad. Welche....	T.	Mad. Ducher	1878	pale yellow	2	mod.
Mad. de Wettstein	H.P.	Levet	1885	cerise	1	mod.
Mad. William	T.	Larty	1857	fawn and white	2	mod.
Mad. Mélanie Willermoz ..	T.	Lacharme	1845	white-salmon	1	vig.
Mad. Wilson.............	H.P.	Vigneron	1884	rose	2	mod.
Mad. Rosalie de Wincop ..	H.P.	Vigneron	1882	rose-lilac	2	vig.
Mad. Charles Wood	H.P.	E. Verdier	1861	rich crimson	1	vig.
Mad. William Wood	H.P.	E. Verdier	1876	rose-red	1	vig.
Mad. Yorke	H.P.	Mor. et Rob.	1882	vermilion	2	vig.
Mad. Zoutman	D.	...	...	pale flesh	2	mod.
Mdlle. Ilona d'Adorjan ..	H.P.	E. Verdier	1874	salmon-rose	2	mod.
Mdlle. Amélie Alphen	H.P.	Margottin	1864	rose-carmine	1	mod.
Mdlle. Juliette Alphen ..	H.P.	Margottin	1869	clear rose	1	vig.
Mdlle. Amand	T.	Lartey	1861	cerise-red	2	mod.
Mdlle. Marie Andre	H.P.	Soup. et Not.	1882	rose-carmine	2	mod.
Mdlle. Thérèse Appert...	H.P.	Trouillard	1866	light rose	1	vig.
Mdlle. Marie Arnaud	T.	Levet	1872	canary-yellow	1	mod.
Mdlle. Louise Aunier ...	H.P.	Liabaud	1884	rose	2	vig.
Mdlle. Berthe Baztheral ..	H.P.	Foutaine	1869	rose-cerise	2	mod.
Mdlle. H. de Beauvau	T.	Lacharme	1886	yellow	1	vig.
Mdlle. Bergier	D.	Pernet	1885	rose	3	mod.
Mdlle. Cécile Berthod	T.	Guillot fils	1871	sulphur-yellow	1	vig.
Mdlle. Marie Berton	T.	Levet	1873	straw-white	2	mod.
Mdlle. Camille Bigotteau..	H.P.	Vigneron	1883	red-cerise	2	mod.
Mdlle. Blanche...	T.	Guillot fils	1877	rosy pink	2	mod.
Mdlle. Bonnaire	H.P.	Pernet	1859	rose-white	2	mod.
Mdlle. Suzanne Bouyer ..	H.P.	Gonod	1879	red-carmine	1	vig.
Mdlle. Alexandrine Bruel..	T.	Levet	1885	white	3	mod.
Mdlle. Germaine Caillot .	H.T.	Pernet	1886	flesh	1	vig.
Mdlle. Charlotte Card	H.P.	Vigneron	1876	red-cerise	1	mod.

Name.	Class.	Raiser.	Year.	Colour.	Size.	Habit.
Mdlle. Marie Castel	H P.	E. Verdier	1877	cherry-red	2	mod.
Mdlle. Elise Chabrier	H. P.	Gautreau		tender rose	2	mod.
Mdlle. Berthe Chaun	H. P.	Fontaine	1886	rose-carmine	1	vig.
Mdlle. Margte. Chatelaine.	B.	Vigneron	1879	pale rose	1	vig.
Mdlle. Marie Chauvet	H. P.	Besson	1882	rose	1	vig.
Mdlle. Louise Chrétien ..	H. P.	Liabaud	1884	rose-salmon	2	mod.
Mdlle Marie Closon	H. P.	E. Verdier	1883	tender rose	2	mod.
Mdlle. Marie Cointet	H P.	Guillot fils	1872	bright rose	1	mod.
Mddle. Annie Cote	H. N.	Guillot fils	1875	lilac-white	1	vig.
Mdlle. Thérèse Conmer ..	H. P.	Liabaud	1866	bright rose	1	vig.
Mdlle. Hélène Croissandeau	H.P.	Vigneron	1883	rose	1	vig.
Mdlle. AnneMarie Danloux	H.P.	Vigneron	1877	rosy white	2	vig.
Mdlle. Marie Deschamps ..	H.P.	Pradel		pink	2	mod.
Mdlle. Louise Dessayre ...	B.	Pradel	1861	tinted white	2	mod.
Mdlle. Marie Digat	H. P.	Levet	1883	crimson	2	vig.
Mdlle. Margte. Dombrain..	H.P.	E. Verdier	1865	satiny rose	1	vig.
Mdlle. Henriette Dubus ...	H.P.	Fontaine	1858	purplish crimsn	1	mod.
Mdlle. Dumaine	H.P.	Pernet	1873	tender rose	2	mod.
Mdlle. Blanche Durr- schmidt	T.	Guillot fils	1877	pink	2	mod.
Mdlle. Julie Dymonier ...	H.P.	Gonod	1879	pale rose	2	mod.
Mdlle. Emain	B.	Pernet	1861	rosy white	1	vig.
Mdlle. Loide de Falloux...	H P.	Trouillard	1864	pale rose	2	mod.
Mdlle. Favart	B.	E. Verdier	1869	rose strip'd wte	2	mod.
Mdlle. Emilie Fontaine ...	H. P.	Fontaine	1882	purple-crimson	1	vig.
Mdlle. F. de la Forest......	H.	Margottnfils	1872	rose-pink	1	vig.
Mdlle. Marie Gapnière......	T.	Nabonnand	1878	salmon-yellow	2	mod.
Mdlle. Julie Gautain	H. P.	Liabaud	1884	rose	1	mod.
Mdlle. Thérèse Genevay ...	T.	Levet	1874	peach-pink	1	vig.
Mdlle. Léonie Giessen	H.P.	Lacharme	1875	rosy white	1	vig.
Mdlle. Julie Grévy	H.P.	Gautrean	1879	deep red	2	vig.
Mdlle. Godard	H.P.	...	1858	lilac-rose	1	vig.
Mdlle. Marie Gonod........	H.P.	Gonod	1871	white	2	mod.
Mdlle. Josephine Gyot ...	B.	Touvais	1863	bright red	2	vig.
Mdlle. Victoire Hélyve ...	H.P.	E. Verdier	1878	tender rose	1	vig.
Mdlle. Nathalie Imbert ...	T.	Nabonnand	1885	salmon	2	mod.
Mdlle. Francisca Kruger...	T.	Nabonnand	1879	yellow-rose	2	mod.
Mdlle. de Labathe	H.P.	Bernède	1856	bright rose	2	mod.
Mdlle. Mathilde Lenaerts .	T.	Levet	1879	rosy white	2	vig.
Mdlle. Alice Leroy	H.P.	Trouillard	1855	delicate rose	2	mod.
Mdlle. Léa Lévêque.........	H.P.	E. Verdier	1884	rose	2	mod.
Mdlle. Berthe Levet..	H.P	Cochet	1865	rose	2	mod
Mdlle. Thérèse Levet	H.P.	Levet	1866	brilliant rose	1	vig.
Mdlle. Gabrielle Loanville	H.P.	Pradel	1861	coppery rose	2	mod.
Mdlle. Lobry	H.P.	Guillot père	1863	rosy white	2	mod.
Mdlle. Malvina	H. P.	Lartay	...	red	1	vig.
Mdlle. Marguerite Manoin	H.P.	Fontaine	1879	cerise-purple	1	vig.
Mdlle. Louise Margerand...	H P.	Liabaud	1876	tender rose	1	vig.
Mdlle. Jeanne Marix	H.P.	Liabaud	1863	deep rose	1	vig.
Mdlle. Lydia Marty.........	H.P.	Liabaud	1878	rose-lilac	2	mod.
Mdlle. Henriette Matthieu	H.P.	Vigneron	1885	satin rose	2	mod.
Mdlle. Claire Merle	T.	Nabonnand	1885	rose	3	mod.

Name.	Class.	Raiser.	Year.	Colour.	Size.	Habit.
Mdlle. Hélène Michel	H.P.	Vigneron	1854	rose	2	vig.
Mdlle. Marguerite Michou	H.P.	Vigneron	1883	red	2	mod.
Mdlle. Marie Moreau	Ben.	Nabonnand	1879	bright rose	2	mod.
Mdlle. Annette Murat......	T.	Levet	1885	yellow	3	mod.
Mdlle. Jeanne Naudin	T.	Nabonnand	1878	bright rose	2	mod.
Mdlle. Claudine d'Offroy...	H.P.	Touvais	1861	clear red	1	vig.
Mdlle. Julie Pereard	H.P.	Pernet	1872	rose	1	mod.
Mdlle. Leonie Persain	H.P.	Fontaine	1864	silvery rose	2	mod.
Mdlle. Gabrielle de Peyronny......	H.P.	Lacharme	1863	bright rose	2	mod.
Mdlle. Lazarine Poizeau ...	T.	Levet	1876	orange-yellow	2	vig.
Mdlle. Portier	H.P.	Guillot père	1864	pale rose	2	mod.
Mdlle. Rachel	T.	Damaizin	1860	yellow	2	mod.
Mdlle. Rachel	T.	Beluze	1841	white	3	mod.
Mdlle. Marie Rady	H.P.	Fontaine	1865	bright red	1	vig.
Mdlle. Caroline Riquet ...	B.	Lacharme	...	white	2	mod.
Mdlle. Suzanne Rodocanachi	H.P.	E. Verdier	1880	rose-carmine	1	vig.
Mdlle. Marie Rodocanachi	H.P.	Lévéque	1884	rose	2	mod.
Mdlle. Marie Roe	H.P.	Liabaud	1875	rose-purple	1	vig.
Mdlle. Berthe Sacaviu	H.P.	E. Verdier	...	satin rose	2	vig.
Mdlle. Eugénie Savary ...	H.P.	Gonod	1872	flesh-white	2	mod.
Mdlle. Catherine Soupert ..	H.P.	Lacharme	1879	delicate rose	1	vig.
Mdlle. Clothilde Soupert	T.	Levet	1884	rose-carmine	1	vig.
Mdlle. Félicité Truillot	B.	E. Verdier	1861	rose	2	vig
Mdlle. Emilie Verdier ...	H.P.	F. Verdier	...	carmine	2	vig.
Mdlle. Eugénie Verdier ...	H.P.	Guillot fils	1869	flesh-rose	1	vig.
Mdlle. Eugénie Verdier ...	P.M.	Schwartz	1872	crimson-red	1	vig.
Mdlle. Marie Verdier	H.P.	E. Verdier	1875	bright rose	1	vig.
Mdlle. Marie Verlot	H.P.	E. Verdier	1884	rose	2	mod.
Mdlle. Marie Villeboisnet .	H.P.	Trouillard	1866	tender rose	1	vig.
Mdlle. Sophie Villeboisnet	H.P.	Touvais	1867	rose	2	mod.
Mdlle. Brigitte Violet...	H.T.	Levet	1878	rose-salmon	1	vig.
Mdlle. Eugénie Wilhelm ..	H.P.	Soup. et Not.	1873	amaranth	2	mod.
Madeline Nonin	H.P.	Ducher	1866	salmon-rose	2	mod.
Madeline de Vauzelles	B.	Vigneron	1882	tender rose	1	mod.
Mafilatre	H.P.	Oger	...	red	2	vig.
Magna Charta	H.P.	W. Paul	1876	carmine-pink	1	vig.
Magna Rosea	H.C.	...	...	blush	3	vig.
Malmaison Rouge.........	B.	Gonod	1880	red	1	vig.
Marcel Grammont	H.P.	Vigneron	1868	deep red	1	vig.
Marcelin Rhoda	T.	Ducher	1872	white-yellow	1	vig.
Marcella . .4......	H.P.	Liabaud	1865	salmon-rose	2	mod.
Marchioness of Exeter	H.P.	Laxton	1877	cherry-rose	1	vig.
Maréchal Bazaine............	H.P.	Defaure	1864	rose-carmine	2	vig.
Maréchal Bugeaud	T.	...	...	bright rose	1	vig.
Maréchal Canrobert	H.P.	Pernet	1863			
Maréchal Forey.............	H.P.	Margottin	1864	red-crimson	1	vig.
Maréchal Niel	N.	Pradel	1864	deep yellow	1	vig.
Maréchal Niel	H.P.	Pradel, jun.	1861	clear rose	1	mod.
Maréchal du Palais	B.	Beluze	1845			
Maréchal Robert	T.	Mad. Ducher	1875	pale lemon	1	vig.

Name.	Class.	Raiser.	Year.	Colour.	Size.	Habit.
Maréchal Souchet	H.P.	Damaizin	1863	rose-carmine	1	vig.
Maréchal Souchet	H.P.	Guillot fils	1863	crimson	1	vig.
Maréchal Vaillant	H.P.	Jamain	1861	purple-crimson	1	vig.
Margarita	N.	Guillot fils	1868	yellow	2	vig.
Marguerite	T.	Guillot fils	1868	bright yellow	2	mod.
Marguerite de St. Amand	H.P.	Sansal	1864	light pink	1	vig.
Marguerite d'Anjou	H.P.	Boyau	1847	satin-rose	2	mod.
Marguerite d'Anjou	H.P.	Trouillard	1862	red edgd. white	1	mod.
Marguerite Bonnet	B.	Liabaud	1864	flesh-white	1	vig.
Marguerite Brassac	H.P.	Brassac	1875	velvety carmine	1	vig.
Marguerite Jamain	H.P.	H. Jamain	1873	flesh-rose	1	vig.
Marguerite Lecureux	H.P.	Cherpin	1853	carmine	3	mod.
Marguerite Marchais	T.	Nabonnand	1878	coppery yellow	1	vig.
Marguerite de Roman	H.P.	Schwartz	1883	flesh	1	vig.
Marie Accary	N.	Guillot fils	1872	rose-yellow	2	vig.
Marie Aviat	H.P.	...	1856	lilac-rose	2	mod.
Marie Baumann	H.P.	Baumann	1863	carmine-crimsn	1	vig.
Marie de Blois	M.	Mor. et Rob.	1852	rose	3	mod.
Marie Boisse	H.P.	Oger	1864	pale rose	2	mod.
Marie de Bourgoyne	P.M.	Mor. et Rob.	1854	deep rose	3	dwf.
Marie Bremond	T.	Guillot fils	1866	purple-red	2	vig.
Marie Charge	N.	...	...	shaded yellow	3	rob.
Marie Cordier	H.P.	Fontaine	...	red-carmine	1	vig.
Marie Debeaux	T.	Guillot	1846			
Marie Débourges	H.P.	Cherpin	1853			
Marie Ducher	T.	Ducher	1868	clear rose	1	mod.
Marie Duncan	H.P.	Lacharme	1872	tender rose	1	mod.
Marie Guillot	T.	Guillot fils	1873	white-yellow	2	vig.
Marie Van Houtte	T.	Ducher	1871	white-yellow	1	vig.
Marie Jaillat	T.	Mad. Ducher	1877	rose	2	mod.
Marie Liabaud	H.P.	Liabaud	1854			
Marie Lafone	H.P.	Pradel	1861	cerise & purple	1	mod.
Marie Larpin	B.	Guillot fils	1867	delicate rose	2	mod.
Marie Leonida	Mac.	...	...	white	1	vig.
Marie Louise Margerand	H.P.	Liabaud	1876			
Marie de Medicis	T.	...	...	fawn	1	mod.
Marie Opoix	T.	Schwartz	1874	white-yellow	2	mod.
Marie Louise Pernet	H.P.	Pernet	1876	bright rose	1	vig.
Marie Perrachon	H.P.	Ducher	1864	violet-purple	2	mod.
Marie Portemer	H.P.	Portemer	1858	purplish red	1	vig.
Marie Rambaux	T.	Rambaux	1879	canary-yellow	2	vig.
Marie de Caroline de Sartoux	T.	Nabonnand	1882	white	2	vig.
Marie Sisley	T.	Guillot fils	1868	yellow-white	1	vig.
Marie Theresa	H.P.	Ducher	1872	pale rose	2	vig.
Marie Thierry	H.P.	...	1858	lilac-rose	1	mod.
Marie Louise de Vitry	H.P.	Masson	1856	rosy carmine	2	mod.
Marietta de Besobrasoff	T.	Nabonnand	1876	rose-carmine	2	mod.
Mariette Biottey	H.P.	Gonod	1875	satiny rose	2	mod.
Marjolin	C.	...	...	crimson	3	mod.
Marquis Balbiano	B.	Lacharme	1855	silvery rose	2	vig.
Marquise de Castellane	H.P.	Pernet	1869	bright rose	1	rob.

Name.	Class.	Raiser.	Year.	Colour	Size.	Habit.
Marquise de Chambou	H.P.	Gautreau	..	salmon-rose	2	mod.
Marquise de Gibot	H.P.	De Sansal	1868	clear rose	1	vig.
Marquise d'Hervey	H.P.	Vigneron	1877	velvety red	1	vig.
Marquise de Lingeris	H.P.	Guenoux	1869	carmine-rose	1	vig.
Marquise de McMahon ...	H.P.	Pernet	1865	bright rose	2	mod.
Marquise de Mortemart ...	H.P.	Liabaud	1868	flesh-white	1	wk.
Marquise de Murat	H.P.	Ducher	1855	carmine	2	vig.
Marquise Adèle de Murinais	H.P.	Schwartz	1876	silvery pink	1	mod.
Marquis of Salisbury	H.P.	Paul & Son	1879	rosy crimson	1	vig.
Marquis de Sanima	T.	Lucher	1875	coppery rose	1	vig.
Marquise de Verdun	H.P.	Oger				
Marshall P. Wilder	H.P.	Ellwanger & Barry	1885	carmine	1	mod.
Mary Bennett	H.P.	Bennett	1884	cerise	1	mod.
Mary Pochin...	H.P.	Pochin	1881	deep crimson	1	vig.
Masterpiece	H.P.	W. Paul	1880	rosy crimson	1	vig.
Mathilde	T.	Granger	1877	white	2	mod.
Mathurin Regnier	H.P.		1855	pink	1	vig.
Maupertuis	P.M.	Mor. et Rob.	1868	velvety red	1	vig.
Maurice Bernardin	H.P.	Granger	1861	vermilion	1	vig.
Maurice Lepelletier	H.P.	Mor. et Rob.	1868	vermilion-red	2	vig.
Maurice Perault	H.P.	Vigneron	1869	cherry-red	1	vig.
Maxime de la Rocheterie .	H.P.	Vigneron	1871	purple-red	1	vig.
Maximilian II....	H.P.	V. Verdier	1858	purplish crmsn.	2	mod.
May Quennell	H.P.	Postans	1878	magenta-carmn	1	mod.
May Turner	H.P.	E. Verdier	1874	rose-pink	1	rob.
Méhul	B.	Guillot	1846			
Melanie Oger...	T.	Oger	1851	white	2	mod.
Melanie Soupert	T.	Nabonnand	1882	white	1	
Mère de St. Louis...	H.P.	Lacharme	1852	blush	2	mod.
Mèrveille d'Anjou	H.P.	Touvais	1867	rosy red	1	vig.
Mèrveille de Lyon	H.P.	Pernet	1883	white	1	vig.
Mesdames Sœurs Chevandier...	H.P.	Pernet	1864	deep red	1	vig.
Meyerbeer	H.P.	E. Verdier	1867	fiery red	1	vig.
Micaela	P.M.	Moreau	1864	cerise	2	mod.
Michael Saunders......	H.T.	Bennett	1878	bright pink	1	vig.
Michael Strogoff	H.P.	Barrault	1883	crimson	1	mod.
Michel Ange	H.P.	Oger	1863	red-purple	2	mod.
Michel Bonnet	B.	Guillot père	1864	lively rose	2	vig.
Mignard...	H.P.	..	1858	crimson-rose	2	mod.
Mignonette	P.	Guillot	1882	rose	3	mod.
Mignonne	T.	Nabonnand	1878	rose-flesh	3	mod.
Minerve...................	H.P.	Gonod	1868	fiery red	2	vig
Miniature	P.	Alegatière	1885	pale rose	3	vig.
Miranda....................	H.P.	Sansal	...	tender rose	3	mod.
Miller Hays	H.P.	E Verdier	1874	crimson	2	mod.
Miss Ethel Brownlow	T.	Dickson & Sn.	1886	salmon-pink	1	vig.
Miss Hassard	H.P.	Turner	1875	delicate pink	1	vig.
Miss Hillier	H.P.	E. Verdier	1873	crimson-red	1	vig.
Miss Ingram	H.C.	Ingram	1868	blush-white	1	vig.
Miss May Paul...............	T.	Levet	1882	tinted white	1	vig.

Name.	Class.	Raiser.	Year.	Colour.	Size.	Habit.
Miss Poole	H.P.	Turner	...	silvery rose	2	vig.
Modèle de Perfection	B.	Guillot fils	1861	bright pink	2	mod.
Moire	T.	Moire	1844	fawn	2	mod.
Mousseline	P.M.	Mor. et Rob.	1882	rose	3	mod.
Mr. Gladstone	H.P.	Paul & Son	1870	rose	2	wk.
Mrs. Baker	H.P.	Laxton	1876	carmine-red	1	vig.
Mrs. J. Berners	H.P.	Ward	1866	magenta-rose	1	vig.
Mrs. George Dickson	H.P.	Bennett	1884	pink	1	vig.
Mrs. Dombrain	H.P.	Trouillard	1862	red and black	1	mod.
Mrs. Elliott	H.P.	Laffay	1840	rose	2	mod.
Mrs. Jowitt	H.P.	Cranston	1880	lake-crimson	1	vig.
Mrs. John Laing	H.P.	Bennett	1886	pink	1	vig.
Mrs. Laing	H.P.	E. Verdier	1872	rosy carmine	1	vig.
Mrs. Laxton	H.P.	Laxton	1878	rosy crimson	1	mod.
Mrs. Opie	T.	Bell & Son	1877	salmon-rose	2	mod.
Mrs. Pierce	P.	Pierce	1850	blush	3	mod.
Mrs. Rivers	H.P.	Guillot	1850	flesh	2	vig.
Mrs. Standish	H.P.	Trouillard	1860	pure crimson	2	mod.
Mrs. Caroline Swailes	H.P.	Swailes	1885	flesh	1	mod.
Mrs. Harry Turner	H.P.	Turner	1880	crimson-scarlet	1	vig.
Mrs. Veitch	H.P.	E. Verdier	1872	bright rose	1	mod.
Mrs. Ward	H.P.	Ward	1866	rose-pink	1	vig.
Molière	B.	Roberts	...	lilac-rose	2	vig.
Monplaisir	T.	Guillot fils	1868	salmon-yellow	1	vig.
Monseigneur Fournier	H.P.	Lévêque	1875	bright red	1	vig.
Mons. Chaix d'Est Auge.	H.P.	Lévêque	1866	bright red	1	mod.
Mons. Loriol de Barny	H.P.	Trouillard	1866	vinous red	2	vig.
Mons. Berthiere	H.P.	Vigneron	1885	crimson	1	mod.
Mons. Paul Bestion	B.	Nabonnand	1879	red-crimson	1	vig.
Mons. Boncenne	H.P.	Liabaud	1864	red-crimson	2	vig.
Mons. Benoit Comte	H.P.	Schwartz	1884	scarlet	1	vig.
Mons. Jean Cordier	H.P.	Gonod	1871	clear rose	1	vig.
Mons. Eugène Delaire	H.P.	Vigneron	1879	fiery red	1	vig.
Mons. Druet	H.P.	Rambaux	1876	rose-carmine	1	vig.
Mons. Alfred Dumesnil	H.P.	Margottin fils	...	deep rose	1	vig.
Mons. Albert Dureau	H.P.	Vigneron	1869	bright red	2	mod.
Mons. Fillion	H.P.	Gonod	1876	rosy magenta	1	vig.
Mons. Furtado	T.	Laffay	1866	sulphur-yellow	2	mod.
Mons. Gerberon	H.P.	Vigneron	1879	brilliant red	2	vig.
Mons. Gourdault	B.	Guillot	1859			
Mons. Hoste	H.P.	Liabaud	1885	crimson	2	mod.
Mons. Jard	B.	Guillot	1857	red	2	mod.
Mons. Joigneaux	H.P.	Liabaud	1861	purple-red	2	mod.
Mons. Journeaux	H.P.	Marest	1863	red-scarlet	1	vig.
Mons. Lapierre	H.P.	Gonod	1878	crimson-red	2	vig.
Mons. Alfred Leveau	H.P.	Vigneron	1881	carmine	2	mod.
Mons. Etienne Levet	H.P.	Levet	1871	carmine	1	vig.
Mons. Françoise Michelon	H.P.	Levet	1871	carmine	1	vig.
Mons. Jules Monges	H.P.	Guillot	1881	rose	1	mod.
Mons. Montigny	H.P.	...	1857	deep rose	1	vig.
Mons. Moreau	H.P.	Guillot père	1864	red-purple	2	vig.
Mons. Noman	H.P.	Guillot père	1867	tender rose	1	vig.

Name.	Class	Raiser.	Year.	Colour.	Size.	Habit.
Mons. Alexandre Palletiere	B.	Duval	1879	bright rose	2	vig.
Mons. Auguste Perrin	H.P.	Schwartz	1887	cherry-red	1	vig.
Mons. Plaisançon	H.P.	Ducher	1866	bright carmine	1	vig.
Mons. de Pontbriant	H.P.	Damaizin	1864	carmine-red	1	vig.
Mons. Ravel	H.P.	Guillot	1856	crimson-scarlet	2	mod.
Mons. Francisque Rive	H.P.	Schwartz	1884	cerise	1	mod.
Mons. Serenye	H.P.	Guillot	1856			
Mons. E. Y. Teas	H.P.	E. Verdier	1874	cerise	1	vig.
Mons. Thiers	H.P.	Trouillard	1866	brilliant red	1	vig.
Mons. Thouvenel	H.P.	Vigneron	1880	velvety red	1	vig.
Mons. Gabriel Tournier	H.P.	Levet	1876	deep rose	1	vig.
Mons. Eugène Vavin	H.P.	Duval	...	cerise	2	vig.
Mons. Woolfield	H.P.	Guillot père	1866	bright rose	1	vig.
Mont d'Or	H.P.	Ducher	1863			
Monte Christo	H.P.	Fontaine	1861	crimson	2	mod.
Monte Rosa	T.	Ducher	1872	rosy salmon	2	vig.
Montozon	H.P.	Pelissier	1850			
Morphée	H.P.	Schwartz	1887	crimson	2	vig.
Murillo	H.P.	Fontaine	1862	velvety purple	2	mod.
Nancy Lee	H.T.	Bennett	1879	satin-rose	3	mod.
Napoléon III.	H.P.	E. Verdier	1866	red-scarlet	1	vig.
Narcisse	N.	..	1845	pale yellow	2	vig.
Narcisse de Salvandy	Prov.	Van Houtte	1845	crimson & whte	2	mod.
Nardy Frères	H.P.	Ducher	1865	purple-rose	1	vig.
Nataschy Metschersky	T.	Nabonnand	1878	rosy salmon	2	mod.
Newton	H.P.	Gonod	1869	red	3	wk.
Nicholas d'Assas	H.P.	...	1854	clear rose	1	vig.
Nina	T.	...	..	blush	2	vig.
Niphetos	T.	Bougère	1844	white	1	vig.
Noémi	H.P.	...	1852	light rose	2	mod.
Notaire Bonnefon	H.P.	Liabaud	1868	red-purple	1	vig.
Notre Dame de Fourvierds	H.P.	Ducher	1861	rose	1	mod.
Nuits de Young	P.M.	Laffay	1845	deep crimson	2	mod.
Octavie	N.	Vibert	1845	bright red	2	vig.
Oderic Vital	H.P.	Oger	1858	rose	2	vig.
Œillet Fantasie	B.	Guillot fils	1871	vel. red, st. wht	2	vig.
Œillet Flamand	B.	Oger	1866	rose, stpd crmn	2	mod.
Œillet Parfait	G.	Foulard	1841	white, stpd crm	3	mod.
Old Blush	C.	...	...	blush	2	vig.
Old Crimson	C.	Evans	1810	crimson	2	mod.
Olga Marix	H.P.	Schwartz	1873	flesh-white	2	mod.
Olivier de Clisson	H.P.	Mor. et Rob.	1866	vermilion	1	vig.
Olivier Delhomme	H.P.	V. Verdier	1861	bright red	1	vig.
Olivier Metra	H.P.	E. Verdier	1885	cerise	1	mod.
Olympe Frecinay	T.	Damaizin	1859			
Ophelia	T.	Ducher	1873	clear yellow	2	vig.
Ophirie	N.	Goubault	1841	coppery yellow	2	vig.
Oriflamme de St. Louis	H.P.	...	1858	carmine	1	vig.
Ornement des Jardius	H.P.	Mor. et Rob.	1855	crimson	2	mod.
Oscar Lamarche	H.P.	Schwartz	1875	amaranth	1	vig.

Name.	Class.	Raiser.	Year.	Colour.	Size.	Habit.
Oscar Leclerc	P. M.	Robert	1853	red	2	mod.
Oxonian	H. P.	Turner	1876	deep rose	1	vig.
Pæonia	Pra.	Lacharme	1855	red	1	vig.
Pallida	H. P.	Feast	1843	blush	3	mod.
Panachée Langrois	H. P.	Rmbaucourt	1873	cherry-red	1	vig.
Panachée de Luxembourg	H. P.	Soup. et Not.	1866	prpl, stpd slmn	2	vig.
Panaché d'Orleans	H. P.	Dauvesse	1854	rose striped	2	vig.
Papillon	T.	Nabonnand	1878	salmon-rose	2	vig.
Pâquerette	P.	Guillot	1875	white	3	mod.
Parmentier	H. P.	Guillot fils	1860	pale rose	2	mod.
Paul Dupuy	H. P.	...	1853	amaranth	1	vig.
Paul de Fabry	H. P.	Liabaud	1879	bright red	1	vig.
Paul Feval	H. P.	Guillot	1861	pink	2	mod.
Paul Floret	T.	Nabonnand	1882	rose	2	mod.
Paul des Grands	H. P.	Liaband	1862			
Paul Jamain	H. P.	Jamain	1878	bright red	1	vig.
Paul Joseph	B.	Portemer	1842	violet-red	2	mod.
Paul de la Meilleraye	H. P.	Guillot fils	1863	cerise-rose	1	vig.
Paul Nabonnand	T.	Nabonnand	1876	satiny rose	2	mod.
Paul Neyron	H. P.	Levet	1869	dark rose	1	vig.
Paul Perras	H. B.	...	...	pale rose	2	vig.
Paul Ricaut	H. B.	Portemer	1845	bright crimson	1	vig.
Paul Verdier	H. P.	C. Verdier	1866	bright rose	1	vig.
Paul's Single Crimson	H. P.	Paul & Son	1882	crimson	2	vig.
Paul's Single White	H. P.	Paul & Son	1882	white	2	vig.
Pauline Buonaparte	H. P.	...	1850	white	3	mod.
Pauline Labonte	T.	...	..	flesh	3	mod.
Pauline Lansezeur	H. P.	Lansezeur	1854	crimson shaded	2	mod.
Pauline Plantier	T.	Plantier	1835	white-lemon	2	mod.
Pauline Talabot	H. P.	E. Verdier	1874	carmine-red	2	mod.
Pavillion de Pregny	H. N.	Guillot père	1863	rosy red	2	vig.
Peach Blossom	H. P.	W. Paul	1873	delicate pink	1	vig.
Pearl	H. T.	Bennett	1878	flesh-white	2	mod.
Penelope Mayo	H. P.	Davis	1878	carmine-red	1	vig.
Perfection de Blanches	H. P.	Schwartz	1873	white	2	mod.
Perfection de Lyon	H. P.	Ducher	1868	rose-lilac	1	vig.
Perfection de Montplaisir	T.	Levet	1871	canary-yellow	2	mod.
Perle d'Angers	H. P.	Mor. et Rob.	1879	pale rose	2	vig.
Perle Blanche	H. P.	Touvais	1862	pale rose	2	mod.
Perle des Blanches	H. N.	Lacharme	1872	white	2	mod.
Perle des Jardins	T.	Levet	1874	canary-yellow	1	vig.
Perle de Lyon	T.	Ducher	1872	apricot-yellow	...	mod.
Perle d'Or	P.	Dubreuil	1884	yellow	3	mod.
Perle de Panachées	G.	...		striped rose	2	mod.
Persian Yellow (from Persia)	A. B.	Willock	1837	deep yellow	1	mod.
Peter Lawson	H. P.	Thomas	..	carmine	2	vig.
Petite Amante	B.	Soup. et Not.	1866	rose-red	2	vig.
Philibert Pellet	H. P.	Gonod	1873	rose	2	mod.
Philippe Bardet	H. P.	Moreau	...	red	2	vig.
Philomene	H. P.	Crozy	1857	pink	2	mod.
Pierre Carnot	H. P.	Levet	1878	deep red	2	vig.

Name.	Class.	Raiser.	Year.	Colour.	Size.	Habit.
Pierre Dunand	H.P.	Pernet	1882	rose	2	vig.
Pierre Guillot	H.T.	Guillot	1879	red	2	mod.
Pierre Isambart	H.P.	Gautreau	1871	red-crimson	2	mod.
Pierre Notting	H.P.	Portemer	1863	blackish red	1	vig.
Pierre Seletzky	H.P.	Levet	1872	bright red	1	vig.
Pitord	H.P.	Lacharme	1867	claret-red	1	mod.
Pius IX	H.P.	Vibert	1849	violet-rose	2	vig.
Pline	H.P.	Guillot fils	1865	vermilion-red	1	vig.
Pluto	s.	...	...	lilac-rose	2	vig.
Pomponette	B.	Soup. et Not	1878	salmon-rose	2	vig.
Pompon Blanc Parfait	A.B.	E. Verdier	1875	flesh-white	3	vig.
Portland Blanche	D.	Vibert	1836	tinted white	2	vig.
Pourpre d'Orleans	H.P.	Dauvesse	1861	purple	2	mod.
Préfet Limbourg	H.P.	Margtn. fils	1878	velvety red	1	mod.
Premier Essai	Mic.	Geschwind	1866	flesh-white	3	vig.
President	T.	Paul & Son	1860	rose-salmon	1	vig.
President Joachim Crespo	H.P.	Lévêque	1885	rose	2	mod.
Président Grévy	H.P.	E. Verdier	1872	purple-red	2	vig.
Président Hardy	H.P.	E. Verdier	1873	purple-carmine	2	mod.
Président Léon de St. Jean	H.P.	Lacharme	1875	dark crimson	1	vig.
Président Lenaertes	H.P.	Soup. et Not.	1883	deep red	2	mod.
President Lincoln	H.P.	Granger	1862	cerise-red	1	vig.
Président Mas	H.P.	Guillot fils	1865	velvety red	1	vig.
Président Menoux	H.P.	Guillot	1854			
Président Porcher	H.P.	Vigneron	1866	rose-carmine	1	vig.
Président Schlachter	H.P.	E. Verdier	1877	crimson-red	2	mod.
Président Senelar	H.P.	Schwartz	1882	cherry-red	2	vig.
President Thiers	H.P.	Lacharme	1871	fiery red	1	vig.
President Willermoz	H.P.	Ducher	1867	bright rose	1	vig.
Pride of Reigate	H.P.	Brown	1885	crmne. stpd. wt.	1	vig.
Pride of Waltham	H.P.	W. Paul	1881	rose-pink	1	vig.
Prince Albert	H.B.	Laffay	1852	crimson	2	mod.
Prince Prosper d'Aremberg	T.	Soup. et Not.	1881	salmon-red	2	mod.
Prince Arthur	H.P.	Cant	1875	deep crimson	2	vig.
Pr. Eugène de Beauharnais	H.P.	Mor. et Rob.	1864	red-scarlet	1	vig.
Prince Charles	C.	...	...	cherry-red	2	mod.
Prince Chipetonzikoff	H.P.	...	1853	deep red	1	mod.
Prince Paul Demidoff	H.P.	Guillot fils	1873	carmine-rose	1	vig.
Prince Humbert	H.P.	Margottin	1867	purple-red	1	mod.
Prince Imperial	H.P.	...	1856	rose-carmine	2	mod.
Prince de Joinville	H.P.	W. Paul	1864	rich rose	1	vig.
Prince Léon	H.P.	Marest	1853	cerise	1	mod.
Prince Leopold	H.P.	W. Paul	1869	deep red	1	rob.
Prince de la Moskowa	H.P.	...	1853	deep red	2	mod.
Prince Napoleon	B.	Pernet	1864	bright rose	1	vig.
Prince Noir	H.P.	...	1854	velvety crimson	2	mod.
Prince Henri de Pays-Bas	H.P.	Soup. et Not.	1862	deep crimson	2	mod.
Prince de Portia	H.P.	E. Verdier	1865	vermilion-red	1	vig.
Prince Cam. de Rohan	H.P.	E. Verdier	1861	velvety crimson	1	vig.
Prince Stirbey	H.P.	E. Verdier	1871	rose-flesh	2	mod.
Prince of Wales	H.P.	Laxton	1871	pink	1	mod.
Princess Adelaide	M.	Laffay	1845	pale rose	2	vig.

Name.	Class.	Raiser.	Year.	Colour.	Size.	Habit.
Princess Alice	M.	Paul	1853	shaded pink	2	mod.
Prncsse. Charles d'Aremberg	H. P.	Soup. et Not.	1876	rose-carmine	1	mod.
Prncsse. Julie d'Aremberg	H. P.	Soup. et Not.	1885	canary	2	mod.
Prncsse. Prspr. d'Aremberg	T.	Soup. et Not.	1881	salmon	2	vig.
Princess Beatrice	H. P.	W. Paul	1872	deep pink	1	vig.
Princess Beatrice	T.	Bennett	1887	yellow	1	vig.
Prncsse. Imperiale du Bresil	H. T.	Soup. et Not.	1882	carmine	1	vig.
Princess Mary of Cambridge	H. P.	Paul & Son.	1866	pale rose	1	vig.
Princess Christian	H. P.	W. Paul	1870	rosy peach	1	vig.
Princesse Clémentine	H. P.	E. Verdier	1876	tender rose	1	vig.
Princesse Mary Dolgorouky	H. P.	Gonod	1878	satiny rose	1	vig.
Princesse Hélène	H. P.	Laffay	1837	rose-purple	2	mod.
Princess Lichtenstein	H. P.	W. Paul	1864	white	1	mod.
Princess Louise	H. P.	Laxton	1871	flesh colour	2	mod.
Princess Louise	E.	Jacques	1828	creamy white	2	mod.
Princesse Mathilde	H. P.	Liabaud	1860	crimson	2	mod.
Princesse de Metternich	H. P.	Sansal	1858	rose	1	vig.
Princesse de Nassau	Musk.	...	...	cream	2	vig.
Princesse Olympe	H. P.	Beluze	1885	white	2	mod.
Princesse Amelie d'Orleans	H. P.	Lévêque	1872	satin-rose	2	mod.
Prncsse. Amélie des Pays-Bas	H. P.	Liabaud	1884	purple-red	1	vig.
Princesse W. des Pays-Bas	P.	Soup. et Not.	1886	white	3	mod.
Princesse Radziwell	H. P.	Lévêque	1846	red	2	vig.
Princess Royal	M.	Portemer	1874	flesh rose	2	mod.
Princesse de Sagan	T.	Dubreuil	1887	crimson	2	vig.
Princesse Ant. Strozzio	H. P.	E. Verdier	1877	tender rose	2	mod.
Princesse C. de la Tremouille	H. P.	Lévêque	1872	bright rose	2	mod.
Princess Louise Victoria	H. P.	Knight	1872	flesh-pink	3	rob.
Princess of Wales	T.	Bennett	1884	yellow	2	vig.
Princess of Wales	H. P.	W. Paul	1864	vivid crimson	1	vig.
Principe Bacciochi	M.	Mor. et Rob.	1885	bright rose	2	vig.
Professor Chevereul	H. P.	C. Verdier	1865	vermilion	1	vig.
Professor Duchartre	H. P.	E. Verdier	1861	clear red	2	vig.
Professor Koch	H. P.	E. Verdier	1884	dark crimson	1	vig.
Professor E. Regel	H. P.	E. Verdier	...	carmine	1	mod.
Prospérité	H. P.	Lartay	...	red	2	mod.
Prosper Laugier	H. P.	E. Verdier	1884	scarlet	2	vig.
Prudence Besson	H. P.	Lacharme	1865	carmine-red	1	vig.
Purpurine	H. P.	Liabaud	1865	red-purple	2	mod.
Queen	Ayr.	Rivers	1836	purple	2	rob.
Queen of Bedders	B.	Noble	1876	crimson	1	vig.
Queen of the Belgians	Ayr.	...	...	white	3	vig.
Queen of Bourbons	B.	Manger	1834	rose	2	mod.
Queen of Denmark	H. P.	Granger	1856	flesh	1	vig.
Queen Eleanor	H. P.	W. Paul	1876	rich pink	1	vig.
Queen of Mosses [syn. Jenny Lind]	H. M.	Laffay	1845	crimson	2	mod.
Queen of the Prairies	Pra.	Feast	1843	rosy red	3	vig.
Queen of Queens	H. P.	W. Paul & Sn.	1883	rose	1	vig.
Queen's Scarlet	Ben.	Hallock and Thorpe	1880	crimson	2	mod.

Name.	Class.	Raiser.	Year.	Colour.	Size.	Habit.
Queen Victoria	H. P.	Fontaine	1850	pale pink	1	vig.
Queen of Waltham	H. P.	W. Paul	1875	cherry-rose	1	vig.
Rampant	E.	..	...	white	2	vig.
R. C. Sutton	H. P.	Frettingham	1882	rose	2	mod.
Red Dragon	H. P.	W. Paul	1878	brilliant crmsn.	1	rob.
Red Gauntlet	H P.	Postans	1881	red-crimson	1	vig.
Red Gauntlet	H. P.	W. Paul & Sn.	1882	crimson	1	vig.
Red Rover	H. P.	W. Paul	1863	fiery red	1	rob.
Regulus	T.	Mor. et Rob.	...			
Reine des Amateurs	H. P.	Oger	1879	salmon-rose	1	vig.
Reine des Belges	H. P.	Cochet	..	red	2	mod.
Reine Blanche	P. M.	Robert	1858	white	2	mod.
Reine Blanche	H. P.	Damaizin	1868	blush-white	1	mod.
Reine de Castile	B.	Pernet	1863	rose-white	1	vig.
Reine de la Guillotière	H. P.	Plantier	1835	tender rose	2	mod.
Reine Marie Henriette	H. T.	Levet	1878	cerise-red	1	vig.
Reine des Massifs	N.	Levet	1874	coppery yellow	2	vig.
Reine du Midi	H. P.	Rolland	1867	bright rose	1	rob.
Reine Emma des Pays-Bas.	T.	Nabonnand	1879	salmon-yellow	2	mod.
Reine Marie Pia	T.	Schwartz	1880	deep rose	1	vig.
Reine du Portugal	T.	Guillot fils	1867	golden yellow	1	vig.
Reine Victoria	B.	Labruyère	1872	bright rose	1	vig.
Reine des Vierges	B.	Beluze	1884	rose	2	mod.
Reine des Violettes	H. P.	Mille-Malet	1860	violet	2	vig.
Reine Olga de Wurtemburg,	H. T.	Nabonnand	1882	red	2	vig.
Rembrandt	H. P.	Mor. et Rob.	1884	vermilion	2	vig.
Rène Daniel	H. P.	Damaizin	1868	cerise-red	1	vig.
Resplandissante	H. P.	Truvais	...	red-rose	2	mod.
Rêve d'Or	N.	Ducher	1869	deep yellow	1	vig.
Rev. J. B. M. Camm	H. P.	Turner	1875	rosy pink	1	vig.
Rev. H. Dombrain	H. B.	Margottin	1863	brilliant red	1	vig.
Rev. Trautmann	H. P.	Soup. et Not.	1877	lake-red	2	mod.
Reveil	B.	Guillot père	1854	purple shd. blk.	1	mod.
Reveil des Printemps	H. P.	Oger	1884	flesh	1	mod.
Reynolds Hole	H. P.	Paul & Son	1872	maroon-crimson	2	vig.
Rhodanthe	B.	Guillot	1847			
R. Dudley Baxter	H. P.	W. Paul	1879	maroon-crimson	1	vig.
Richard Laxton	H. P.	Laxton	1878	red-crimson	1	vig.
Richard Smith	H. P.	E. Verdier	1061	purple-red	2	mod.
Richard Wallace	H P.	Lévêque	1871	bright rose	1	mod.
Richesse de Couleur	H. P.	Touvais	1861	purple & violet	1	vig.
Rivers	H. P.	Laffay	1839	rose	1	vig.
Rivers' Musk	Musk	...		pink	3	vig.
Robert Burns	H. P.	Paul	1850	bright crimson	2	vig.
Robert de Brie	H. P.	Granger		salmon-rose	2	mod.
Robert Fortune	H. P.	Ducher	1861	bright rose	2	mod.
Robert Marnock	H. P.	Paul & Son	1878	deep crimson	2	mod.
Robusta	B.	Soup. et Not.	1877	fiery red	2	rob.
Roi de Bavière	H. P.	...	1857	maroon-crimsn.	2	mod.
Roi d'Espagne	H. P.	Fontaine	1864	bright red	2	vig.
Rosa Bonheur	H. P.	Fontaine	1871	rose-carmine	1	vig.

Name.	Class.	Raiser.	Year.	Colour.	Size.	Habit.
Rosa Mundi	H.P.	Ducher	1864	rosy blush	2	mod.
Rosalie	T.	Hallock and Thorpe	1885	pink	3	mod.
Rose à Bois Jape	H.P.	Brassac	1877	bright cerise	1	vig.
Rose Button	Lucida	Veitch & Sons	1885	rose	3	mod.
Rose Perfection	H.P.	Touvais	1866	bright rose	1	vig.
Rose du Roi	D.	Lelieur	1812	crimson	2	mod.
Rosieriste Harms	H.P.	E. Verdier	1879	velvety red	1	vig.
Rosieriste Jacobs	H.P.	Mad. Ducher	1880	blackish red	1	vig.
Rosine Margottin	H.P.	Margottin	1856	pink & white	2	mod.
Rosine Parou	H.P.	Fontaine	...	cerise	2	mod.
Rosy Morn	H.P.	W. Paul	1878	rose-peach	1	vig.
Royal Epoux	H.P.	Damaizin	1859	bright rose	1	mod.
Royal Standard	H.P.	Turner	1874	satiny rose	1	vig.
Rubens	T.	Robert	1859	rose-white	1	vig.
Rubens	H.P.	C. Verdier	1864	velvety red	2	mod.
Ruga	Ayr.	...	...	pale flesh	2	vig.
Rugosa alba	Mic.	...	...	white	2	vig.
Rugosa rubra	Mic.	...	...	deep rose	2	mod.
Rugosa rubra fl. pl.	Mic.	...	...	deep rose	2	mod.
Rushton Radclyffe	H.P.	E. Verdier	1864	red-cerise	1	vig.
Russelliana	Mult.	...	...	rose	2	vig.
Safrano	T.	Beauregard	1839	bright apricot	3	vig.
Safranot à Fleur Rouges	T.	Oger	1869	red-yellow	3	mod.
Salet	P.M.	Lacharme	1854	pale rose	2	vig.
St. George	H.P.	W. Paul	1874	dark crimson	1	vig.
Secretaire Nicolais	H.P.	Schwartz	1884	purple-red	1	vig
Semiramis	H.P.	Touvais	1864	flesh-rose	1	mod.
Sénateur Chevreau	H.P.	Pernet	1869	bright red	1	vig.
Sénateur Favre	H.P.	Rousseau	...	vermilion	1	mod.
Sénateur Reveil	H.P.	Damaizin	1863	bright rose	1	vig.
Sénateur Vaisse	H.P.	Guillot père	1859	brilliant red	1	vig.
Setina	B.	Henderson	1859	rose	2	mod.
Shirley Hibberd	T.	Levet	1873	yellow-buff	3	mod.
Silver Queen	H.P.	W. Paul & Sn.	1887	crimson	1	vig
Simon St. Jean	H.P.	Liaband	1861	purple	3	mod.
Sir Joseph Paxton	B.	Laffay	1852	deep red	2	mod.
Sir John Sebright	Musk.	...	...	crimson	3	vig.
Sir Garnet Wolseley	H.P.	Cranston	1875	vermilion-red	1	vig.
Snowball	S.	...	...	white	2	vig.
Socrates	T.	Mor. et Rob.	1858	fawn	2	mod.
Sœur des Anges	H.P.	Oger	1862	flesh-white	1	vig.
Sœur Athanase	H.P.	Fontaine	...	carmine	1	vig.
Sœur Thècle	H.P.	Fontaine	1866	rose-carmine	1	vig.
Soleil d'Austerlitz	H.P.	Lacharme	1850	crimson	2	vig.
Solfaterre	N.	Boyau	1843	sulphur-yellow	?	vig.
Sombreuil	T.	Robert	1850	rose-white	1	vig.
Soupert et Notting	P.M.	Pernet	1874	rosy red	2	vig.
Souv. d'un Ami	T.	Defougere	1846	salmon-rose	1	vig.
Souv. de la Reine d'Angleterre	H.P.	Cochet	1854	bright rose	1	mod.

Name.	Class.	Raiser.	Year.	Colour.	Size.	Habit.
Souv. de l'Arquebuse	B.	...	1854	crimson	2	mod.
Souv. d'A. Bahivet	H.P.	Cochet	1867	velvety crimson	1	vig.
Souv. de la Reine des Belges	H.P.	Cochet	1850	bright carmine	2	mod.
S. du Pr. Royal de Belgique	H.P.	Gautreau	1869	red	2	mod.
Souv. de Bellanger	H.P.	Eude	1871	red-purple	2	mod.
Souv. de Mad. Berthier ...	H.P.	Berthier	1882	red	1	vig.
Souv. de Mons. Boll	H.P.	Boyau	1866	cerise-red	1	vig.
Souv. de Lord Brougham..	Ben.	Nabonnand	1879	rich red	1	vig.
Souv. de Caillat	H.P.	E. Verdier	1867	violet-purple	2	mod.
Souv. de Petit Caporal ...	H.P.	Guillot père	1854	lilac shd crm.	2	mod.
Souv. de Comte Cavour ...	H.P.	Margottin	1861	velvety crimsn	1	vig.
Souv. de Comte Cavour ...	H.P.	Mor. et Rob.	1861	red	2	mod.
Souv. de Mad. Auguste Charles	B.	Mor. et Rob.	1866	flesh colour	2	mod.
Souv. de Henry Clay	S.	Boll	1854	pale rose	2	mod.
Souv. de Madame Corval...	H.P.	Gonod	1867	salmon-rose	2	vig.
Souv. de l'Amiral Courbet.	T.	Pernet père	1885	bright red	2	vig.
Souv. de l'Expos. de Darmstadt	H.P.	Soup. et Not.	1871	dark crimson	1	vig
Souv. de Romain Desprez	H.P.	Jamain	1872	flesh-rose	2	mod.
Souv. de Mdlle. Marie Detry	T.	Mad. Ducher	1877	salmon-rose	1	mod.
Souv. de Général Douai ...	H.P.	Peruet	1871	satiny-rose	2	mod.
Souv. de Mons. Droche ...	H.P.	Mad. Ducher	1881	rose	2	mod.
Souv. de G. Drevet	T.	Guillot	1885	salmon	1	vig.
Souv. de Ducher	H.P.	E. Verdier	1874	bright red	2	vig.
Souv. de Pierre Dupuy ...	H.	Levet	1876	rich red	2	vig.
Souv. de Lady Eardley ...	H.P.	Guillot père	1861	amaranth	1	vig.
Souv. de Victor Emmanuel	H.P.	Mor. et Rob.	1878	vermilion-red	1	vig.
Souv. de Victor Emmanuel	H.P.	Pernet	1878	pale rose	2	mod.
Souv. de Mons. Faivre ...	H.P.	Levet	1879	rosy red	1	vig.
Souv. d'Aline Fontaine .	H.P.	Fontaine	1879	carmine-rose	2	vig.
Souv. de Mère Fontaine ...	H.P.	Fontaine	1874	rose-carmine	1	vig.
Souv. de Leon Gambetta...	H.P.	Gonod	1884	carmine	2	mod.
Souv. de Louis Gaudin ...	B.	Trouillard	1864	red-purple	1	mod.
Souv. de Leon Gonod	H.P.	Gonod	1871	rich rose	1	vig.
Souv. de Mdll. Marie Gourdin	T.	Nabonnand	1879	rose-yellow	2	mod.
Souv. de Leveson Gower...	H.P.	Guillot père	1852	ruby-red	1	mod.
Souv. de Louis van Houtte	H.P	E. Verdier	1876	bright crimson	1	vig.
Souv. de Dr. Jamain	H.P	Lacharme	1865	velvety crimson	1	mod.
Souv. de l'Ami Labruyere	H.P.	Gonod	1885	pink	2	vig.
Souv. de Mons. Laffay ...	H.P.	E. Verdier	1878	crimson-red	2	vig.
Souv. de Victoire Laudeau	H.P.	Mor. et Rob.	1885	rose	2	mod.
Souv. d'Adèle Launay	P.M.	Mor. et Rob.	1872	bright rose	1	vig.
Souv. Alphonse Lavallée...	H.P.	C. Verdier	1885	red	1	vig.
Souv. de Rène Lévequé ...	H.P.	Lévéque	1884	red-purple	2	vig
Souv. de T. Levet	T.	Levet	1883	red	1	vig.
Souv. d'A. Lincoln	H.P.	E. Verdier	1865	crimson-purple	2	vig.
Souv. de l'Ex de Londres .	B.	Guillot père	1851	amaranth	1	mod
Souv. de la Malmaison ...	B.	Beluze	1843	flesh-colour	1	vig.
Souv. du Capt. Marc	H.P.	Oger	1874	crimson-red	2	mod.
Souv. de Champ de Mars..	H.P.	Fontaine	1867	red-purple	1	vig.
Souv. de Maximilian	T.	Mor. et Rob.	1867	red-white	2	vig

Name.	Class.	Raiser.	Year.	Colour.	Size.	Habit.
Souv. d'une Mère	H. P.	Touvais	1864	tender rose	2	mod.
Souv. de Mad. A. Michaut	H. P.	Vigneron	1873	deep red	1	vig.
Souv. de Charles Montault	H. P.	Mor. et Rob.	1863	fiery red	2	vig.
Souv. de Nemours	B.	Hervé		rose	2	vig.
Souv. de Paul Neyron......	T.	Levet	1871	salmon-yellow	1	vig.
Souv. de l'Ami Pancher ...	H. P.	E. Verdier	1879	rich crimson	2	vig.
Souv. de Mdlle. Jenny Pernet	T.	Pernet	1863	rose-red	1	vig.
Souv. de Mad. Pernet	T.	Pernet	1875	salmon-pink	1	vig.
Souv. de B. St. Pierre......	H. P.	Guillot fils	1864	velvety red	2	mod.
Souv. de Mons. Poiteau ...	H. P.	Margottin	1868	salmon-pink	1	vig.
Souv. de François Ponsard	H. P.	Touvais	1867	bright rose	1	vig.
Souv. de Mons. Ponsard	H. P.	Liabaud	1867	clear rose	1	vig.
Souv. de President Porcher	H. P.	Granger	1881	rose	2	mod.
Souv. de Redoute...	H. P.	Fontaine	1867	red-purple	2	vig.
Souv. d'Auguste Rivière .	H. P.	E. Verdier	1877	brilliant crimsn	1	vig.
Souv. de Mad. Robert.....	H. P.	Mor. et Rob.	1877	salmon-pink	2	mod.
Souv. du Petit Roi de Rome	H. P.	Beluze	1850			
Souv. de Baron de Roths- child	B.	Crozy	1868	red-crimson	2	vig.
Souv. de Mons. Rousseau...	H. P.	Lévèque	1861	red & carmine	1	vig.
Souv. de Georges Sand ...	T.	Mad. Ducher	1876	rosy salmon	1	vig.
Souv. d'Arthur Sansal ...	H. P.	Guenoux	1876	bright rose	1	vig.
Souv. de Baron Semur .	H. P.	Lacharme	1874	purple-red	1	vig.
Souv. du Maréchal Serrurier	H. P.	Fontaine	...	red	1	vig.
Souv. de Spa	H. P.	Gantreau	1873	crimson-red	1	vig.
Souv. de Charles Sumner .	H. P.	E. Verdier	1874	carmine-red	1	mod.
Souv. d'Adolphe Thiers .	H. P.	Mor. et Rob.	1877	deep crimson	1	mod.
Souv de Toulouse	H. P.	Brassac	...	red	1	mod.
Souv. d'Elise Vardon ..	T.	Marest	1854	creamy white	1	vig.
Souv. de J. G. Veitch	H. P.	E. Verdier	1872	bright crimson	1	vig.
Souv. de Pierre Verdier ...	P. M.	Mor. et Rob.	1867	red-carmine	1	vig.
Souv. Mad. Victor Verdier	H. P.	E. Verdier	1884	rose	1	mod.
Souv. de Victor Verdier ..	H. P.	E. Verdier	1878	crimson-violet	1	vig.
Souv. de Pierre Vibert ...	P. M.	Moreau Rob	1867	dark red	1	vig.
Souv. de Mad. W. Wood	H. P.	E. Verdier	1877	deep rose	2	vig.
Souv. de William Wood ...	H. P.	E. Verdier	1864	violet-purple	1	vig.
Splendeus	Ayr	...	...	white	2	vig.
Spintarus .... ·	B.	Guillot	1845			
Spong....................	P.	...	...	pale rose	2	mod.
Standard of Marengo	H. P.	Guillot père	1851	scarlet-red	1	vig.
Stanwell Perpetual	P. S.	...	...	rosy blush	2	mod.
Star of Waltham	H. P.	W. Paul	1875	deep crimson	1	mod.
Sulphureux	T.	Ducher	1869	sulphur	2	mod.
Sultan of Zanzibar	H. P.	Paul & Son	1876	dark maroon	2	mod.
Sunset	T.	Henderson	1884	red striped	2	mod.
Superba	P.	Feast	1843	pink	3	vig.
Surpasse Comice de Seine- et-Marne	B.	Guillot	1852	crimson	2	vig.
Susanna Wood	H. P.	E. Verdier	1869	bright rose	1	vig.
Sydonie	H. P.	Dorisy	1846	rose	2	vig.
Tantine	T.	Pradel	...	cerise	2	mod.

Name.	Class.	Raiser.	Year.	Colour.	Size.	Habit.
Tatiana Onequine............	H.P.	Lévèque	1882	carmine-red	1	mod.
Théocrite	H.P.	..	1851	rosy pink	1	vig.
Théodore Buchelet	H.P.	E. Verdier	1873	violet-purple	1	mod.
Théodore Bullier	H.P.	E. Verdier	1879	purple-carmine	1	vig.
The Garland	Musk	...	...	white	3	vig.
The Meteor	H.T.	W. Paul&Son	1887	dark crimson	1	vig.
The Puritan	H.P.	Evans	1887	white	1	vig.
The Shah	H.P.	Paul & Son	1876	dark crimson	2	mod.
Thérèse Coumer	H.P.	Liabaud	1866			
Thérèse Genevay	T.	Levet	1875	rose	2	mod.
Thérèse Loth	T.	Liabaud	1874	blush-pink	2	mod.
Thomas Methven	H.P.	E. Verdier	1869	bright carmine	1	vig.
Thomas Mills	H.P.	E. Verdier	1873	rosy carmine	1	vig.
Thomas Rivers	B.	..	1858	lilac	1	mod.
Thorin	H.P.	Lacharme	1866	bright rose	1	vig.
Thunberg	H.P.	E. Verdier	1867	purple-violet	1	vig.
Thyra Hammerich	H.P.	V. Verdier	1868	rosy flesh	1	vig.
Toujour Fleuri	H.P.	Cherpin	1855	purple-crimson	2	mod.
Tour Bertrand	T.	Ducher	1869	clear yellow	1	mod.
Tourrefort..................	H.P.	Liabaud	1867	bright rose	1	vig.
Tourville	H.P.	Mor. et Rob.	1879	rose-carmine	1	vig.
Townsend ...	S.		...	blush	2	vig.
Triomphe d'Alencon	H.P.	Chauvet	...	red	1	mod.
Triomphe d'Amiens	H.P.	Mille-Malet	1861	crimson	2	vig.
Triomphe d'Angers	H.P.	Mor. et Rob.	1863	purple-crimson	2	mod.
Triomphe d'Avrauches ...	H.P.	...	1855	bright red	1	mod.
Triomphe des Beaux Arts .	H.P.	Fontaine	1857	crimson	2	mod.
Triomphe de Beauté	H.P.	Oger	1853	crimson	2	vig.
Triomphe de Caen	H.P.	Oger	1861	purple-crimson	2	mod.
Triomphe de l'Exposition .	H.P.	Margottin	1855	reddish crmsn.	2	mod.
Triomphe des Français ..	H.P.	Pernet	1864	crimson	2	vig.
Triomphe de France	H.P.	Margottin	1875	deep carmine	1	vig.
Triomphe de Guillot fils	T.	Guillot fils	1861	white and rose	1	vig.
Triomphe de la Guillotière	Mic.	Guillot père	1864	clear rose	2	mod.
Triomphe de Lyon	H.P.	Cordier	1859	velvety crmsn.	2	mod.
Triomphe de Luxembourg.	T.	Hardy	1836	buff	1	mod.
Triomphe de Milau ...	T.	Mad. Ducher	1876	white-yellow	1	vig.
Triomphe de Montrouge ..	H.P.	...	1858	crimson	1	vig.
Triomphe de Nancy........	H.P.	Crousse	...	crimson	1	vig.
Triomphe de Paris	H.P.	...	1852	dark crimson	1	vig.
Triomphe de Rennes	S.	Lansezeur	1857	canary-yellow	1	vig.
Triomphe de Rouen ...	H.P.	Garçon	...	rose	2	mod.
Trphe. de la Terre des Roses	H.P.	Guillot père	1864	violet-rose	2	mod.
Triomphe de Rosomanes .	H.P.	Gonod	1873	dark crimson	1	vig.
Triomphe de Soissons	H.P.	Fontaine	1866	salmon-rose	1	vig.
Triomphe de Toulouse.....	H.P.	Brassac	1873	carmine	1	vig.
Triumphant	Pra.	Pierce	1850	deep rose	3	vig.
Turenne..................	H.P.	V. Verdier	1861	bright crimson	1	vig.
Ulrich Brunner fils	H.P.	Levet	1882	cerise	1	vig.
Unique	T.	Guillot fils	1869	white-purple	2	mod.
Unique	P.	Grimwood	1777	white	2	mod.

Name.	Class.	Raiser.	Year.	Colour.	Size.	Habit.
Unique Jaune	N.	Mor. et Rob.	1872	red-yellow	2	vig.
Vainqueur de Goliath	H.P.	Pernet	1872	cherry-red	2	vig.
Validé	P.M.	Laffay	1858	rosy carmine	2	mod.
Vallée de Chamounix	T.	Ducher	1872	coppery	2	mod.
Vandermersch Mertens	T.	Nabonnand	1882	yellow	2	mod.
Vase d'Election	H.P.	Ducher	1864	clear rose	2	vig.
Vaucanson	H.P.	Schwartz	1871	vinous red	2	mod.
Velours Pourpre	H.P.	E. Verdier	1866	velvety purple	1	mod.
Vicomte Maison	H.P.	Fontaine	1868	cerise-carmine	1	vig.
Vicomte Vigier	H.P.	V. Verdier	1861	violet-red	1	vig.
Vicomtesse de Cazès	T.	Pradel	1844	deep yellow	1	vig.
Vicomtesse Folkestone	H.T.	Bennett	1886	pink	1	vig.
Vicomtesse de Montesquieu	H.P.	Quetier	1861	flesh	1	mod.
Vicomtesse du Terrail	B.	Vigneron	1884	flesh	2	mod.
Vicomtesse de Vezins	H.P.	Gautreau	1868	bright rose	1	vig.
Victor le Bihan	H.P.	Guillot père	1859	rose-carmine	2	mod.
Victor Emmanuel	B.	Guillot père	1867	purple-crimson	1	mod.
Victor Hugo	H.P.	Schwartz	1885	crimson	2	mod.
Victor Puillat	T.	Ducher	1870	yellow-white	1	vig.
Victor Trouillard	H.P.	Trouillard	1855	deep crimson	1	dwf.
Victor Trouillard père	H.P.	Trouillard	1868	violet-red	1	vig.
Victor Verdier	H.P.	Lacharme	1859	rose-carmine	1	vig.
Victor Verne	H.P.	Damaizin	1871	deep red	1	vig.
Victorine Helfenbein	H.P.	Guillot	1851			
Village Maid	G.		..	white, red stpd	2	mod.
Villaret de Joyeuse	H.P.	Damaizin	1874	carmine-rose	1	vig.
Ville de Clamart	H.P.	Fontaine	1879	bright rose	2	vig.
Ville de Lyon	H.P.	Ducher	1866	silvery rose	1	mod.
Vincent Duval	H.P.	Duval	1879	rosy carmine	1	vig.
Violette Bouyer	H.P.	Lacharme	1882	flesh	1	vig.
Viridiflora	C.		...	green	3	mod.
Virgile	H.P.	Guillot père	1871	salmon-rose	1	mod.
Virginal	H.P.	Lacharme	1858	white	2	mod.
Viscountess Falmouth	H.T.	Bennett	1878	rose-pink	1	vig.
Vivid	H.B.	W. Paul	1853	bright red	1	vig.
Vorace	B.	Lacharme	1852	velvety crimsn.	1	vig.
Vulcain	H.P.	V. Verdier	1850	purple-red	1	mod.
Waltham Climbers, Nos. 1, 2, 3	H.T.	W. Paul &Sn.	1885	crimson	1	vig.
White Baroness	H.P.	Paul & Son	1882	white	1	vig.
White Bath	M.	Slater	1810	white	1	vig.
William Francis Bennett	T.	Bennett	1885	purple	2	vig.
William Bull	H.P.	E. Verdier	1861	rosy cerise	1	vig.
William Griffith	H.P.	Portemer	1854	satiny rose	1	rob.
William Jesse	H.C.	Laffay	1850	rosy crimson	1	vig.
William Koelle	H.P.	Pernet	1878	bright red	1	vig.
William Lobb	M.	Laffay	1855	red	2	mod.
William Paul	H.P.	Guillot père	1862	red-crimson	2	mod.
William Pützer	H.P.	E. Verdier	1861	brilliant red	2	vig.
W. A. Richardson	N.	Mad. Ducher	1878	orange-yellow	1	vig.

Name.	Class.	Raiser.	Year.	Colour.	Size.	Habit.
William Rollisson	H.P.	E. Verdier	1865	cherry-rose	2	mod.
William Warden	H.P.	Mitchell	1879	rose-pink	1	vig.
Wilson Saunders	H.P.	Paul & Son	1874	vivid crimson	2	mod.
Woodland Marguerite	N.	Pentland	1859	blush	2	vig
Xavier Olibo	H.P.	Lacharme	1864	blackish crmsn.	1	mod.
Yellow Austrian	A.B.	...	...	bright yellow	3	mod.
Yellow Scotch	S.	...	...	straw-yellow	2	vig.
Yellow Tea	T.	...	1824	yellow	2	mod.
Ye Primrose Dame	T.	Bennett	1886	yellow	2	vig.
Yolande d'Aragon	H.P.	Vibert	1843	lilac-rose	2	mod.
York & Lancaster............	D.	...	...	red & white stpd	2	vig.

H. M POLLETT & Co., Horticultural Printers, Fann Street, Aldersgate Street, London, E.C.